SUPER FOODS
SUPER EASY

SUPER FOODS
SUPER EASY

JG
PRESS

CONTENTS

Welcome to the NEXT STAGE OF
the healthy food revolution

Put down your health books, take up your knife and fork and discover how to eat your way to a healthier lifestyle, easily, quickly and deliciously. So, savour our recipes and move into the super food nutritional fast lane.

Super Foods Super Easy is a cookbook with a difference – a fantastic selection of tasty, modern and easy recipes for everyday living, each of them packed with foods that have been demonstrated to promote long-term health, aid healing, and even help to fight some diseases. And all this can be done without fuss, complicated preparation and lengthy cooking time – and with supermarket staples.

WHAT IS A SUPER FOOD?

Super foods, such as broccoli, blueberries and salmon, contain natural ingredients with exceptional nutritional values or protective qualities. They contain natural chemicals, compounds and nutrients that, for example, may help to protect against the impact of diseases such as cancer and Type 2 diabetes, as well as fight the effects of ageing, help to lower cholesterol levels and improve mental alertness.

Here are five top reasons for including more super foods in your daily diet:

● Super foods will help you to meet the seven-a-day fruit and vegetable target that health professionals recommend as a minimum daily amount to protect your body and maintain wellbeing.

● Many super foods such as lentils and oats have a low glycaemic index (GI) value, which means that their carbohydrates are absorbed slowly into the bloodstream. Such foods stave off hunger and keep you feeling full for longer, so helping with weight control.

● Many super foods such as wholewheat pasta and carrots are a good source of fibre. This helps your digestive system to work effectively, and some forms of fibre can help to lower cholesterol.

● All super foods are low in, or free from, the 'bad' fats, such as saturates and trans fats, which can increase the risk of heart disease.

● Super foods naturally provide high levels of the essential vitamins and minerals that your body needs for a healthy nervous system, a fully functioning brain and other key bodily processes, such as the regulation of blood clotting and the efficient working of your cells and organs.

Turn to the Super Food Benefits Chart (see pages 10–11) for a list of the main super foods featured in our recipes and the conditions they can help to reduce and possibly even prevent, as well as their positive health benefits in the body.

MAKING YOURS A **BALANCED DIET**

Super foods should form a large part of a healthy, well-balanced diet. Follow this checklist of what food types to include regularly to keep your mind and body performing at their best.

Protein
Essential for building and maintaining muscles and internal organs, protein is also needed to build new cells and repair damaged tissue in your body. High-protein foods include lean meat, poultry, fish, seafood, low-fat dairy foods, eggs and legumes.

Carbohydrate
The staple of most diets, starchy carbohydrates provide energy for your body throughout the day and as you sleep. About 50 per cent of your daily energy should come mainly from starchy wholegrain foods, such as brown rice, wholewheat pasta and wholegrain bread. Within this total, no more than 10 per cent should come from sugary foods. The best type of sugar is found naturally in fruit and vegetables, not added.

Fat
Providing your body with energy and fat-soluble vitamins, and protecting your vital organs, are among the many roles fat has to play. Eating too much fat, though, especially saturated fat, can lead to weight problems and heart disease. The good fats are unsaturated fats, such as olive oil or canola oil. Other healthy fats include omega-3, found in oily fish, nuts and seeds.

Vitamins and minerals
Vitamins A, the B group, C, D, E and K are the essential nutrients for keeping your body in good working order. Major minerals (those found in relatively large amounts in the body) are iron, calcium, zinc, selenium, magnesium and potassium. Vitamins and minerals appear in small quantities in lots of different foods, so a varied diet is the best way to obtain them all.

Dietary fibre
You need about 30 g of fibre per day to keep your digestive system in good working order. Some types of fibre also help to lower cholesterol levels, which is vital if you want to maintain a healthy heart. Unrefined (unprocessed) plant-based foods contain the highest amounts of fibre. Good examples include wholegrains, legumes such as lentils and beans, dried fruit and fresh fruit and vegetables.

Fluids
Water is vital for physical wellbeing. An average adult needs to drink almost 2 litres of fluid every day. Water is the best thirst quencher, but tea, coffee and low-fat milk are also included. Food can also supply some of your fluid requirements – many fruit and salad ingredients have a high water content.

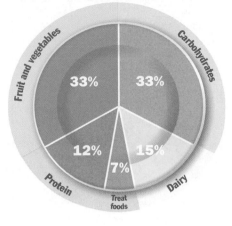

EATING WELL

Build your food intake around the main food groups for healthy living. The optimum amount of nutrients needed to maintain health varies from person to person – depending on sex, age, height, weight and activity levels – but as a rule of thumb, about one-third of the food you eat should come from high fibre, starchy foods such as wholegrains, pulses and potatoes, another third from fruit and vegetables, with the rest made up from fish, poultry, lean meat and low-fat dairy foods, with only limited amounts of processed fatty or sugary foods.

A NOTE ON SEASONING

Salt Avoid adding salt to your cooking and when serving – too much can lead to high blood pressure. Choose salt-reduced stock, or make your own stock. Salt is not added to the cooking water of vegetables, rice and pasta in our recipes. We have not seasoned the recipes needlessly either.

Herbs Use herbs and spices to boost flavour – many have their own health properties. Fresh is best but use dried, if preferred.

Sugar Replace processed sugar with natural sweetness whenever you can from fresh and dried fruit.

FREEZING SUPER FOODS

Using a freezer to store food ready to use at any time is a great idea – vegetables, fruit, meat, poultry, fish and even some fresh herbs and spices retain their nutritional value when frozen.

Freeze meat, poultry and fish on the day of purchase and do not store it for longer than 3 months. Never re-freeze meat, fish or poultry.

Frozen vegetables are very handy – either when shop-bought or fresh from the garden. If freezing your own produce, always freeze as soon as possible after picking to avoid losing essential vitamins and minerals. Wash and chop the vegetables ready for freezing, then blanch in a saucepan of boiling water for 2–3 minutes. Lift out with a slotted spoon, refresh under cold water, drain and pack into labelled containers. Once opened, reseal bags of frozen vegetables with a tie. Salad vegetables cannot be frozen.

Always defrost food thoroughly in the refrigerator before cooking. Do not cook raw poultry or meat from frozen as it may not cook right through. Some seafood and fish can be cooked from frozen – follow the recipe instructions.

SUPER EASY **PLANNING** AND **SHOPPING**

Healthy cooking does not mean costly lists of little-known ingredients. Much of it is about making a few easy changes to your usual routine and planning ahead, such as making best use of your freezer (see left).

A WELL-STOCKED PANTRY
Build up your super food pantry staples and you will always be able to make delicious, healthy food even if you forget to plan ahead. These are the staples that should always be on your shelves:
- grain products such as brown rice, rolled oats, burghul, couscous, quinoa, a few different wholewheat pasta shapes, noodles and flour
- dried and canned legumes, including lentils, cannellini beans, kidney beans and chickpeas
- a variety of unsalted nuts and seeds
- oils for cooking and salads – canola oil and olive oil are best
- natural sweeteners such as agave syrup, honey and maple syrup
- whole and ground spices, plus a selection of seasonings, such as low-salt soy sauce, stock cubes, herbs and pepper.

THE SAVVY SHOPPER
All the ingredients in our recipes are easy to find in supermarkets. If your local store has a fish or meat counter, ask the fishmonger or butcher to prepare the food fresh for you. You are likely to end up with less waste – and even save money.

Also try specialty shops either at shopping centres or online, and make use of local farmers' markets for top-quality produce that is locally and ethically farmed. Choose organic ingredients whenever possible as they should be free from pesticides and artificial additives.

Fish When buying fish, look for sustainable sources – try to avoid endangered bluefin tuna, orange roughy (ocean perch) and flake, and use more abundant varieties such as snapper, bream and whiting.

Poultry Choose free-range chicken and turkey where possible. They are slightly more expensive than 'basic' ranges but will have a better flavour.

Meat Beef, pork and lamb are sold ready cubed, sliced or minced, which will save on preparation time. Steaks, chops and tenderloin are best for quick cooking. Always choose lean mince. Choose grass-fed or wild meat where available.

Fruit and vegetables Fresh is best, but ready-prepared packs will save you time.

LET'S GET COOKING

Super Foods Super Easy contains 184 health-boosting recipes, and all include at least one super food. Each recipe page offers clear step-by-step cooking instructions, ingredient information and invaluable tips.

● **Ingredients** Each ingredient is listed on the page in the order that it is needed in the recipe, with exact quantities given, either in weight or numbers. Unless otherwise stated, all ingredients such as eggs, fruit and vegetables are medium in size.

● **Alternative ingredients** The majority of recipes in this book include different ingredient suggestions so you can include the foods you prefer – or adapt the recipe to what you have available.

● **Nutritional values** If you need to keep an eye on the kilojoules or your intake of fat, protein and fibre, these values supply guidance at a glance.

● **Cook's tips** Expert practical advice to get the most from our recipes, from how to remove seeds from a cardamom pod to which cut of lamb to choose for a stir-fry and the best way to cook raw beetroot.

● **Super food information** Every recipe page tells you about the health benefits of one super food ingredient. Refer to the Glossary (right) if there are any terms that are unfamiliar to you. Also, special features on 14 major super foods appear throughout the book. Each provides information on the food's health-promoting benefits and includes five simple mouth-watering recipes.

CONVERSION CHART

We have supplied this conversion chart for those people who feel more confident with imperial measures than with metric measures. Remember to use either metric or imperial – do not mix the two together or the recipes may not work.

Weight

Metric	Imperial (approx)	Metric	Imperial (approx)
10 g	¼ oz	55 g	2 oz
15 g	½ oz	60 g	2¼ oz
20 g	¾ oz	70 g	2½ oz
25 g	1 oz	75 g	2¾ oz
35 g	1¼ oz	85 g	3 oz
40 g	1½ oz	90 g	3¼ oz
50 g	1¾ oz	100 g	3½ oz
		1 kg	2 lb 4 oz

Volume

Metric	Imperial (approx)	Metric	Imperial (approx)
30 ml	1 fl oz	90 ml	3¼ fl oz
50 ml	2 fl oz	100 ml	3½ fl oz
75 ml	2½ fl oz	1 litre	1¾ pints
85 ml	3 fl oz		

GLOSSARY

anthocyanin: a type of plant pigment that may help to protect the body against heart disease (see also flavonoid).

anti-oxidant: a substance that helps to protect against and destroys harmful free radicals that can damage the body's cells.

beta-carotene: part of a family of natural anti-oxidants found in many fruit and vegetables. It can be converted to vitamin A in the body.

cholesterol: fatty substance made predominantly by the body from saturated fat in the diet. Too much cholesterol in the blood can increase the risk of heart disease.

ellagic acid: a plant chemical that may have anti-cancer properties.

flavonoid: a plant pigment with beneficial anti-oxidant properties.

folate: form of B vitamin folic acid that occurs naturally in food. Folate helps to produce and maintain new red blood cells in the body.

glycaemic index (GI): a ranking of carbohydrate foods based on the rate at which they raise blood glucose levels after eating. A low GI rating means only a gradual rise in blood glucose levels, which may help with weight control and reduce the risk of heart disease and diabetes.

immune system: the body's defence system, composed of cells, tissues and organs, which protects the body against infection.

monounsaturated fat: can help to lower harmful cholesterol in the blood and keep the heart healthy.

phytochemical: describes a wide variety of compounds produced by plants that may help to reduce the risk of cancer.

polyunsaturated fat: heart-healthy fats that lower harmful cholesterol in the bloodstream. They provide essential fatty acids.

saturated fat: can raise harmful cholesterol in the blood, increasing the risk of heart disease.

vitamin: a substance found in food that is essential to maintain a healthy body.

SUPER FOOD BENEFITS CHART

	Ageing (skin)	Cancer	Cholesterol lowering	Depression	Diabetes (Type 2)	Digestive health	Eye health	Fatigue	Heart health	Immune function	Menopause	Mental alertness	Osteoporosis	Rheumatoid arthritis	Stroke prevention	Weight control
Apples	•	•	•	•	•	•	•		•	•	•	•		•	•	•
Apricots	•	•	•	•	•	•	•		•	•	•	•	•	•	•	•
Avocados	•	•	•	•	•	•	•		•	•	•	•	•	•	•	
Bananas	•	•	•	•	•	•		•	•	•	•	•	•	•	•	•
Beans		•		•	•	•		•	•	•		•		•	•	•
Beef (lean)	•			•				•		•		•	•	•		•
Beetroot	•	•	•	•	•	•	•		•	•		•			•	•
Berries	•	•	•	•	•	•	•		•	•	•	•	•	•	•	•
Broccoli	•	•	•	•	•	•	•		•	•	•	•	•	•	•	•
Cabbage	•	•	•	•	•	•	•		•	•	•	•	•	•	•	•
Carrots	•	•	•	•	•	•	•		•	•	•	•	•	•	•	•
Capsicums	•	•	•	•	•	•	•		•	•	•	•	•	•	•	•
Cauliflower	•	•	•	•	•	•			•	•	•	•		•	•	•
Cherries	•	•	•	•	•	•			•	•		•	•	•	•	•
Chicken		•		•	•		•	•	•	•		•	•	•	•	•
Chicken livers		•		•	•		•	•	•	•		•	•	•	•	•
Citrus	•	•	•	•	•	•	•		•	•	•	•	•	•	•	•
Dried fruit	•	•	•	•	•	•		•	•	•	•	•	•	•	•	•
Eggplant	•	•	•	•	•	•			•	•	•	•			•	•
Eggs		•		•			•	•	•	•	•		•		•	•
Garlic		•	•		•	•			•						•	•
Grains		•	•	•	•	•		•	•	•	•	•			•	•
Grapes	•	•	•	•	•	•			•	•	•	•		•	•	•
Lentils		•	•	•	•	•		•	•	•	•	•	•		•	•

The chart below lists top super foods and shows you where they may be particularly beneficial when eaten as part of a balanced diet for the health issues, diseases and conditions indicated in the headings. Use this chart as a guide only – always talk to your doctor if you have any concerns about your health.

	Ageing (skin)	Cancer	Cholesterol lowering	Depression	Diabetes (Type 2)	Digestive health	Eye health	Fatigue	Heart health	Immune function	Menopause	Mental alertness	Osteoporosis	Rheumatoid arthritis	Stroke prevention	Weight control
Low-fat dairy	•	•		•	•	•		•	•	•	•	•	•	•	•	•
Mangoes	•	•	•	•	•	•	•		•	•	•	•	•	•	•	•
Mushrooms	•	•	•	•	•	•	•	•			•	•		•	•	•
Nuts	•	•	•	•	•		•		•	•	•	•	•	•	•	•
Oats		•	•	•	•			•	•	•	•	•				•
Oily fish	•	•	•	•	•				•	•	•	•	•	•	•	
Olive oil	•	•	•		•				•	•		•	•	•	•	
Onion		•	•		•	•			•	•	•	•				•
Pears	•	•	•	•	•	•			•	•		•			•	•
Peas	•	•	•	•	•	•	•	•	•	•	•	•	•	•	•	•
Pineapples	•	•	•	•	•	•			•	•	•	•			•	•
Pomegranates	•	•	•	•	•	•	•		•	•	•	•	•	•	•	•
Pumpkin, butternut	•	•	•	•	•	•	•	•	•	•	•	•		•	•	•
Seafood	•	•	•	•	•		•	•	•	•	•	•	•	•	•	•
Seeds	•	•	•	•	•	•	•	•	•	•	•	•	•	•	•	•
Soybeans	•	•	•	•				•	•	•	•	•	•	•	•	•
Spinach	•	•	•	•	•	•	•	•	•	•	•	•	•		•	•
Sweet potatoes		•	•	•	•	•	•	•	•	•	•	•		•		•
Tomatoes	•	•	•	•	•	•	•		•	•	•	•	•	•	•	•
Turkey		•				•			•	•	•					•
White fish		•	•	•	•				•	•		•	•	•	•	•
Wholegrain bread		•	•	•	•	•			•	•	•	•	•	•	•	•
Wholegrain rice		•	•	•	•			•	•	•	•	•	•	•	•	•
Zucchini	•	•	•	•	•	•			•	•	•	•		•	•	•

SOUPS,
STARTERS
and
SNACKS

CHUNKY **VEGETABLE** SOUP WITH **PASTA**

A real Italian-inspired meal in a bowl – nutritious wholewheat spaghetti in a rich minestrone-style soup chock-full of tender vegetables. Serve with warmed olive focaccia for a heartening treat.

Serves 4
Preparation 10 minutes
Cooking 30 minutes

Each serving provides
- 1130 kJ • 270 kcal • 11 g protein
- 13 g fat of which 4 g saturates
- 29 g carbohydrates of which
13 g sugars • 7 g fibre

1 onion
1 carrot
1 stick celery
1 yellow capsicum
1 parsnip
100 g mushrooms
2 tablespoons olive oil
1 bay leaf
1 clove garlic, crushed
400 g can chopped tomatoes
2 cups (500 ml) hot chicken
  or vegetable stock
75 g wholewheat spaghetti
½ cup (50 g) grated parmesan,
  to serve

ALTERNATIVE INGREDIENTS
• For a meaty version of this soup, dry-fry 50 g diced smoked bacon, chorizo or pancetta for 1 minute before starting step 1.
• Leave out the parsnip and add 150 g fresh or frozen green beans or broad beans with the pasta.

1 Finely chop the onion. Dice the carrot, celery, capsicum and parsnip, and chop the mushrooms. Heat the oil in a large saucepan over a high heat. Add the bay leaf, onion, carrot, celery and garlic, reduce the heat to low, then cover and cook for 2 minutes.

2 Stir in the capsicum and mushrooms, re-cover and cook for a further 2 minutes. Add the parsnip and tomatoes, then pour in the hot stock and bring back to the boil. Reduce the heat and simmer, covered, for 20 minutes, or until the vegetables are tender.

3 Snap the spaghetti into 4 cm pieces and stir them into the soup. Bring back to the boil, reduce the heat and simmer for 5 minutes, or until the pasta is tender. Ladle the soup into four bowls and sprinkle with parmesan.

COOK'S TIP
● Frozen vegetables are great for everyday meals, saving time on shopping and preparation. There is a wide variety of mixtures, some with capsicums, celery and mushrooms as well as the usual carrots, peas and beans. Use fresh onion and garlic, then add frozen mixed vegetables in step 2 in place of the fresh ingredients. Reduce the cooking time by 5 minutes.

SUPER FOOD

WHOLEWHEAT PASTA
Most of the goodness of wholegrains is concentrated in the outer bran layer. Wholewheat pasta retains that bran and so contains up to 75 per cent more nutrients than pasta made from refined grains. Regularly eating wholewheat pasta protects against heart disease and may lower the risk of some forms of cancer of the digestive tract.

CHILLED **CARROT** AND **ORANGE** SOUP

For a refreshing and healthy cold soup, try a fusion of yogurt, herbs and two juices whose vibrant orange colour is the product of the cancer-fighting pigment beta-carotene.

Serves 4
Preparation 10 minutes
Cooking 2 minutes

700 ml carrot juice, chilled
150 ml natural yogurt
grated zest of ½ orange and juice
    of 1 orange, about 75 ml
4 tablespoons snipped fresh chives
2 tablespoons chopped fresh
    tarragon
1 tablespoon olive oil
4 slices wholemeal bread

Each serving provides
• 757 kJ • 181 kcal • 7 g protein
• 6 g fat of which 1 g saturates
• 26 g carbohydrates of which
11 g sugars • 3 g fibre

ALTERNATIVE INGREDIENTS
• For a slightly thicker soup with
a 'nutty' flavour, cut the crusts off
3 extra slices of wholemeal bread,
about 100 g, and whizz the bread in
a blender with the carrot juice, yogurt
and chives.
• Fresh coriander works well instead
of tarragon.
• Try tomato juice in place of carrot
juice and add a dash of chilli sauce
for a piquant tomato soup.

1 Preheat the grill to the hottest setting. Pour the carrot juice into a large bowl and whisk in the yogurt until smooth. Add the orange zest, juice and chives, then whisk again. Ladle into four soup bowls.

2 Mix the tarragon with the oil. Toast the bread for 1 minute on one side under the grill, then turn and lightly brush the untoasted side with the tarragon oil. Toast for a further 1 minute, or until golden and crisp. Season the soup with ground black pepper to taste, and serve.

COOK'S TIPS
● You can make this soup in advance and chill for several hours in the fridge before serving. Add chopped tarragon to the oil well in advance to infuse it with the herb flavour and then store it in an airtight jar in the fridge until needed.
● If you cannot get carrot juice from your supermarket, make it with an electric juicer or in a blender. For this recipe you will need 1 kg of peeled or scrubbed carrots. Either juice the carrots according to the juicer instructions or whizz them in a blender until finely mashed. Add a little water if the mixture becomes too dry and the blades stick. Pour the carrot juice into a jug and add 2 cups (500 ml) water. Leave it to stand for 30 minutes, then strain through a fine-meshed sieve.

SUPER FOOD

CARROTS
Beta-carotene, found in abundance in carrots and other brightly coloured fruits and vegetables, has strong anti-oxidant properties and may help to protect against cancer. It is converted to vitamin A in the body, which helps to promote healthy skin and improve vision in dim light.

CARROTS

It is no myth that carrots help you to see in the dark, thanks to their high level of beta-carotene, which the body converts to vision-enhancing vitamin A. Yet carrots offer much more – cell-protecting properties for great-looking skin, plenty of fibre to aid digestion, and a low fat and low kilojoule count to make them a healthy any-time snack.

HERBED CARROT AND CORIANDER SOUP

Serves 4
Preparation 10 minutes Cooking 45 minutes

Each serving provides • 469 kJ • 112 kcal
• 2 g protein • 5 g fat of which 1 g saturates
• 16 g carbohydrates of which 13 g sugars • 4 g fibre

Heat **1 tablespoon olive oil or canola oil** in a saucepan over a medium–low heat and then add **5 chopped carrots** and **1 large chopped onion**. Stir-fry for 5 minutes, or until softened. Add **2 crushed cloves garlic** and **1 teaspoon ground coriander**, and stir occasionally for 1 minute. Pour in **4 cups (1 litre) hot vegetable stock** and bring to a simmer. Cover and cook for 30 minutes. Take off the heat, leave to cool a little then purée in a blender or in the pan with a stick blender until smooth. Stir in the **juice of ½ lemon**, and season to taste. Gently reheat the soup but do not boil. Just before serving, stir in **4 tablespoons chopped fresh coriander**. Ladle into four bowls and drizzle **1 teaspoon natural yogurt** over each one before serving.

COOK'S TIP

● Give the soup a slightly different flavour by using ground cumin instead of ground coriander.

LAYERED VEGETABLE CASSEROLE

Serves 4
Preparation 15 minutes Cooking 60 minutes

Each serving provides • 1594 kJ • 381 kcal
• 13 g protein • 8 g fat of which 2 g saturates
• 62 g carbohydrates of which 20 g sugars • 3 g fibre

Heat **1 tablespoon olive oil** in a flameproof casserole dish and cook **1 large thinly sliced onion** over a medium–low heat for 5 minutes to soften, stirring occasionally. Add **1 tablespoon chopped fresh parsley, 1 tablespoon snipped fresh chives** and **2 crushed cloves garlic**, and stir through the onions. Remove the onion mixture from the casserole dish with a slotted spoon. Cover the bottom of the dish with **500 g thickly sliced potatoes** then sprinkle over **40 g dried split peas** and a third of the onion mixture. Add the next layer of **5 sliced carrots** and cover with **40 g dried split peas** and one-third of the onion mixture. Top with a layer of **2 sliced parsnips** then **40 g dried split peas** and the remaining third of the onion mixture. Pour in **4 cups (1 litre) hot vegetable stock** and bring to the boil. Reduce the heat, cover and simmer for

30 minutes. Remove the lid and cook for a further 20 minutes, or until the vegetables are tender and the sauce has thickened. Serve each portion with **1 tablespoon sour cream** on top.

COOK'S TIPS

● The dried split peas cook in the casserole stock, so there is no need to pre-soak or pre-cook them.

● Serve the casserole with a steamed green vegetable such as broccoli, spinach or savoy cabbage.

HONEY-BRAISED CARROTS WITH BABY PEAS

Serves 4
Preparation 5 minutes Cooking 12 minutes

Each serving provides • 573 kJ • 137 kcal
• 3 g protein • 8 g fat of which 3 g saturates
• 15 g carbohydrates of which 14 g sugars • 5 g fibre

Place **500 g whole baby carrots** in a saucepan and add **15 g butter, 1 tablespoon olive oil, 3 tablespoons hot vegetable stock, ½ teaspoon grated nutmeg** and **1½ tablespoons runny honey**. Bring to a simmer, cover and cook for 8 minutes, or until the carrots are just tender. Add **1 cup (125 g) frozen baby peas** to the pan and heat through for 1–2 minutes. Serve the carrots garnished with **1 tablespoon snipped fresh chives**.

COOK'S TIPS

● If baby carrots are not available, use large ones and cut them in half widthwise and lengthwise.

● Serve as a side dish to roast beef or venison to complement their rich meat flavours.

BROWN RICE, LENTIL AND CARROT SALAD

Serves 4
Preparation 10 minutes Cooking 35 minutes

Each serving provides • 1577 kJ • 377 kcal
• 9 g protein • 21 g fat of which 3 g saturates
• 38 g carbohydrates of which 6 g sugars • 6 g fibre

Cook **150 g brown rice** in a saucepan in **300 ml hot vegetable stock** and boil, covered, for 30 minutes, or until tender and the stock is absorbed. Cut **3 carrots** into 1–2 cm chunks and boil with **200 g broccoli florets** for 10 minutes, or until tender. Remove the rice from the heat and add **150 g canned green lentils** to the rice. Stir in gently and allow to cool. Stir the cooked vegetables into the rice with **1 tablespoon finely**

chopped sun-dried tomatoes. Make a dressing with **2 tablespoons olive oil, 2 tablespoons sesame oil, 1 tablespoon balsamic vinegar, 2 teaspoons finely grated fresh ginger** and a dash of **shop-bought hot pepper sauce**. Stir the dressing and **2 tablespoons chopped parsley** into the rice mixture. Sprinkle **1 tablespoon sesame seeds** over the salad and serve.

COOK'S TIPS

● If you want to use dried lentils rather than canned, put 150 g green lentils in boiling water and simmer for 25 minutes until tender. Drain before adding to the rice.

● If the rice is not cooked through by the time the stock is absorbed, add a little more hot stock or boiling water and continue cooking until tender. Rice varies in cooking time according to the age and variety of the grains.

● Handy for a buffet, this salad can be stored overnight in the fridge. It will taste even better when brought back to room temperature and the flavours have infused.

SWEET AND SOUR NOODLES

Serves 4
Preparation 10 minutes Cooking 10 minutes

Each serving provides • 1397 kJ • 334 kcal
• 7 g protein • 12 g fat of which 2 g saturates
• 52 g carbohydrates of which 16 g sugars • 5 g fibre

Cook **200 g medium egg noodles** for 4 minutes, or according to the packet instructions. In another pan, heat **2 tablespoons olive oil or canola oil** over a high heat and add **3 thinly sliced carrots** and **1 sliced leek**. Stir-fry for 3 minutes. Diagonally slice **6 spring onions** and add to the pan with **2 chopped cloves garlic** and **1 chopped mild green chilli**. Stir-fry for 1 minute. Add **1 teaspoon ground cumin, 1 tablespoon light soy sauce** and **2 teaspoons runny honey** and stir for a further 1 minute. Add the noodles and stir gently to heat through. Add **1 teaspoon whole cumin seeds** before serving.

COOK'S TIPS

● Adjust the level of chilli heat to your preference with mild, medium or hot chillies.

● For a heartier meal add leftover cooked meat, or thin slices of pork or chicken fillet stir-fried in 1 tablespoon olive oil or canola oil, when adding the noodles.

CHICKEN AND RICE BROTH WITH SHREDDED OMELETTE

Sesame oil, juicy chicken and vitamin-rich bok choy are just three of the good-for-you ingredients in this delectable soup. Laced with strips of protein-packed omelette, it is a perfect light meal.

Serves 4
Preparation 15 minutes
Cooking 35 minutes

Each serving provides
- 1318 kJ • 315 kcal • 22 g protein
- 16 g fat of which 3 g saturates
- 22 g carbohydrates of which
5 g sugars • 2 g fibre

ALTERNATIVE INGREDIENTS
- Ready-prepared stir-fry chicken strips are available in the chiller cabinets at supermarkets. If you cannot find any, use the same quantity of chicken breast and cut it into small slices.
- Choi sum, or mustard greens, is a good substitute for bok choy. Alternatively, replace with purple sprouting broccoli and allow an extra 1 minute cooking time in step 4.

SUPER FOOD

EGGS

Two medium eggs will provide 100 per cent of your recommended daily amount of vitamin B_{12}. Researchers believe this vitamin may help to retain mental alertness and protect against Alzheimer's disease. Eggs are also rich in protein and other key nutrients.

1 small onion
2 sticks celery
2 carrots
2 tablespoons olive oil or canola oil
1 tablespoon sesame oil
250 g stir-fry chicken strips
75 g brown rice

2 cloves garlic, crushed
1.2 litres hot chicken stock
2 eggs
250 g bok choy
2 spring onions

1 Thinly slice the onion and chop the celery into 1 cm chunks. Cut the carrots into 5 mm sticks. Heat 1 tablespoon of the olive oil or canola oil and the sesame oil in a large saucepan. Add the chicken and cook over a high heat for 1 minute. Stir in the rice, garlic, onion, celery and carrots. Cook for a further 1 minute.

2 Add the hot stock and bring back to the boil, then reduce the heat. Cover and simmer for 30 minutes, or until the chicken and vegetables are cooked and the rice is tender.

3 Meanwhile, heat the remaining 1 tablespoon of olive oil or canola oil in a frying pan over a high heat. Beat the eggs together and pour them into the pan. Cook over a high heat for 1 minute, tilting the pan and lifting the edges of the omelette as the egg sets. Remove from the pan, roll up the omelette and slice into 1 cm wide strips.

4 Slice the bok choy and shred the spring onions. When the soup is cooked, add the bok choy and spring onions, bring back to a simmer and cook for a further 1 minute. Season to taste, add the omelette rolls and ladle into four bowls to serve.

COOK'S TIP
● To wash and prepare bok choy, swish the head in a bowl of water. Rinse between the leaves with running water then shake well. This keeps the head intact and makes slicing easy. Trim off the base and slice as required.

BEETROOT AND CRANBERRY BORSCHT

Cranberry juice brings sweetness and fruity goodness to red cabbage and purple beetroot in a soup that is full of vitamins and anti-oxidants. Wholemeal bread makes a tasty accompaniment.

Serves 4
Preparation 5 minutes
Cooking 15 minutes

1 onion
2 sticks celery
1 tablespoon olive oil
2 cloves garlic, crushed
pinch of ground mace or nutmeg
300 g red cabbage
500 g cooked beetroot
600 ml hot salt-reduced
   chicken stock
600 ml cranberry juice drink
1 teaspoon red wine vinegar
   or cider vinegar
4 tablespoons low-fat natural yogurt
2 tablespoons snipped chives

Each serving provides
• 944 kJ • 225 kcal • 8 g protein
• 5 g fat of which 1 g saturates
• 37 g carbohydrates of which
34 g sugars • 7 g fibre

ALTERNATIVE INGREDIENTS
• Use fresh beetroot instead of cooked. Wash, trim, peel and dice 500 g fresh beetroot and add it to the onion mixture instead of the cabbage in step 2. Add the stock and water, bring to the boil then reduce the heat, cover and simmer for 10 minutes. Add the cabbage and cranberry juice drink and continue from step 2.
• Try pomegranate juice drink instead of cranberry for a stronger sweet–sour soup. Increase the quantity of vinegar to 2–3 teaspoons, tasting as you add, to balance the sweeter fruit juice.

1 Chop the onion and dice the celery. Heat the olive oil in a large saucepan over a high heat and add the onion, celery, garlic and mace. Stir the vegetables and reduce the heat to medium, then cover and cook for 4 minutes, or until the vegetables begin to soften.

2 Finely shred the red cabbage and dice the beetroot. Add the cabbage to the pan and cook, stirring, for 1 minute. Add the hot stock and the cranberry juice drink. Stir in the beetroot and bring to the boil. Reduce the heat to low, so that the soup simmers steadily. Cover and cook for 10 minutes.

3 Stir in the vinegar, season to taste and ladle the soup into four bowls. Top each serving with 1 tablespoon yogurt and sprinkle with chives.

COOK'S TIPS
● Cut red cabbage into short fine shreds by slicing it into slim wedges and then finely slicing the wedges – the cabbage should then fall apart.
● Vacuum-packed cooked beetroot, available from some specialist food stores, is a brilliant pantry ingredient with a long shelf life. It works well in this recipe – just make sure it is not the kind preserved with vinegar or acetic acid. Otherwise, boil or bake unpeeled beetroot until tender, rub off the skins, and use as directed in the recipe.

SUPER FOOD

RED CABBAGE
Cabbage belongs to the brassica family, along with brussels sprouts, broccoli and watercress. It is bursting with anti-oxidant nutrients, and also provides vitamin C and B vitamins, such as folate. There is some evidence to link brassicas with a reduced risk of getting cancer, especially cancer of the digestive tract.

SPRING **VEGETABLE** SOUP

The gentle aniseed flavour of fennel, the firm texture of new potatoes and a kick of fresh parsley merge temptingly in a hearty soup inspired by a Polish recipe. Serve with bread and cheese.

Serves 4
Preparation 15 minutes
Cooking 25 minutes

1 bulb fennel
2 large onions
2 carrots
1 tablespoon olive oil
1 small sprig rosemary
3 cloves garlic, crushed
500 g small new potatoes
900 ml hot vegetable stock
4 tablespoons chopped fresh parsley

Each serving provides
• 845 kJ • 202 kcal • 5 g protein
• 5 g fat of which 1 g saturates
• 36 g carbohydrates of which
13 g sugars • 6 g fibre

ALTERNATIVE INGREDIENTS
• Add 4–6 diced sticks of celery instead of the fennel for a milder flavour with less aniseed.
• If new potatoes are out of season, use regular potatoes that are recommended for boiling. Peel them and cut into bite-sized chunks.
• For some extra colour, add the tips of 200 g broccolini spears to the soup for the final 5 minutes of cooking. Bring the soup back to a simmer before covering the pan to ensure that the broccolini cooks.
• Boost the flavour of the soup by adding 100 g diced bacon or pancetta in step 2.

1 Trim and chop the stalk and feathery leaves of the fennel and set aside. Cut the bulb into slim wedges, remove the core from the base and thinly slice the wedges into bite-sized pieces.

2 Chop the onions and coarsely dice the carrots. Put the oil, fennel stalk and leaves, rosemary, onions, carrots and garlic in a large saucepan and cook, stirring occasionally, over a high heat for about 3 minutes. Stir in the diced fennel bulb, cover and reduce the heat to low. Cook for a further 5 minutes, or until the vegetables have softened, stirring once.

3 Scrub the potatoes, cut in half and add them to the pan, then add the hot stock. Bring back to the boil and adjust the heat so that the soup simmers steadily. Cover and cook for 10–15 minutes, or until the potatoes are tender. Season to taste and stir in the parsley just before serving.

COOK'S TIPS
● Use good-quality cubed, powdered or packaged stocks for the best flavour when making soup.
● If making your own stock, simmer the leftovers of a roast chicken (minus any stuffing) with an onion, carrot and celery stick.

SUPER FOOD

PARSLEY
Though usually served and eaten only in small amounts, parsley is highly nutritious. It contains fibre for a healthy digestive system, the anti-oxidant vitamin C for cancer prevention and folate (a B vitamin) for heart health.

CREAMY **LENTIL** SOUP WITH **CROUTONS**

Perk up the rich flavours of hearty lentil soup with an unexpected zingy topping of avocado, spring onion and lemon zest. Crisp wholemeal croutons add crunch appeal.

Serves 4
Preparation 15 minutes
Cooking 22 minutes

Each serving provides
• 1421 kJ • 340 kcal • 13 g protein
• 22 g fat of which 4 g saturates
• 25 g carbohydrates of which
9 g sugars • 8 g fibre

1 onion
2 sticks celery
1 large carrot
200 g swede
1 tablespoon olive oil
1 clove garlic, crushed
½ cup (100 g) red lentils
1 bay leaf
2 sprigs fresh thyme
1 tablespoon tomato purée
900 ml hot salt-reduced chicken
    or vegetable stock

Croutons
2 slices wholemeal bread
1 tablespoon olive oil
1 avocado or 1 cooked potato, peeled
1 spring onion
finely pared zest of 1 lemon

ALTERNATIVE INGREDIENTS
• As a change from red lentils, use 150 g green or brown lentils and increase the quantity of stock to 1.2 litres. Simmer the soup for 30–35 minutes, or until the lentils are tender. Do not blend, but serve as a chunky soup.
• Add 1 large diced parsnip instead of the swede for a sweeter flavour.

1 Chop the onion then dice the celery, carrot and swede into 3 cm pieces. Heat the oil in a large saucepan over a high heat. Add the onion, celery, carrot, swede and garlic. Reduce the heat to low, cover and cook for 2 minutes.

2 Rinse the lentils in a sieve under cold running water. Add the lentils, bay leaf, thyme and tomato purée to the pan. Pour in the hot stock, stir and bring back to the boil. Reduce the heat, cover and simmer for 20 minutes, or until the lentils have disintegrated.

3 Meanwhile, make the croutons. Preheat the grill to high. Brush one side of the bread slices with ½ tablespoon of the olive oil and grill for 1 minute or until golden. Turn them over, brush with the remaining oil and grill for a further 1 minute. Cut the toast into 2 cm croutons.

4 Dice the avocado or cooked potato and place in a bowl. Finely chop the spring onion and add it to the avocado or potato. Stir in the lemon zest. Remove the thyme and bay leaf from the soup. Purée the soup in a blender or in the pan with a stick blender until smooth. Season to taste and ladle the soup into four bowls. Top with the croutons and avocado or potato mixture.

COOK'S TIPS
● If using a blender, return the soup to the pan after blending and reheat for 1–2 minutes to make sure that it is piping hot when served.
● Use a potato peeler or zester to remove, or pare, the lemon zest. Make sure that you remove only the yellow skin and not the white pith as well, as this tastes bitter.

SUPER FOOD

LENTILS
Rich in starchy carbohydrates, lentils have a low glycaemic index (GI) rating, so are great for keeping hunger at bay. Their high fibre content is good news for the digestive system, and with iron, B vitamins and immunity-boosting zinc, lentils are an all-round healthy choice.

SPINACH AND PEA SOUP WITH MINTY YOGURT

This beautiful, garden-fresh soup is just bursting with the flavours of energy-boosting spinach and peas. It is quick to make, too – simply add a refreshing yogurt swirl and then serve.

Serves 4
Preparation 10 minutes
Cooking 18 minutes

Each serving provides
- 713 kJ • 170 kcal • 13 g protein
- 5 g fat of which 1 g saturates
- 17 g carbohydrates of which 8 g sugars • 3 g fibre

1 onion
1 large potato
1 spring onion
200 g low-fat natural yogurt
2 tablespoons chopped fresh mint
1 tablespoon olive oil
1 clove garlic, crushed
600 ml hot salt-reduced chicken stock
350 g frozen peas or baby peas
200 g fresh spinach

ALTERNATIVE INGREDIENTS
- Silverbeet, Chinese leaves or lettuce work well in this recipe as an alternative to the spinach.
- Use a peeled and diced whole cucumber instead of the spinach.
- As a change from the yogurt topping, dice the flesh from 2 ripe avocados and toss them with 2 tablespoons chopped fresh coriander and the grated zest and juice of ½ lime. Spoon over the soup just before serving.

1 Chop the onion and dice the potato into 2 cm cubes. Finely chop the spring onion. Spoon the yogurt into a bowl and add the spring onion and mint. Heat the oil, garlic, onion and potato in a large saucepan over a medium heat. Cook for 2 minutes, or until the onion softens slightly, stirring occasionally. Add the hot stock, stir, bring the contents of the pan back to the boil, then cover and simmer for 10 minutes.

2 Add the frozen peas, bring back to the boil, cover and simmer for 2 minutes. Stir in the spinach, cover and cook for a further 3 minutes.

3 Remove the pan from the heat and leave the soup for 1 minute to cool slightly. Purée using a blender. Reheat for 1–2 minutes, if necessary. Pour the soup into four bowls and serve with generous helpings of the mint yogurt.

COOK'S TIP
● This soup freezes well, without the yogurt topping, for up to 3 months. Make twice the quantity and store half immediately in a lidded container. Thaw completely, then reheat to boiling point, stirring frequently, before serving with the yogurt swirl.

SUPER FOOD

SPINACH

Rich in nutrients, spinach is an excellent source of folate – a vitamin needed for good blood circulation and a healthy pregnancy. The vegetable also contains fibre to promote digestive health and iron to help to prevent anaemia.

COCK-A-LEEKIE SOUP WITH KALE

This traditional Scottish recipe includes chunks of tender chicken, sweet kale, soft leeks and vitamin-filled prunes to keep you energised throughout the day. Serve with a crusty baguette.

Serves 4
Preparation 15 minutes
Cooking 20 minutes

400 g boneless, skinless chicken breast
350 g leeks
1 tablespoon olive oil or canola oil
2 carrots, about 150 g
1.2 litres hot chicken stock
350 g kale
100 g pitted prunes

Each serving provides
• 1004 kJ • 240 kcal • 24 g protein
• 7 g fat of which 1 g saturates
• 15 g carbohydrates of which
14 g sugars • 7 g fibre

ALTERNATIVE INGREDIENTS
• Fresh savoy cabbage or spring greens make good alternatives to kale.

1 Cut the chicken breast fillets into 3 cm cubes. Trim, slice and rinse the leeks. Heat the oil in a large saucepan over a high heat. Add the chicken and leeks and cook for 5 minutes, reducing the heat to medium after the first 1–2 minutes. Stir occasionally.

2 Slice the carrots. Pour the hot stock into the pan. Add the carrots and bring to the boil over a high heat, stirring, then reduce the heat to low. Cover and simmer for 10 minutes, or until the carrots are tender.

3 Finely shred the kale and stir into the pan. Bring back to the boil then reduce the heat, re-cover and simmer for 4 minutes. Chop the prunes into quarters and stir them into the soup. Simmer for 1 minute, season to taste and then ladle into four bowls to serve.

COOK'S TIPS
● To shred leafy green vegetables such as kale, tightly roll up a few leaves together and slice them thinly with a sharp knife. For short shreds, cut the slices in half. Alternatively, ready-prepared vegetables, especially frozen, are a labour-saving option for everyday cooking.
● Organic chicken stock is a good choice as it has a light flavour and is not too high in salt.
● If fresh vegetables are not to hand, use mixed frozen broccoli and cauliflower instead of kale. Add the florets with the prunes in step 3 so that they remain crunchy.

SUPER FOOD

LEEKS
Among a leek's many phytochemicals is a rich amount of carotenoids, especially beta-carotene, a natural anti-oxidant. With potassium to help to regulate blood pressure, and B vitamins, including folate, leeks are a good all-rounder for heart and digestive health.

CAPSICUM AND TOMATO SOUP WITH A SPICY EGG

For a bowl of sunshine, try a rustic soup packed with the vivid goodness of tomato and red capsicum, topped with a chilli-flecked fried egg. It makes a filling snack or tasty light supper.

Serves 4
Preparation 10 minutes
Cooking 25 minutes

1 onion
1 stick celery
2 red capsicums
3 tablespoons olive oil
400 g can chopped tomatoes
600 ml hot chicken stock
1 spring onion
4 eggs
pinch of chilli flakes

Each serving provides
• 1050 kJ • 251 kcal • 10 g protein
• 19 g fat of which 4 g saturates
• 11 g carbohydrates of which
10 g sugars • 3 g fibre

ALTERNATIVE INGREDIENTS
• To boost the fibre content of this dish, drain a 400 g can of cannellini beans or red kidney beans and add them in step 2.
• For a meaty soup, slice 100 g chorizo sausage and add it to the soup at the end of step 3 to warm through while the eggs are frying.
• For a complete meal in a bowl, add 50 g miniature pasta shapes in step 2 during the final 5 minutes of cooking.

1 Chop the onion and dice the celery and capsicums. Put 1 tablespoon of the oil in a large saucepan over a high heat. Add the onion, celery and capsicums and cook for about 30 seconds, or until sizzling. Reduce the heat to medium–high, cover with a lid and cook for 5 minutes, shaking the pan occasionally, until the vegetables are softened.

2 Add the tomatoes and stir in the hot stock. Bring back to the boil. Reduce the heat, re-cover and simmer the soup for 15 minutes. Trim and finely chop the spring onion.

3 Heat the remaining 2 tablespoons of oil in a large frying pan over a medium-high heat. Break in the eggs and fry for 1–2 minutes, or until the whites are set but the yolks are soft. Season the soup to taste and ladle into bowls. Float an egg on each portion and sprinkle with the chopped spring onion and chilli flakes.

COOK'S TIP
● An alternative is break the eggs directly into the soup and allow them to poach for 1–1½ minutes. The trick is to have the soup bubbling steadily when the eggs are added, then regulate the heat to keep the liquid simmering gently. Use a slotted spoon to transfer the eggs to each bowl before ladling in the soup.

SUPER FOOD

TOMATOES
The anti-oxidant lycopene in tomatoes gives them their wonderful rich colour. Lycopene is more easily absorbed by the body from processed or cooked tomatoes, so it pays to enjoy them canned or in a paste, as well as fresh. As a rich source of potassium, tomatoes can help to regulate blood pressure, reducing the risk of stroke.

CHUNKY FISH AND VEGETABLE SOUP

Aromatic lemon and herbs blend brilliantly with leeks and broad beans to make a perfect match for pieces of succulent white fish. This robust soup is low in fat and really satisfying.

Serves 4
Preparation 10 minutes
Cooking 20 minutes

Each serving provides
- 1305 kJ • 312 kcal • 28 g protein
- 10 g fat of which 1 g saturates
- 29 g carbohydrates of which
9 g sugars • 7 g fibre

1 large leek
2 tablespoons olive oil
2 cloves garlic, crushed
4 sprigs fresh thyme
2 bay leaves
2 x 400 g cans chopped tomatoes
600 ml hot fish stock
450 g skinless firm white fish, such
   as bream, snapper, cod or hapuka
¼ cucumber
200 g frozen baby broad beans
grated zest of 1 lemon
100 g shop-bought croutons

ALTERNATIVE INGREDIENTS
• Try a mixture of salmon and white fish or mixed seafood. If using frozen mixed seafood, add an extra 1 minute of cooking time in step 3.
• For a subtle aniseed flavour, add 1 large bulb fennel and cut it into slim wedges, then slice these across into shreds. Cook the fennel with the leek in step 1.
• Frozen peas or sweetcorn can be used instead of the broad beans.
• For a more substantial soup, add a drained 400 g can of cannellini or black-eyed beans with the broad beans.

1 Finely chop the leek. Heat the oil in a large saucepan over a high heat, then add the leek, garlic, thyme and bay leaves. Cover and cook for 2 minutes, reducing the heat if the vegetables begin to brown too quickly.

2 Stir in the tomatoes and the hot stock. Bring back to the boil, cover, reduce the heat to low and simmer for 15 minutes. Meanwhile, cut the fish into 3 cm square chunks and dice the cucumber.

3 Add the broad beans to the pan, cover and bring back to the boil. Reduce the heat so that the soup is bubbling gently then add the fish, lemon zest and cucumber. Cover and simmer for 3 minutes, or until the fish is cooked through. Ladle into four bowls, add a sprinkling of croutons to each one and serve.

COOK'S TIPS
● When buying fresh fish, choose fillets or steaks that are firm and translucent. Fish that smells fishy is probably past its best. If you are concerned about sustainability, buy fish that is responsibly caught or farmed. If buying supermarket fish, look out for a logo stating that the fish has come from a sustainable source.
● Croutons are available in different sizes and flavours, so you can add your own twist to the presentation and taste. Alternatively, make your own: toast four thick slices of wholemeal bread and cut into chunks just before serving.

SUPER FOOD

WHITE FISH
Government guidelines recommend that we eat more fish – at least one serving of white fish per week – to maintain good health. White fish is low in fat, high in protein and rich in iodine, vital for a healthy metabolism.

FRESH **TUNA** AND **BEAN** SALAD

What better way could there be to get those all-important omega-3 oils? Arrange strips of lightly seared tuna next to a lemony bean salad infused with garlic and basil for a tangy lunch or starter.

Serves 4
Preparation 20 minutes
Cooking 1 minute

Each serving provides
• 920 kJ • 220 kcal • 17 g protein
• 15 g carbohydrates of which
2 g sugars • 10 g fat of which
2 g saturates • 5 g fibre

1 small red onion
400 g can cannellini beans
1 small clove garlic, chopped
zest of 1 lemon
4 tablespoons chopped fresh parsley
8 fresh basil leaves, finely shredded, plus extra whole leaves, to garnish
2 tablespoons olive oil
150 g tuna steak
4 lemon wedges, to garnish

ALTERNATIVE INGREDIENTS
• Use 200 g smoked mackerel, boned and flaked, instead of the tuna.
• Grilled haloumi cheese is a delicious vegetarian alternative with the bean salad. Brown the slices under a hot grill for 30 seconds on each side.
• This salad also makes a good base for grilled salmon fillet. Cook the fillets, flesh side up, under a very hot grill for about 1 minute until just firm.

1 Thinly slice the onion. Drain and rinse the cannellini beans. In a bowl, mix the cannellini beans with the garlic, onion, lemon zest, parsley, shredded basil and oil. Cover and leave to stand for 15 minutes.

2 Meanwhile, cut the tuna steak into slices about 5 mm thick. Heat a heavy non-stick frying pan over a high heat, add the tuna slices and fry for 30 seconds to brown. Turn the fish over and fry for a further 30 seconds. Remove from the heat immediately.

3 Divide the bean salad among four plates. Arrange 3–4 tuna slices on one side and garnish each portion with a lemon wedge and whole basil leaves.

SUPER FOOD

TUNA
Unlike canned tuna, fresh tuna is rich in health-promoting omega-3 oils. In addition to their proven heart benefits, these oils can alleviate inflammatory conditions such as rheumatoid arthritis and joint stiffness. One weekly serving of oily fish, such as herring, salmon, mackerel or fresh tuna, provides your daily requirement.

COOK'S TIPS
● The frying pan must be very hot so that the tuna browns and cooks almost immediately. If you do not have a non-stick pan, add 1 tablespoon olive oil or canola oil before adding the tuna. Use tongs for turning the tuna, or try a spatula and fork.
● For rare tuna still pink in the middle, cook the steak whole, browning it for 30–60 seconds on each side, then remove from the heat and slice. This method is best suited to really fresh tuna. Pre-packed or frozen tuna is better cooked until opaque.

BEANS

In all its forms, from tender garden-fresh green beans to robust dried kidney beans, this humble vegetable soaks up flavours while contributing a generous helping of fibre for gut health and enriching the blood with iron. Beans fill you up but are low in fat, and as most beans contain at least 20 per cent protein they are an excellent alternative to meat for vegetarians.

WARM CITRUS BEAN SALAD

Serves 4
Preparation 10 minutes Cooking 15 minutes

Each serving provides • 435 kJ • 104 kcal
• 6 g protein • 5 g fat of which 1 g saturates
• 9 g carbohydrates of which 2 g sugars • 7 g fibre

Boil **400 g frozen baby broad beans** in a saucepan of boiling water for 3 minutes, or until just tender, then drain and set aside. Heat **1 tablespoon olive oil** in a frying pan and add **2 finely chopped French shallots** and **1 crushed clove garlic**. Stir-fry over a medium heat for 8 minutes, or until softened. Add the beans to the onions in the pan with **2 tablespoons finely chopped fresh mint, 2 tablespoons finely chopped fresh parsley** and the **juice of ½ lemon**. Cook for 2 minutes, stirring occasionally, before serving.

COOK'S TIPS

● If the broad beans are large, remove the outer pale green cases. Pour boiling water over them, leave for 2–3 minutes, then drain and refresh with cold water. Pop the beans out of the cases.

● This dish works really well with grilled chicken or smoky bacon.

● Use the juice of 1 lemon to sharpen the flavour and serve with steamed white fish fillets.

SUMMER BEAN RISOTTO

Serves 4
Preparation 5 minutes Cooking 30 minutes

Each serving provides • 2494 kJ • 596 kcal
• 19 g protein • 12 g fat of which 4 g saturates
• 110 g carbohydrates of which 5 g sugars • 7 g fibre

Heat **1 tablespoon olive oil** in a large frying pan and add **1 thinly sliced large onion**. Cook over a medium–low heat for 5 minutes, or until softened. Stir in **2 finely chopped cloves garlic**. Add **400 g risotto rice**, turn up the heat to medium–high, and stir to coat all the rice with oil. Add **1 tablespoon fresh thyme** and the **juice of 1 lemon**. Begin to add **4 cups (1 litre) hot vegetable stock** to the pan in 200 ml batches, allowing the rice to absorb each amount of stock before adding more. Drain and rinse **600 g canned cannellini beans** and add to the pan when half the stock is used up. Season to taste with plenty of **ground black pepper**. After about 25 minutes, or when all the liquid is absorbed, the rice grains should be soft and creamy. If the rice is not tender, continue to add more hot vegetable stock or water until cooked. Divide the risotto among four bowls and top each portion with **1 tablespoon shaved parmesan**.

COOK'S TIPS

● Replace 100 ml of the stock with dry white wine for a more sophisticated flavour.

● Add 150 g chopped cooked green beans towards the end of the cooking time to boost colour and nutrition.

● Serve the risotto with a crisp green salad.

MEDITERRANEAN GREEN BEANS

Serves 4
Preparation 5 minutes Cooking 15 minutes

Each serving provides • 427 kJ • 102 kcal
• 3 g protein • 7 g fat of which 1 g saturates
• 8 g carbohydrates of which 6 g sugars • 4 g fibre

Top and tail **450 g green beans** and boil in a saucepan for 3 minutes, or until just cooked but still firm. Refresh the beans under cold running water, drain and pat dry. Heat **1 tablespoon olive oil** in a frying pan and stir-fry **1 thinly sliced onion** over a medium heat for about 8 minutes, or until softened. Stir **16 whole red cherry tomatoes** and **2 teaspoons olive oil** into the onions. Cook for 2 minutes, turning the tomatoes gently once or twice. Add the cooked green beans to the pan and stir for 1 minute over the heat to warm through.

COOK'S TIPS

● This tasty and healthy side dish goes very well with beef or chicken. Add 200 g diced cooked potatoes to the pan with the onions for a main dish.

● For extra crunch, add 30 g flaked toasted almonds to the dish before serving.

SPICY CARIBBEAN RICE

Serves 4
Preparation 15 minutes Cooking 45 minutes

Each serving provides • 2259 kJ • 540 kcal
• 16 g protein • 19 g fat of which 9 g saturates
• 81 g carbohydrates of which 15 g sugars • 10 g fibre

Heat **2 tablespoons olive oil or canola oil** in a large frying pan over a medium heat and add **2 finely chopped red onions** and **2 sliced red capsicums** to the pan. Cook for 5 minutes to soften the vegetables, then add **2 finely chopped cloves garlic** and **1 or 2 finely chopped chillies, 1 teaspoon medium pepper sauce** and

2–3 teaspoons paprika. Stir for 1 minute, or until the aromas are released, then add **200 g long-grain brown rice**. Stir to coat all the grains of rice with oil. Pour in **1 cup (250 ml) hot vegetable stock** and **400 ml light coconut milk**. Bring to a simmer then reduce the heat, cover and cook for 15 minutes. Drain and rinse **200 g canned red kidney beans** and **200 g canned black-eyed beans**. Add to the rice with **2 teaspoons dried thyme** and **2 teaspoons dried oregano**. Cover again, simmer for 10 minutes then stir in **4 chopped tomatoes**. Cook uncovered for a further 15 minutes, or until the rice is tender. To serve the dish moist, you may need to add more hot stock or water to leave a small amount of liquid in the pan by the time the rice is cooked.

COOK'S TIP

● For a heartier dish, add small pieces of cooked chicken or bacon to the pan with the tomatoes.

RICH CHICKEN AND BEAN HOTPOT

Serves 4
Preparation 10 minutes Cooking 1 hour

Each serving provides • 1301 kJ • 311 kcal
• 37 g protein • 8 g fat of which 1 g saturates
• 24 g carbohydrates of which 11 g sugars • 7 g fibre

Heat **2 teaspoons olive oil** in a flameproof casserole dish and add **4 boneless, skinless chicken breasts**. Cook for 5 minutes, turning occasionally, until browned on both sides. Remove from the dish and keep warm. Add **1 tablespoon olive oil** to the dish with **2 sliced onions** and **1 chopped celery stick**. Cook over a medium–low heat for 5 minutes, or until softened. Stir in **4 chopped garlic cloves, 200 ml hot chicken stock, 1 bay leaf, 1 teaspoon dried rosemary, 5 skinned chopped tomatoes** (see page 56, No-cook tomato pasta sauce, for how to skin tomatoes) and **100 ml tomato passata**. Cover and cook over a low heat for 20 minutes. Drain and rinse **250 g canned borlotti beans** and add them to the casserole dish with the browned chicken fillets. Simmer for a further 30 minutes with the lid off, stirring occasionally, until the chicken is cooked through and a thick, rich sauce has formed. Serve sprinkled with **2 tablespoons chopped fresh parsley**.

COOK'S TIP

● Sides of crusty bread and a green salad add extra dimensions of flavour and texture.

CARROT PANCAKES WITH PROSCIUTTO AND MANGO

Freshen up these golden pancakes and high-protein prosciutto slivers with delicious slices of firm, ripe mango. Bursting with anti-oxidants and vitamin C, it tastes fabulous, too.

Serves 4
Preparation 10 minutes
Cooking 10 minutes

Each serving provides
- 2067 kJ • 494 kcal • 11 g protein
- 39 g fat of which 6 g saturates
- 27 g carbohydrates of which
8 g sugars • 3 g fibre

For the pancakes
1 small carrot
⅔ cup (100 g) self-raising flour
1 egg
100 ml low-fat milk
2 tablespoons chopped fresh parsley
1 tablespoon olive oil or canola oil

For the mango salad
1 ripe mango
8 slices prosciutto
4 sprigs fresh basil, to garnish
2 tablespoons olive oil

ALTERNATIVE INGREDIENTS
- Try other types of air-dried ham such as westphalian or serrano instead of prosciutto.
- Use papaya either as an alternative to mango or combined with it. Halve the fruit, scoop out and discard the seeds, then peel and slice the papaya.
- For a lighter fruit flavour with a contrasting crunchy texture, slice 1 starfruit instead of mango, sprinkle the ham with 1 teaspoon lightly toasted pine nuts per portion and drizzle over walnut oil instead of olive oil.

1 First make the pancakes. Finely grate the carrot. Sift the flour into a bowl, add the egg and 25 ml of the milk, then stir the mixture to form a thick paste and beat until smooth. Gradually beat in the remaining 75 ml milk to make a thick batter. Stir in the carrot and parsley.

2 Heat a griddle pan or heavy-based frying pan and brush with a little of the oil. Drop 4 separate dessertspoonfuls of batter into the pan, spacing them well apart. Cook for 2 minutes, or until browned underneath and bubbling on top. Turn and cook the second side for about 1 minute. Transfer the pancakes to a plate lined with a tea towel and wrap them to keep warm. Repeat twice more to make 12 small pancakes.

3 Peel the mango and cut the flesh off the stone in small neat slices (see Cook's Tip). Divide the mango among four plates. Trim away any fat from around the edges of the prosciutto, arrange the slices on the plates then scatter over the basil leaves. Drizzle 2 teaspoons olive oil over each portion of prosciutto and serve with the pancakes.

COOK'S TIP
- To slice mango flesh, use a large knife to make one cut straight down into the stone, then cut the fruit at an angle to remove the first slice. Work outwards, cutting off slices at an angle until the fruit is removed from one flat side. Turn the stone over and repeat for the second half. Peel each slice before serving.

SUPER FOOD

MANGOES
Thanks to its high vitamin C and carotenoid content, the mango is a great source of anti-oxidants, good for boosting immunity and offering protection from heart disease and some cancers.

BEETROOT AND MOZZARELLA WITH RASPBERRY DRESSING

A piquant fruit dressing spices up this salad of creamy mozzarella cheese and earthy beetroot. The raspberries contain natural anti-oxidants that may help to protect against heart disease.

Serves 4
Preparation 10 minutes

100 g raspberries
2 teaspoons runny honey
2 teaspoons cider vinegar
500 g peeled cooked beetroot
150 g mozzarella
50 g fresh flat-leaf parsley
a few whole raspberries, to garnish

Each serving provides
• 699 kJ • 167 kcal • 10 g protein
• 8 g fat of which 5 g saturates
• 15 g carbohydrates of which
14 g sugars • 4 g fibre

ALTERNATIVE INGREDIENTS
• Blackberries taste as good with beetroot as raspberries do.
• For a contrasting flavour, use a cheese with a more pronounced taste, such as roquefort or goat's cheese.
• For a tangy flavour, use fetta instead of mozzarella and tender basil leaves instead of parsley.
• Add orange slices to the beetroot for a citrus kick. Drizzle with a little olive oil, then add the mozzarella. A few fresh oregano leaves make a tasty garnish.

1 Put the raspberries in a bowl and crush them with a fork. Drizzle in the honey then mix in the vinegar to make a thick dressing.

2 Thinly slice the beetroot and arrange the slices on four plates. Dice the mozzarella into 1 cm cubes. Spoon the raspberry dressing over the beetroot and add the mozzarella. Strip the leaves from the parsley, roughly chop and sprinkle over the dish, then garnish with whole raspberries and serve.

COOK'S TIPS
● Make this salad as close to serving time as possible because the raspberries (and raspberry vinegar) will lose their flavour if left for more than an hour.
● Frozen raspberries are ideal for this dressing. Either microwave them on high for 30 seconds, or let them defrost naturally at room temperature for a couple of hours.
● For a more substantial salad, serve with boiled new potatoes – they are great for soaking up the lovely salad juices.
● You can cook beetroot from fresh or, to save time, buy it ready-cooked (see Cook's Tips on page 22).

SUPER FOOD

BEETROOT
Known for its distinctive, deep purple colour, beetroot contains a range of essential vitamins and minerals, including vitamin C, magnesium, potassium and folate. Betaine, a compound important for heart health, is also abundant in beetroot.

TANGY **SARDINE** PÂTÉ

Lemon, garlic and dill deliver flavour punches to a robust fish pâté that is great as a tasty starter or snack. Serve with vine-ripened tomatoes, thin cucumber sticks and a round of crunchy toast.

Serves 4
Preparation 5 minutes

120 g can sardines in olive oil
  or canola oil, drained
1 clove garlic, crushed
grated zest of 1 lemon and juice
  of ½ lemon
125 g low-fat ricotta or low-fat
  cream cheese
1 small spring onion
2 tablespoons chopped fresh dill

Each serving provides
• 348 kJ • 83 kcal • 7 g protein
• 5 g fat of which 3 g saturates
• 1 g carbohydrates of which
1 g sugars • no fibre

ALTERNATIVE INGREDIENTS
• For a fabulous, firm-textured mustard and dill pâté, reduce the quantity of low-fat ricotta or low-fat cream cheese to 50 g and omit the spring onion. Use 2 tablespoons wholegrain mustard instead of the garlic and reduce the zest to ½ lemon and the juice to 1 tablespoon.
• Use canned mackerel in oil instead of sardines. Canned smoked mackerel also makes a tasty alternative to sardines.
• A number of herbs complement sardines. Try chopped fresh parsley as an alternative to dill, adding 4 finely shredded fresh basil leaves to the parsley for a distinctive aroma.

1 Use a fork to mash the sardines with the garlic and lemon zest in a bowl. Stir in the lemon juice when the sardines have a smooth consistency. Add the low-fat ricotta or cream cheese and beat the mixture until all the ingredients are combined.

2 Season to taste and divide the pâté among four ramekins, or spoon it onto plates. Finely chop the spring onion and sprinkle a little over each portion together with the dill.

COOK'S TIPS
● Use leftover pâté to fill rolls or sandwiches. The pâté will keep for up to 2 days in the fridge; store in a sealed container to prevent the strong smell of garlic and fish from contaminating other food.
● Make double the quantity of pâté and freeze half of it to use on another occasion. Store in an airtight container for up to 2 months.

SUPER FOOD

SARDINES
One of the few foods rich in vitamin D, sardines help to boost dietary intake of this essential vitamin. Vitamin D is needed for the formation and maintenance of bones and the absorption of calcium into the body. It may also play a role in protecting against breast, prostate and colon cancers, and heart disease.

ASPARAGUS AND HAM GRILL

Quick to prepare and with a no-fuss cheesy sauce, this grill is sure to become a favourite for a tasty hot lunch. Asparagus provides a host of health benefits, so make the most of it when it is in season.

Serves 4
Preparation 5 minutes
Cooking 12 minutes

Each serving provides
- 713 kJ • 170 kcal • 17 g protein
- 10 g fat of which 6 g saturates
- 3 g carbohydrates of which
2 g sugars • 1 g fibre

12 asparagus spears
4 large slices cooked ham, about 150 g
150 g low-fat ricotta or low-fat cream cheese
1 teaspoon cornflour
50 g parmesan
3 tablespoons milk
2 tablespoons snipped fresh chives

ALTERNATIVE INGREDIENTS
- Try baby leeks instead of asparagus. Allow 2–3 leeks per portion and poach them in a pan of boiling water for 3–5 minutes, or until tender.
- Use crumbled blue cheese instead of parmesan.

1 Trim any tough ends off the asparagus (see Cook's Tip) and lay the spears in a large frying pan. Add just enough boiling water to cover, then bring back to the boil over a high heat. Reduce the heat, cover the pan and simmer for about 5 minutes, or until the spears are just tender.

2 Meanwhile, lay the ham on a board. Preheat the grill to medium–high and have a large ovenproof dish or four gratin dishes ready for step 3. In a bowl, mix the ricotta or low-fat cream cheese and cornflour. Finely grate the parmesan. Reserve 1 tablespoon of the parmesan and stir the rest into the mixture. Whisk in the milk.

3 Drain the asparagus and lay three spears over each slice of ham. Roll up and place in the prepared dish. Spoon the cheese mixture over the ham and sprinkle with the remaining 1 tablespoon of parmesan. Cover any protruding asparagus tips with foil.

4 Grill the asparagus and ham rolls for 5–6 minutes, or until the cheese topping is bubbling and browned. Sprinkle over the snipped chives before serving.

COOK'S TIP
● If the spears have slightly tough ends, trim them off with a knife or snap them off – the stems will break at their weakest point, where the tender spear meets the woody end. Use the woody parts to flavour a stock, straining and discarding them before use.

SUPER FOOD

ASPARAGUS
This colourful vegetable is a good source of energy-releasing B vitamins, including folate, which lowers the risk of heart disease and stroke. With calcium and magnesium to maintain strong bones, asparagus is an all-round super food.

GARLIC **MUSHROOMS** WITH **SUN-DRIED TOMATOES**

Great for soaking up the garlic flavour and as a contrast to the intense sweet tomatoes, mushrooms are also low in kilojoules and a good source of fibre. It all adds up to a mouth-watering, satisfying dish, wonderful hot or cold.

Serves 4
Preparation 5 minutes
Cooking 5 minutes

Each serving provides
• 858 kJ • 205 kcal • 5 g protein
• 16 g fat of which 2 g saturates
• 10 g carbohydrates of which
7 g sugars • 6 g fibre

500 g button mushrooms
4 tablespoons olive oil
4 cloves garlic, crushed
12 sun-dried tomato halves
20 g chopped fresh flat-leaf
** parsley**
lemon wedges, to garnish

ALTERNATIVE INGREDIENTS
• Use Swiss brown mushrooms instead of button mushrooms for a slightly stronger flavour.
• Try nut oils instead of olive oil. Cook the garlic in the olive oil then add walnut or hazelnut oil in step 2.
• Add sunflower seeds to the ingredients. Roast 2–3 tablespoons sunflower seeds in a dry pan and remove them before adding the oil and garlic. Sprinkle the seeds over the mushrooms before serving.

1 Halve the mushrooms and trim any long stalks. Heat 1 tablespoon of the oil in a large saucepan. Add the garlic and cook for 1 minute over a high heat until it begins to sizzle.

2 Add the mushrooms and continue to cook, stirring occasionally, for 4 minutes. When the mushrooms begin to brown, remove the pan from the heat and toss them in the remaining oil.

3 Slice the sun-dried tomatoes and stir them into the mushrooms together with the parsley. Season to taste and garnish with lemon wedges before serving.

COOK'S TIPS
● To serve cold, add the sun-dried tomatoes in step 3, then transfer the mushroom mixture to a bowl, cover and marinate for 15 minutes. Add the parsley just before serving.
● Larger mushrooms also work well in this recipe if they are quartered, but do not use open-cap mushrooms, with the soft gills exposed, as they are not firm enough.

SUPER FOOD

MUSHROOMS
A useful source of fibre, mushrooms contain energy-releasing B vitamins and minerals, too. They are rich in selenium, an important anti-oxidant that may help to prevent heart disease and cancer, as well as being high in folate for healthy blood and circulation.

GINGER AND APRICOT RAREBIT

Here is a lively and unusual version of an old favourite that combines the zing of ginger and the succulence of apricots with a high-calcium cheese for a really nutritious snack.

Serves 4
Preparation 10 minutes
Cooking 5 minutes

50 g fresh ginger
75 g dried apricots
4 thick slices wholegrain bread
125 g grated cheddar
50 g rocket
50 g watercress
lemon wedges, to garnish

Each serving provides
• 1138 kJ • 272 kcal • 13 g protein
• 12 g fat of which 7 g saturates
• 29 g carbohydrates of which
9 g sugars • 3 g fibre

ALTERNATIVE INGREDIENTS
• To help you achieve your seven serves of fruit and vegetables per day, dice 1 eating apple and add it to the toast in addition to the ginger and apricots.
• Leave out the ginger and use 50 g chopped dates instead of the apricots.
• Top with crumbled fetta instead of cheddar.

1 Preheat the grill to the hottest setting. Cut the ginger into fine strips and slice the apricots. Toast the bread slices on one side under the grill. Turn the slices and lay them close together in the grill pan.

2 Scatter the ginger and apricots evenly over the bread, then sprinkle with the cheese, right up to the edges. Toast for 5 minutes, or until the cheese is bubbling and golden.

3 Divide the rarebits among four plates and serve with the rocket and watercress leaves garnished with lemon wedges.

COOK'S TIPS
● Adding the topping to the untoasted side of the bread means that the crusts do not burn before the cheese has melted. The result is a crisp base with a moist top.
● Instead of grating the cheese, pare off thin slices using a potato peeler to get a more even covering.

SUPER FOOD

GINGER
Ginger has traditionally been used to stimulate appetite and soothe the digestive system, promoting normal gut movement and reducing nausea.

MINTED **CELERY** HUMMUS

Celery gives a lovely light crunch to this high-fibre chickpea dip, while mint imparts a clean, fresh flavour. Serve with vegetable sticks and warm pita bread for a quick, healthy low-fat snack.

Serves 4
Preparation 10 minutes

Each serving provides
• 1050 kJ • 251 kcal • 7 g protein
• 19 g fat of which 3 g saturates
• 13 g carbohydrates of which
1 g sugars • 1 g fibre

400 g can chickpeas, drained
4 large leaves fresh mint
1 clove garlic
1 tablespoon tahini
4 tablespoons olive oil
1 stick celery
grated zest and juice of 1 lemon
mint sprigs, to garnish

1 Put the chickpeas, mint, garlic and tahini in a food processor and reduce to a crumbly mixture.

2 With the processor motor running, gradually pour in the oil until the mixture forms a thick paste. Continue to process, adding 2 tablespoons of water to soften the hummus if it is very thick.

3 Dice the celery and add it to the processor with the lemon zest and half of the lemon juice. Process for 3 seconds to avoid crushing the celery. Stir in the remaining lemon juice, season to taste and transfer the hummus to a bowl. Serve garnished with mint sprigs.

COOK'S TIPS
● Tahini is a sesame seed paste. It is thick and pale, usually with a layer of oil on the surface when the ground seeds have sunk. Stir well before use.
● If you do not have a food processor, make the hummus in a blender. Use a spatula to scrape the mixture down the sides occasionally so that it processes evenly. Stir in the celery with the remaining lemon juice.
● This hummus will keep in a sealed container in the fridge for 3 days.

ALTERNATIVE INGREDIENTS
• Fennel is delicious and delicate in hummus instead of celery. Use a quarter of a fennel bulb, finely diced, and do not use mint. For a more pronounced flavour, slice off the top of the fennel bulb – the remains of the stalk and any feathery leaves – chop and add them to the hummus with the garlic and chickpeas.
• For a hummus with a rich tomato flavour, finely chop 4 sun-dried tomatoes (drained if stored in olive oil) and add them with the celery in step 3. Leave out the mint leaves and stir in a finely shredded basil sprig. Leave the hummus to stand for 30 minutes and stir before serving.

SUPER FOOD

CHICKPEAS
A low-fat, starchy, high-fibre food, chickpeas are good for digestive health. They also contain calcium, which helps to maintain healthy bones and teeth, and are a useful source of iron, making them a great alternative to red meat.

CHEESY **VEGETABLE** FRITTATA

Tender baby turnips add peppery punch, and plenty of fibre, to zucchini and tomatoes in a layered set omelette. A topping of slices of toasted brie adds a delectable creaminess.

Serves 4
Preparation 10 minutes
Cooking 25 minutes

Each serving provides
- 1623 kJ • 388 kcal • 21 g protein
- 31 g fat of which 13 g saturates
- 8 g carbohydrates of which
7 g sugars • 3 g fibre

1 onion
250 g baby turnips
2 zucchini
2 tablespoons olive oil
1 clove garlic, crushed
5 eggs
3 tablespoons chopped fresh parsley
2 large roma (plum) tomatoes
200 g brie

ALTERNATIVE INGREDIENTS
- Use 250 g small cauliflower florets instead of the baby turnips. When cooking, check that they are tender, but not soft, by piercing with the tip of a sharp knife before adding the zucchini.
- Celeriac makes a change from turnips. Use 250 g diced celeriac and top the frittata with roquefort, gorgonzola or smoked cheese.
- Butternut pumpkin goes well with turnip instead of zucchini. Peel and dice 300 g pumpkin and add it with the turnips in step 1.

1 Finely chop the onion. Peel, halve and thinly slice the turnips. Finely slice the zucchini. Heat 1 tablespoon of the oil in a large lidded frying pan over a high heat. Add the onion, garlic and turnips then turn down the heat to medium–low. Cover and cook for 5 minutes, stirring occasionally, until the turnip slices are tender. Stir in the zucchini, cover and cook for a further 4 minutes, or until the zucchini are tender and beginning to brown in places.

2 Preheat the grill to the hottest setting. Beat the eggs with salt and pepper to taste and the parsley. Add the remaining oil to the pan with the vegetables and heat for a few seconds until sizzling. Pour in the eggs, cover and cook for 10 minutes. After 2 minutes of cooking, using a slice or spatula, lift the set egg off the pan.

3 Slice the tomatoes and cut the brie into four wedges. Place the frying pan under the grill, with the handle sticking out, and grill the frittata for 1 minute to set any uncooked egg. Arrange the tomatoes and the brie slices on top. Grill for a further 4 minutes, or until the brie is lightly golden. Cool for 2–3 minutes before cutting into wedges.

COOK'S TIPS
● The trick with set omelettes – Italian frittata or Spanish tortilla – is to cover the pan to keep in the heat, which helps to set the egg mixture and prevent the underneath from overbrowning on the pan. Regulate the heat – and be patient – for good results.
● This frittata is also great cold for picnics or in lunchboxes. Cool the cooked frittata for 20–30 minutes, cover and chill in the fridge until needed or for up to 24 hours.

SUPER FOOD

TURNIPS
A winter root crop, turnips contain more starchy energy-giving carbohydrates than many other vegetables. They are a good source of fibre, which makes them beneficial for digestive health, and their potassium content can help to regulate blood pressure.

TOMATOES

Fruit or vegetable? Who cares, when tomatoes are jam-packed with health-giving nutrients? Eat just one large tomato and you get over half of your daily vitamin C needs, potassium to aid the control of high blood pressure, a rich supply of carotenes and lycopene, which may help to reduce the risk of cancer.

CHEESY-CRUST BAKED TOMATOES

Serves 4
Preparation 10 minutes Cooking 45 minutes

Each serving provides • 753 kJ • 180 kcal
• 6 g protein • 7 g fat of which 2 g saturates
• 26 g carbohydrates of which 8 g sugars • 3 g fibre

Preheat the oven to 190°C (170°C fan-forced). Cook **75 g brown rice** in a saucepan of boiling water with **½ teaspoon saffron threads** for 20 minutes, or until tender. Slice the tops off **4 large tomatoes** and scoop out the insides, leaving the walls intact. Reserve any juice. Heat **1 tablespoon olive oil** in a frying pan and fry **1 small finely chopped onion** for 5 minutes over a medium heat, or until softened. Add **150 g chopped Swiss brown mushrooms** and stir-fry for 1 minute. When the rice is cooked, drain and combine with the onion and mushroom mixture, **2 tablespoons chopped fresh parsley** and the **reserved tomato juice**. Fill the tomatoes with the mixture. Combine **2 tablespoons fresh breadcrumbs** with **2 tablespoons grated parmesan**, then sprinkle over the tomato tops. Place on a lightly oiled baking tray and brush the tomato skins with a little olive oil or canola oil. Bake in the oven for 20 minutes, or until the tomatoes are tender.

COOK'S TIP
● The stuffed tomatoes are ideal as a starter, or a light lunch served with salad leaves.

NO-COOK TOMATO SAUCE WITH PASTA

Serves 4
Preparation 10 minutes, plus 15 minutes standing
Cooking 12 minutes

Each serving provides • 1701 kJ • 406 kcal
• 11 g protein • 15 g fat of which 2 g saturates
• 56 g carbohydrates of which 5 g sugars • 6 g fibre

Skin **6 ripe tomatoes**. The best way to do this is to remove any stalks, make a cross with a sharp knife on the stalk end and blanch (submerge the tomatoes in boiling water) for 1–2 minutes, or until the skins start to split. Drain and peel off the skins. Chop the tomatoes and transfer to a bowl. Crush **2 cloves garlic** with **1 teaspoon sea salt** in a mortar and pestle or small bowl and mix until you have a paste, then add this to the tomatoes. Stir in **2 tablespoons chopped fresh parsley, 2 tablespoons finely shredded fresh basil leaves, 3 tablespoons olive oil, 1 tablespoon red**

wine vinegar and add **ground black pepper** to taste. Leave to stand for 15 minutes at room temperature, covered, then stir again. Cook **300 g pasta** for 12 minutes, or according to the packet instructions. Drain the pasta, return to the pan and stir in the tomato sauce. The heat of the pasta will warm the sauce.

COOK'S TIP

● If you prefer, you can heat the sauce for a short while in a bowl in the microwave or in a saucepan.

SUMMER SEAFOOD SALAD

Serves 4
Preparation 10 minutes Marinating 30 minutes

Each serving provides • 1460 kJ • 349 kcal
• 15 g protein • 28 g fat of which 5 g saturates
• 9 g carbohydrates of which 7 g sugars • 4 g fibre

Thaw **300 g frozen mixed cooked seafood** overnight in the fridge or, if available, use the equivalent weight of fresh cooked mussels, prawns and sliced squid. Halve **350 g ripe cherry tomatoes** and place in a large bowl. Rinse and drain the seafood and add to the bowl with **1 thinly sliced small red capsicum** and **2 peeled sliced ripe avocados**. In a small bowl combine **3 tablespoons olive oil** with **2 teaspoons chilli sauce** (optional), **2 teaspoons white wine vinegar, a pinch of paprika** and **ground black pepper** to taste. Cover and set aside in a cool place for 30 minutes to allow the flavours to develop at room temperature. Place a handful of salad leaves on four plates then spoon a quarter of the seafood mixture onto each plate. Garnish with **1 tablespoon chopped fresh coriander** per portion.

COOK'S TIPS

● Using a mixture of golden, orange and red tomato varieties will make this salad look even more appetising.
● Replace the seafood with the same quantity of prawns or dressed crab for a more conventional salad.

CLASSIC TOMATO SOUP

Serves 4
Preparation 35 minutes Cooking 30 minutes

Each serving provides • 607 kJ • 145 kcal
• 4 g protein • 7 g fat of which 2 g saturates
• 16 g carbohydrates of which 15 g sugars • 3 g fibre

Skin and chop **1 kg firm ripe tomatoes** (see opposite, No-cook tomato sauce with pasta, for how to skin tomatoes). Heat **1 tablespoon olive oil** over a medium heat and add **1 finely chopped onion**. Stir-fry the

onions for 3 minutes, or until just softened. Add **1 large chopped clove garlic** and **1 teaspoon paprika** and continue to stir-fry for 1 minute. Stir in **2 tablespoons tomato purée**, then cook for a further 2 minutes. Add the chopped tomatoes, without the juice if watery, **2 teaspoons caster sugar, 1 bay leaf, 600 ml hot vegetable stock** and **½ cup (125 ml) low-fat milk**. Bring the soup to a simmer and cook, uncovered, for 20 minutes. Remove the bay leaf, allow the soup to cool a little, then purée in a blender (or in the pan using a stick blender) until smooth. Reheat, season to taste and ladle into four bowls. Sprinkle each serving with **1 teaspoon snipped fresh chives**.

COOK'S TIPS

● Classic tomato soup is often made with cream instead of milk, but the low-fat milk still gives a creamy texture to the finished soup and is lower in fat.
● Drizzle 1–2 teaspoons of pouring cream into each bowl for a touch of indulgence.

TRICOLOUR TOMATO TOWERS

Serves 4
Preparation 15 minutes

Each serving provides • 1870 kJ • 447 kcal
• 25 g protein • 35 g fat of which 17 g saturates
• 8 g carbohydrates of which 8 g sugars • 3 g fibre

Lightly crush **2 tablespoons pine nuts** in a bowl and combine with **3 tablespoons shop-bought basil pesto** and **4 finely chopped spring onions**. Rinse and pat dry **2 soft Italian mozzarella balls (about 200 g)** then carefully cut each one into 8 thin slices. Slice the bottom off each of **4 large tomatoes** to make a flat base, then cut each tomato into five horizontal layers. Reassemble each tomato on a serving plate, spreading a little pesto mixture and adding a slice of mozzarella between each tomato layer. Slowly drizzle **½ teaspoon olive oil** over each tomato and garnish with **2–3 small fresh basil leaves**.

COOK'S TIPS

● Make sure that the tomatoes are ripe yet firm, or they will be hard to slice evenly and will not retain their shape when stacked.
● If you are concerned about the layers slipping, insert a cocktail stick down through the centre of the tomato, but tell your diners before serving.

WALNUT AND BASIL PESTO PASTA

Packed with Italian flavour and the intense aroma of basil, pesto sauce makes a brilliant partner for wholewheat pasta. For a tasty twist, the pesto uses walnuts instead of the more usual pine nuts.

Serves 4
Preparation 5 minutes
Cooking 15 minutes

25 g parmesan
1 small clove garlic
50 g walnuts
10 g fresh basil leaves
4 tablespoons olive oil
300 g wholewheat pasta, such as fusilli, penne or spaghetti

Each serving provides
• 2134 kJ • 510 kcal • 13 g protein
• 27 g fat of which 4 g saturates
• 58 g carbohydrates of which 2 g sugars • 3 g fibre

ALTERNATIVE INGREDIENTS
• For a traditional pesto, replace the walnuts with 50 g pine nuts.
• Rather than serving the pesto with pasta, use it in rolls, sandwiches or wraps. Spread the pesto thinly instead of butter or mayonnaise as a base for salad-leaf fillings, tomatoes, sliced hard-boiled eggs or cooked, diced chicken.
• For a more substantial meal with added protein, grill four plain fish steaks, such as cod, salmon or tuna, and place one on top of each portion of pesto pasta just before serving.

1 Cut the parmesan into 1 cm pieces. Mix the garlic, parmesan, walnuts and basil (reserving a few leaves to garnish) in a food processor until reduced to a crumbly paste. Alternatively, use a blender or a vegetable chopper.

2 With the motor running, gradually pour in the oil to create a coarse, thick paste.

3 Fill a large saucepan with boiling water. Add the pasta, bring back to the boil and cook for 12–15 minutes, or refer to the packet instructions for specific cooking times.

4 Drain the pasta in a colander and return it to the pan. Add the pesto and toss to coat evenly. Transfer the pesto pasta to four warmed plates, garnish with the reserved basil leaves and serve.

COOK'S TIPS
● To test if the pasta is cooked, carefully remove a piece with a slotted spoon, cool under cold running water and taste. It should be firm but not crunchy or chalky in the middle – and certainly not mushy.
● Pesto freezes well and is a great way of preserving home-grown basil leaves. Freeze the pesto in pots that contain sufficient sauce for one meal. Thaw it in the fridge overnight or at room temperature for 2–3 hours before use.

SUPER FOOD

OLIVE OIL
Eighty per cent of the fats in olive oil are heart-healthy monounsaturated and polyunsaturated fats, containing vitamin E, which helps protect against heart disease. Virgin olive oil, and particularly extra virgin, is high in anti-oxidants. Like all oils, olive oil is high in kilojoules, so should be used sparingly for weight control.

BANANA AND DATE
BREAKFAST BAGEL

Bananas and wholemeal bagels release energy slowly, so here is a satisfying snack guaranteed to keep you alert and to stave off hunger until lunchtime. The mixed seeds are full of protein.

Serves 4
Preparation 10 minutes
Cooking 5 minutes

4 wholemeal bagels
120 g low-fat ricotta or low-fat
   cream cheese
2 large bananas
12 pitted dates, about 85 g
8 tablespoons mixed seeds
   (see Cook's Tips)
4 teaspoons runny honey

Each serving provides
• 1895 kJ • 453 kcal • 17 g protein
• 17 g fat of which 4 g saturates
• 60 g carbohydrates of which
33 g sugars • 9 g fibre

ALTERNATIVE INGREDIENTS
• Allow 2 stoned and sliced fresh apricots per bagel instead of banana.
• Ring the changes by using different bread bases. English muffins have a similar soft bready texture to bagels, while French brioche rolls are richer and slightly sweet. Thin slices of dark rye bread or linseed bread also work well. Increase the quantity of honey to 6 teaspoons when using firmer breads.
• For added fibre, include 1 tablespoon each of rye grain and whole flaked oats in the seed mix before sprinkling over the bagels.

1 Preheat the grill to the hottest setting. Cut the bagels in half horizontally and toast them, cut sides down, for 2 minutes until warm but not overly browned.

2 Spread the untoasted sides of the bagels with ricotta or cream cheese, then place them, cheese side up, in a large ovenproof dish. Alternatively, cover the grill pan with foil before adding the bagels, but be careful as the pan will be hot.

3 Slice the bananas at a slight angle and arrange the slices over the bagels. Chop the dates into thirds and place the pieces on and around the banana. Sprinkle each bagel half with seeds then drizzle with honey. Grill the bagels for 3 minutes, or until the topping is hot. Watch carefully to ensure that the seeds do not burn.

COOK'S TIPS
● There are many brands of mixed seeds in shops and supermarkets and most contain sunflower, sesame and pumpkin seeds as the main ingredients. Store any leftover seeds in an airtight container.
● Buy raw seeds and toast them lightly in a dry, heavy-based frying pan over a medium heat, stirring frequently until lightly browned. Cool completely before storing in an airtight container.

SUPER FOOD

BANANAS
Ripe bananas are great energy boosters, and with their low to moderate glycaemic index (GI) rating provide a sustained energy supply. Full of essential potassium, bananas can help to regulate blood pressure, reducing the risk of a stroke.

RASPBERRY, BANANA
AND **OAT** SMOOTHIE

Beautiful to look at and delightful to taste, this feel-good high-fibre drink provides both quick-release and slow-burning energy that lasts for hours. Raspberries are high in anti-oxidants, too.

Serves 4
Preparation 5 minutes

2 large bananas
60 g rolled oats
200 g raspberries
1 tablespoon honey
8 raspberries, to garnish

Each serving provides
• 628 kJ • 150 kcal • 3 g protein
• 2 g fat (no saturates)
• 32 g carbohydrates of which
20 g sugars • 3 g fibre

ALTERNATIVE INGREDIENTS
• Use 200 g blackberries, redcurrants or blackcurrants instead of the raspberries for an equally refreshing and good-for-you smoothie.
• For a chilled smoothie, substitute frozen mixed berries for fresh raspberries.

1 Peel the bananas and cut them into 3 cm chunks. Put the bananas, oats and raspberries in a blender. Pour in the honey and 1 cup (250 ml) cold water. Purée until smooth, then add another 1 cup (250 ml) water and blend for a further 4–5 seconds.

2 Pour the smoothie into four tall glasses. Garnish with 2 raspberries per glass and serve immediately.

COOK'S TIPS
● For a refreshing raspberry drink that is tangy rather than sweet, use just-ripe bananas, which contain less sugar than very ripe fruit.
● Rolled oats are large flakes often sold as traditional or original porridge oats. Do not buy fine, medium or coarse oatmeal as it will not amalgamate into the drink.

SUPER FOOD

RASPBERRIES
Raspberries are full of nutrient goodness – they are a valuable source of fibre, contain potassium, which helps to regulate blood pressure, and pack an anti-oxidant punch thanks to their high levels of vitamin C and flavonoids.

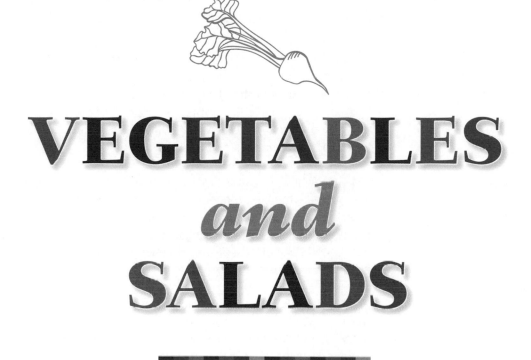

VEGETABLES
and
SALADS

GOLDEN **PUMPKIN** WITH **CAPSICUM** AND **ALMONDS**

Succulent is the word for a sunny medley of vitamin-rich butternut pumpkin and yellow capsicum in a nut and honey glaze. It's ideal as a side dish or a vegetarian main course with country-style bread.

Serves 4
Preparation 10 minutes
Cooking 20 minutes

½ butternut pumpkin, about 600 g
2 cloves garlic
2 tablespoons olive oil
8 sprigs fresh thyme
2 large yellow capsicums
¼ cup (40 g) whole almonds
1 tablespoon honey
finely pared zest and juice of
   1 lemon

Each serving provides
• 809 kJ • 195 kcal • 6 g protein
• 9 g fat of which 1 g saturates
• 25 g carbohydrates of which
17 g sugars • 6 g fibre

ALTERNATIVE INGREDIENTS
• When in season, use 2–3 small yellow button squash, halved, per portion instead of the butternut pumpkin slices. Add 10 minutes to the cooking time.
• Eggplant slices work well in place of butternut pumpkin. Allow 3 large slices per portion or 2 large eggplant in total. When available, use white-skinned eggplant for a change.
• Try pistachios instead of almonds and add 50 g sliced pitted black olives.

1 Preheat the oven to 200°C (180°C fan-forced). Peel the pumpkin and scoop out the seeds. Cut the pumpkin into 12 slices, each about 1 cm thick. Transfer the slices to a shallow roasting tin. Slice the garlic. Drizzle the pumpkin slices with 1 tablespoon of the oil and add the garlic and thyme. Roast in the oven for 20 minutes, or until softened and beginning to brown.

2 Meanwhile, slice the capsicums into 1 cm strips. When the pumpkin has just 5 minutes of cooking time left, heat the remaining 1 tablespoon of oil in a frying pan over a medium–high heat. Add the capsicum strips and fry for 5 minutes, stirring frequently, until they are tender and beginning to brown. Transfer the capsicum and pumpkin to a warmed serving dish.

3 Add the almonds, honey and lemon zest and juice to the frying pan. Stir-fry over a high heat for a few seconds until the mixture is bubbling and the lemon juice and honey have thickened to form a glaze. Spoon over the vegetables and serve.

COOK'S TIPS
● Butternut pumpkin will continue to soften after it has been removed from the oven. To test if it is cooked, carefully prick with a fork – it should be tender but firm.
● Use either set or runny honey. To measure out set honey, use a knife to fill a tablespoon measure. With runny honey, dip the spoon into the jar then scrape off the excess honey from the sides of the spoon and level the top with a knife.

SUPER FOOD

BUTTERNUT PUMPKIN
A source of both types of fibre – soluble and insoluble – butternut pumpkin helps to promote digestive health and lower blood cholesterol. The nutrient-packed orange flesh is bursting with anti-oxidants alpha- and beta-carotene, as well as vitamin E.

HERBED **ASPARAGUS** OMELETTES

The delicate flavour of asparagus combines perfectly with light fluffy eggs in a nutritious dish that can be rustled up in minutes. Serve with a salad and sliced tomato drizzled with olive oil.

Serves 2
Preparation 5 minutes
Cooking 8 minutes

8 asparagus spears
4 eggs
4 tablespoons chopped fresh dill
10 g butter

Each serving provides
• 1075 kJ • 257 kcal • 20 g protein
• 18 g fat of which 3 g saturates
• 5 g carbohydrates of which
4 g sugars • 3 g fibre

ALTERNATIVE INGREDIENTS
• If you are concerned about your cholesterol levels, use 1 tablespoon of olive oil per omelette instead of butter. Heat it in the pan until hot rather than adding it to a hot pan.
• Use chopped mixed fresh herbs instead of dill – fennel, parsley, chives, thyme and tarragon all go nicely with eggs.
• For a fish and herb omelette, add 25 g chopped smoked salmon per portion, sprinkling it over the egg in step 3 before adding the asparagus.

1 Trim or snap any tough ends from the asparagus (see Cook's Tip on page 47) and lay the spears in a frying pan. Add just enough boiling water to cover, bring back to the boil then reduce the heat. Cover and simmer for 3 minutes, or until the asparagus is just tender. Drain.

2 Meanwhile, beat 2 eggs in a bowl with 1 tablespoon of water and 2 tablespoons of dill. Heat a frying pan or omelette pan until very hot. Add 5 g of the butter and swirl it around the pan. Over a high heat, pour the beaten eggs into the pan and cook for 1–2 minutes, lifting the edge of the omelette as it cooks to allow the egg to run onto the hot pan.

3 When the egg is almost set, add 4 asparagus spears. Fold the omelette over the asparagus, turn out onto a plate and keep warm. Repeat with the remaining ingredients to cook the second omelette.

COOK'S TIPS
● To ensure that your omelettes are hot when you eat them, prepare warm plates for serving and have accompaniments ready on the table.
● Use a heavy pan to make the omelettes, ensuring that it is evenly coated with the butter to prevent the eggs from sticking.

SUPER FOOD

EGGS
The ultimate natural fast food, eggs are easy to cook, nutritious and versatile. Rich in vitamins A and D for eye and bone health, eggs also contain the pigments zeaxanthin and lutein, which may help to prevent degenerative eye disease.

TOFU-STUFFED CAPSICUMS

Sweet grilled capsicum shells contain bite-sized tomatoes and marinated tofu pieces for a vivid, juicy Mediterranean-style dish. Serve with baked new potatoes.

Serves 4
Preparation 5 minutes
Marinating 1 hour
Cooking 15 minutes

3 tablespoons olive oil
pinch of grated nutmeg
¼ tablespoon paprika
¼ tablespoon dried marjoram
2 large cloves garlic, crushed
400 g packet firm tofu
4 large green capsicums
24 cherry tomatoes
1 teaspoon fennel seeds
75 g herbed mixed salad, such
   as rocket, watercress and basil

Each serving provides
• 912 kJ • 218 kcal • 10 g protein
• 17 g fat of which 2 g saturates
• 8 g carbohydrates of which
7 g sugars • 5 g fibre

ALTERNATIVE INGREDIENTS
• Add a pinch of dried chilli flakes to the tomatoes for a hint of heat.
• Use cumin seeds instead of fennel and sprinkle the tofu with tandoori seasoning or good-quality curry powder rather than nutmeg.
• Ring the changes with haloumi or Indian paneer cheese instead of tofu, although this will increase the amount of saturated fat per portion.
• For delicate flavours, try yellow capsicums with yellow cherry tomatoes and basil leaves in place of garlic.

1 Mix the oil, nutmeg, paprika, marjoram and 1 crushed clove garlic in a shallow dish just large enough to hold the block of tofu. Add the tofu and turn it to coat both sides, then cover and set aside to marinate for 1 hour.

2 Preheat the grill to the hottest setting. Cut each capsicum in half and remove the seeds. Grill, cut sides down, for 3–4 minutes, until blistered but not blackened. Turn the pieces, cut sides up, and grill for a further 2 minutes, or until juicy and just tender.

3 Cut each tomato in half and mix them with the fennel seeds and remaining crushed clove garlic in a bowl. Remove the tofu from the marinade and slice it into eight strips, then cut these across in half.

4 Divide the tomatoes among the capsicum halves and grill for 2 minutes. Place two pieces of tofu in each capsicum half, nestling them at an angle among the tomatoes. Drizzle the remaining marinade over the tofu and grill for a further 4–5 minutes, or until the tofu is just beginning to brown. Divide the salad among four plates, place the capsicum halves on top and serve.

COOK'S TIPS
● Before cutting the capsicums in half, sit them on your chopping board or work surface to check the best place for slicing through so that they stand steadily.
● As well as chilled tofu, used in this recipe, which has a relatively short shelf-life and must be stored in the fridge, look out for long-life packs of tofu, which make a good pantry ingredient. Smoked tofu pieces also work well in this recipe.

SUPER FOOD

TOFU
Also known as soybean curd, tofu is a low-fat, high-protein food. Soy protein helps to lower blood cholesterol levels, so tofu is good for heart health. A source of calcium, tofu can also play a role in maintaining strong bones.

SPRING **GREENS** STIR-FRY WITH **HAM** AND TOASTED **ALMONDS**

Simply stir-fry leeks, cucumber and snow peas with lime zest, heart-friendly toasted almonds and lean ham and you have a super-quick light dish, great with couscous.

Serves 4
Preparation 10 minutes
Cooking 12 minutes

350 g snow peas
50 g flaked almonds
2 leeks
½ cucumber
200 g lean cooked ham
2 tablespoons olive oil
grated zest of 1 lime
4 lime wedges, to garnish

Each serving provides
• 1255 kJ • 300 kcal • 21 g protein
• 21 g fat of which 4 g saturates
• 7 g carbohydrates of which
5 g sugars • 5 g fibre

ALTERNATIVE INGREDIENTS
• Sugarsnap peas make a good substitute for snow peas. They are more substantial and often have a fuller flavour.
• Try pastrami or smoked pork loin, chicken or turkey as an alternative to the ham.
• For a vegetarian meal, leave out the ham and add 100 g frozen soybeans or shelled broad beans in step 3. Use cashew nuts instead of almonds, increasing the quantity to 75 g.

1 Put the snow peas in a large frying pan and add just enough boiling water to cover. Bring back to the boil, cover and cook over a high heat for 1 minute until the snow peas are bright green and slightly puffed. Drain and set aside.

2 Roast the almonds in a dry frying pan over a medium-high heat for 2 minutes. Shake the pan frequently so that the nuts cook evenly and do not burn. Transfer to a plate.

3 Slice the leeks. Peel the cucumber and cut it into 1 cm wide sticks. Cut the ham into 2 cm strips. Add the oil to the frying pan and stir-fry the leeks over a medium-high heat for 3 minutes. Add the lime zest and cucumber and cook for a further 5 minutes, or until the leeks are reduced and the cucumber is cooked.

4 Stir in the snow peas, ham and almonds and stir-fry for 1 minute to heat through. Serve garnished with lime wedges.

COOK'S TIPS
● Carefully zest the lime using a parer so you can use the leftover lime, minus the zest, as a garnish rather than buying two limes.
● Do not cook the snow peas for too long or they will go soft and turn a dull green colour. They should be bright green with a crunchy texture.
● Air-dried, uncooked ham, such as westphalian, prosciutto, parma or serrano, is not recommended for a stir-fry.

SUPER FOOD

ALMONDS
With high levels of cholesterol-lowering monounsaturated fats, almonds are especially good for keeping the heart healthy. They are also rich in essential vitamin E, an important anti-oxidant that may help to fight the free radical damage that can eventually lead to cancer or heart disease.

BROCCOLI MASH
WITH POACHED EGG

Melt-in-the-mouth mash teamed with vitamin C-rich broccoli and tangy black olives makes a great alternative to plain potato. Top with a poached egg for extra protein and flavour.

Serves 4
Preparation 15 minutes
Cooking 25 minutes

Each serving provides
- 1427 kJ • 341 kcal • 15 g protein
- 16 g fat of which 3 g saturates
- 36 g carbohydrates of which 3 g sugars • 5 g fibre

1 kg potatoes
2 cloves garlic
200 g tender broccoli spears
40 g pitted black olives
4 eggs
2 tablespoons olive oil
4 tablespoons low-fat milk
grated zest of 1 lemon
4 tablespoons chopped fresh parsley

ALTERNATIVE INGREDIENTS
• Use sweet potatoes instead of regular potatoes, or a mixture of half sweet and half regular.
• Add 200 g swede and 200 g carrot to the potatoes as a change from the broccoli. Cut the swede into 3 cm chunks and cook for 5 minutes before adding the carrot and potatoes.

1 Peel the potatoes and cut them into 2 cm cubes. Peel the garlic. Roughly chop the broccoli and slice the olives. Put the potatoes and garlic in a large saucepan and pour in just enough boiling water to cover. Bring back to the boil over a high heat, reduce the heat to low, cover and simmer for 15 minutes, or until tender.

2 Meanwhile, pour 3 cm of boiling water into a large pan set over a medium heat. Bring back to the boil and carefully break the eggs, one at a time, into the water, keeping them separate until the white is set. Simmer for 8–10 minutes, or until set.

3 Drain the potatoes in a colander. Pour the oil into the potato pan, add the broccoli and stir-fry over a medium–high heat for 2 minutes before adding the milk. Bring to the boil, cover and cook for a further 2 minutes. Transfer the broccoli mixture to a bowl.

4 Return the potatoes to the saucepan (off the heat) and mash them. Stir in the broccoli and milk once the potatoes are thoroughly mashed. Gently mix in the lemon zest, olives and parsley. Carefully remove the eggs from the pan with a slotted spoon and place one on top of each portion of mash before serving.

SUPER FOOD

BROCCOLI

An original super food hero, broccoli is one of the top-scoring anti-oxidant vegetables. It contains sulforaphane, a phytochemical known to activate enzymes that may destroy cancer-causing chemicals. Also, it takes only one 85 g serving of lightly cooked broccoli to provide up to 100 per cent of your daily vitamin C requirements.

COOK'S TIPS
● Use potatoes suitable for boiling, such as king edward or desiree.
● To poach an egg successfully, keep the water at a bare simmer throughout cooking. Cook until the white is set – this will take 5–10 minutes over a low heat. Alternatively, use an egg poacher to help to give a uniform shape.

BROCCOLI

A versatile vegetable in the kitchen, broccoli is also rich in a number of nutrients. These include phytochemicals, or plant chemicals, which may help to prevent some cancers and heart disease as well as protect against the signs of ageing. Broccoli contains plenty of vitamin C, too, boosting the immune system.

BROCCOLI PÂTÉ

Serves 4
Preparation 15 minutes Cooking 28 minutes

Each serving provides • 657 kJ • 157 kcal
• 1 g protein • 11 g fat of which 3 g saturates
• 3 g carbohydrates of which 2 g sugars • 3 g fibre

Preheat the oven to 180°C (160°C fan-forced). Cook **350 g broccoli florets** in a pan of boiling water for 3 minutes, or until barely cooked. Drain, refresh under cold running water and pat dry with paper towel. Transfer the broccoli to a large bowl and lightly mash. Stir in **3 beaten eggs, 50 ml low-fat milk, 3 tablespoons grated parmesan** and **2 finely chopped spring onions**. Season to taste. Lightly brush four ramekins with **olive oil or canola oil** and fill each with a quarter of the broccoli mixture. Place the ramekins on a baking tray and bake in the oven for 25 minutes, or until set and golden. Allow to cool, then serve.

COOK'S TIP

● Garnish with cherry tomatoes or basil leaves and serve with wholegrain bread or oatcakes.

SUMMER BROCCOLI AND LEMON SOUP

Serves 4
Preparation 10 minutes Cooking 32 minutes

Each serving provides • 628 kJ • 150 kcal
• 8 g protein • 6 g fat of which 1 g saturates
• 18 g carbohydrates of which 6 g sugars • 5 g fibre

Heat **1 tablespoon olive oil** in a large frying pan. Add **1 finely chopped onion** and fry gently over a low heat for 5 minutes, or until softened. Add **2 crushed cloves garlic** and stir for 1 minute before adding **500 g broccoli florets**, cut in half if large, and **250 g finely diced potato**. Pour in **4 cups (1 litre) vegetable stock**, bring to the boil, then lower the heat immediately, cover and simmer for 25 minutes. Cool a little then purée in a blender. Return the soup to the pan, add the **juice of ½ lemon** and reheat gently. Stir **1 tablespoon natural yogurt** into each bowl of soup and sprinkle each with **½ tablespoon finely snipped fresh chives** before serving piping hot.

COOK'S TIP

● Do not boil the soup, except to bring the stock up to temperature, otherwise it will lose its vibrant green colour and may look unappetising.

ITALIAN PASTA WITH PINE NUTS

Serves 4
Preparation 10 minutes Cooking 15 minutes

Each serving provides • 2310 kJ • 552 kcal
• 20 g protein • 27 g fat of which 5 g saturates
• 62 g carbohydrates of which 4 g sugars • 10 g fibre

Cook **300 g wholewheat spaghetti** in a saucepan of boiling water for 12 minutes, or according to the packet instructions, until tender. Add **400 g broccoli florets**, cut in half if large, to the pan for the last 5 minutes of cooking. Meanwhile, heat **3 tablespoons olive oil** in a small frying pan and add **4 crushed cloves garlic** and **1 finely chopped red chilli**. Stir over a medium heat for 2 minutes. Drain the pasta and broccoli and transfer them to a serving dish. Pour the garlic and chilli oil over the hot pasta and toss thoroughly to coat. Mix **4 tablespoons toasted pine nuts, 2 tablespoons grated parmesan** and **2 tablespoons breadcrumbs**. Sprinkle the topping over the pasta before serving.

COOK'S TIP

● To make breadcrumbs, put 1 slice of wholemeal bread into a food processor and blend until it turns to crumbs. Transfer to a baking tray and toast under the grill for about 5 minutes, turning regularly, or until golden.

SWEET POTATO, BROCCOLI AND LENTIL SALAD

Serves 4
Preparation 15 minutes Cooking 25 minutes

Each serving provides • 1975 kJ • 472 kcal
• 14 g protein • 28 g fat of which 4 g saturates
• 43 g carbohydrates of which 9 g sugars • 9 g fibre

Preheat the oven to 200°C (180°C fan-forced). Peel **400 g sweet potatoes** and cut into 2.5 cm cubes. Toss the cubes in **3 tablespoons olive oil** and arrange on a baking tray. Bake for 25 minutes, or until cooked through and golden. Meanwhile, cook **150 g brown** or **French-style green (puy) lentils** in a pan of boiling water for 25 minutes, or until tender, then drain. Cook **300 g broccoli florets** in a pan of boiling water for 5 minutes. Transfer to a colander and refresh under cold running water, then pat dry. Halve **150 g cherry tomatoes** and then chop **1 small bunch fresh coriander leaves**. Make a dressing by mixing **2 tablespoons olive oil, 2 tablespoons sesame oil, 2 tablespoons light soy**

sauce, **½ teaspoon chilli sauce** and **½ teaspoon finely grated fresh ginger**. Toss the broccoli, potato and lentils with the tomatoes, coriander and dressing. Serve warm or cold.

COOK'S TIP

● This salad is ideal as a starter or part of a buffet. Alternatively, serve it as an accompaniment to grilled chicken breasts.

BROCCOLI, CARROT AND MUSHROOM STIR-FRY

Serves 4
Preparation 10 minutes Cooking 6 minutes

Each serving provides • 841 kJ • 201 kcal
• 6 g protein • 13 g fat of which 2 g saturates
• 15 g carbohydrates of which 13 g sugars • 4 g fibre

Heat **1 tablespoon olive oil or canola oil** in a wok or non-stick frying pan. Add **200 g broccoli florets** and **150 g carrots**, cut into thin julienne strips (see Cook's Tip). Stir-fry over a high heat for 2 minutes and add **8 spring onions**, sliced lengthwise, and cook for a further 2 minutes. Stir in another **1 tablespoon olive oil or canola oil**, plus **100 g sliced button mushrooms** and **2 crushed cloves garlic**. Stir-fry for 1 minute and then pour in **2 tablespoons light soy sauce, 2 teaspoons runny honey** and **1 tablespoon rice vinegar**. Heat through for 1 minute and serve sprinkled with **4 tablespoons cashew nuts**.

COOK'S TIP

● To make julienne strips, first peel the carrots. Trim four sides of each carrot to create a rectangle. Cut the rectangle lengthwise into 3 mm slices then stack the slices and cut lengthwise to make more 3 mm strips.

RATATOUILLE WITH FETTA GRATIN

A light version of a classic dish that contains all the goodness of eggplant, zucchini and tomatoes. The topping of bread and Greek fetta turns a side dish into a vegetarian main meal.

Serves 4
Preparation 20 minutes
Cooking 20 minutes

1 eggplant, about 300 g
1 onion
2 tablespoons olive oil
1 clove garlic, crushed
2 zucchini
4 large tomatoes
2 tablespoons tomato purée
4 tablespoons chopped fresh parsley
4 fresh basil sprigs

Topping
2 slices wholemeal bread
150 g fetta
1 tablespoon olive oil

Each serving provides
• 1230 kJ • 294 kcal • 10 g protein
• 20 g fat of which 7 g saturates
• 19 g carbohydrates of which
11 g sugars • 5 g fibre

ALTERNATIVE INGREDIENTS
• For a more traditional ratatouille, add 1 diced green capsicum with the onion in step 1.
• Use a 400 g can of chopped tomatoes instead of fresh tomatoes.

1 Trim and discard the stalk end of the eggplant and cut the flesh into 1 cm cubes. Chop the onion. Heat the oil in a large saucepan over a high heat, add the onion and garlic and cook for 1 minute. Add the eggplant, reduce the heat to medium and cook for 5 minutes, stirring occasionally, until softened.

2 Meanwhile, cut the zucchini into 1 cm cubes. Add them to the pan and continue to cook for a further 2 minutes, stirring occasionally until the vegetables start to brown.

3 Preheat the grill to the hottest setting. Dice the tomatoes then add them along with the tomato purée to the pan. Stir in 90 ml of cold water. Heat the mixture until simmering, cover and cook over a medium to medium–low heat for 8–10 minutes. Stir in the parsley and transfer to a shallow ovenproof dish or gratin dish.

4 For the topping, cut the bread into 1 cm cubes. Crumble the fetta into a bowl, add the bread then pour over the oil and toss to coat. Sprinkle the topping over the ratatouille and grill for 1–2 minutes, or until the cheese softens and the bread browns. Strip the leaves from the basil sprigs and sprinkle them over the ratatouille before serving.

COOK'S TIP
● Do not worry about salting the eggplant before use. In the past, eggplant cultivars were bitter and had to be salted (known as degorging) to draw out the sour juices, but varieties available in supermarkets today have been bred to avoid this and can therefore be added straight into the ratatouille.

SUPER FOOD

EGGPLANT
Rich in anti-oxidants, eggplant may help to protect against cancer and heart disease. They also contain vitamin K, needed to regulate blood clotting, some folate for heart health and a useful amount of fibre.

MIXED GRILL WITH TOMATOES

Ripe tomatoes have unbeatable flavour and are crammed with anti-oxidants to help to protect cells. Combine with green beans, mushrooms, a fried egg and bread for a tasty meat-free big breakfast.

Serves 4
Preparation 10 minutes
Cooking 20 minutes

200 g green beans
4 tablespoons olive oil
1 garlic clove, crushed
½ teaspoon mixed dried herbs
12 slices baguette
6 tomatoes
8 large flat mushrooms
4 eggs
2 tablespoons snipped fresh chives
2 tablespoons chopped fresh parsley

Each serving provides
• 1770 kJ • 423 kcal • 16 g protein
• 24 g fat of which 4 g saturates
• 37 g carbohydrates of which
7 g sugars • 5 g fibre

ALTERNATIVE INGREDIENTS
• Serve two spoonfuls of baked beans instead of green beans.
• Try poached or scrambled eggs as a change from fried eggs.
• For a main meal, omit the fried bread and serve with mashed potato.
• Top each mushroom with a slice of haloumi cheese or tofu 1 cm thick and leave out the egg.

1 Preheat the grill to the hottest setting and line the grill pan with foil. Trim the beans and put them in a saucepan. Pour in boiling water to cover, then bring back to the boil, reduce the heat, cover and cook for 5 minutes, or until tender. Drain and keep warm.

2 Mix the oil, garlic and herbs and brush a little over one side of the baguette slices. Fry, oiled sides down, in a dry frying pan over a medium heat for 4 minutes, or until browned underneath. Set aside.

3 Halve the tomatoes and place them on the grill pan, cut sides down. Place the mushrooms on the grill pan, stalk sides up. Brush everything with the flavoured oil and grill for 3 minutes. Turn over, brush with more oil and grill for a further 3 minutes. Add the bread, untoasted sides up, and brush sparingly with the oil. Grill for 1–2 minutes.

4 Meanwhile, heat the remaining garlic and herb oil in the frying pan over a high heat. Break in the eggs and cook for 1–2 minutes. Transfer the eggs to four plates. Add the mushrooms, tomatoes and beans. Sprinkle with chives and parsley before serving with the bread.

COOK'S TIP
● Slice tomatoes in half horizontally rather than down through the stalks. This way they sit flat on the grill pan and cook evenly.

SUPER FOOD

TOMATOES
The anti-oxidants in tomatoes may help to combat the effects of oxygen free radicals in the body. These molecules can damage cells, which researchers think may lead to cancer and some other diseases. Anti-oxidants are able to 'mop up' the free radicals and so protect cells.

AVOCADO AND EGGPLANT STACKS

A topping of haloumi cheese adds a taste of Cyprus to little towers of tender sun-ripened vegetables for an enticing mix of textures and flavours. Just add a tomato salad.

Serves 4
Preparation 10 minutes
Cooking 12 minutes

1 large eggplant, about 400 g
2 tablespoons olive oil
1 clove garlic, crushed
grated zest of 1 lemon and
  juice of ½ lemon
2 firm ripe avocados
250 g haloumi cheese
25 g flaked almonds

Each serving provides
• 1946 kJ • 465 kcal • 16 g protein
• 42 g fat of which 15 g saturates
• 6 g carbohydrates of which
4 g sugars • 6 g fibre

ALTERNATIVE INGREDIENTS
• Try Indian paneer or mozzarella cheese instead of the haloumi. Paneer retains a similarly firm texture during cooking, but the mozzarella will melt.
• If you do not have a fresh lemon, use 2 tablespoons of bottled lemon juice. The recipe will taste just as good but with a slightly less zingy flavour.
• Use pine nuts instead of the flaked almonds.
• Sliced tomatoes can be grilled on top of the eggplant – include them instead of the almonds or the avocado slices. Use 1–2 tomato slices for each slice of eggplant.

1 Preheat the grill to the hottest setting and line the grill pan with foil. Trim and cut the eggplant into 12 slices. Place the eggplant on the foil. Mix the oil and garlic and brush sparingly over the eggplant. Grill for 4 minutes, or until just beginning to brown in places. Turn over, brush with more oil and grill for a further 4 minutes, or until tender.

2 Put the lemon zest and juice in a shallow non-metallic dish. Cut the avocados into quarters. Peel and cut each quarter into three slices, coating them in the lemon juice to prevent discolouration. Cut the haloumi into 12 slices.

3 Sprinkle the almonds over the eggplant and arrange three avocado slices, with the lemon zest, on each. Top each stack with a slice of haloumi and brush with any remaining oil. Grill for 4 minutes, or until the cheese browns.

COOK'S TIPS
● For a balanced stack, layer up a large slice of eggplant, then a medium slice of avocado and finally a small slice of cheese. If top-heavy, the stacks will topple over.
● If the heat is not evenly distributed under the grill, rearrange the eggplant slices when turning them so that they brown all over.

SUPER FOOD

AVOCADOS
Unusually for a fruit, avocados are high in fat – 20 g in half an avocado – though most of the fat is the healthy, monounsaturated kind that helps to lower blood cholesterol and keep hearts healthy. Avocados are also rich in fibre. Half an avocado provides one-quarter of your total daily fibre needs.

GLAZED **PEARS** WITH **FETTA**

Salty fetta offsets the sweetness of honey-glazed pears for a refreshingly different and healthy salad. Toasted pumpkin seeds add extra bite, and zinc and selenium to boost the immune system.

Serves 4
Preparation 10 minutes
Cooking 10 minutes

½ crunchy lettuce, such as cos
   or iceberg
60 g rocket
juice of 2 limes and grated zest
   of 1 lime
1 tablespoon honey
4 firm, just-ripe pears, about 600 g
4 tablespoons pumpkin seeds
200 g fetta

Each serving provides
- 1368 kJ • 327 kcal • 13 g protein
- 17 g fat of which 8 g saturates
- 32 g carbohydrates of which
23 g sugars • 5 g fibre

ALTERNATIVE INGREDIENTS
- Blue cheese, such as stilton, is a delicious alternative to fetta here. Or try dolcelatte for a creamy texture.
- Firm apples with a sweet-sharp flavour can be used instead of the pears for a crunchier salad. Use lemon zest with apples rather than lime.
- Pine nuts make a good substitute for pumpkin seeds.
- Peppery rocket is delicious with the lime and fetta, but watercress also works well, as do the slightly bitter red leaves of radicchio.

1 Coarsely shred the lettuce and divide it among four large plates together with the rocket. Stir the lime juice, honey and 4 tablespoons of water together in a frying pan.

2 Peel, core and slice the pears, removing the stalks. Add to the frying pan and bring to the boil over a high heat. Cook, turning the pear slices, for 3–5 minutes, or until the liquid has evaporated and the slices are slightly golden. Remove the pan from the heat, add 2 tablespoons of water and stir to glaze the pears.

3 Toast the pumpkin seeds by sprinkling them into a separate dry frying pan and cooking over a medium heat for 3–4 minutes. Stir occasionally to prevent the seeds from blackening.

4 Arrange the pears on top of the leafy salad. Crumble the fetta and divide it among the plates of salad leaves. Sprinkle the lime zest and toasted pumpkin seeds over the top, then serve.

COOK'S TIPS
- Peel the pears whole, quarter them lengthwise and then you will be able to cut the core out easily. Then cut each quarter lengthwise into neat slices. Have the juices ready in the pan and add the pears as they are prepared so they do not discolour.
- Use a spatula and fork to turn the pears in the frying pan. The cooking time will depend on the type of pan. For instance, the juices may evaporate and begin to caramelise more quickly in a thin metal pan. Take care when adding water to a hot pan as it may spit.
- A zester is a useful kitchen tool for removing the zest from citrus fruit, such as lime, but if you don't have one use a vegetable peeler.

SUPER FOOD

PEARS
Like most fruits, pears are excellent for effective weight control. They are low in kilojoules, yet have a good 'fullness factor', great for staving off hunger. Pears also have a low glycaemic index (GI) rating, so they help to keep blood glucose steady.

WARM **POTATO** AND **BROAD BEAN** SALAD

For an elegant, flavour-drenched warm salad, take nutty new potatoes and high-fibre broad beans, drizzle them with a herby vinaigrette, then serve up on salad leaves.

Serves 4
Preparation 15 minutes
Cooking 15 minutes

Each serving provides
- 1033 kJ • 247 kcal • 7 g protein
- 13 g fat of which 2 g saturates
- 28 g carbohydrates of which
4 g sugars • 6 g fibre

500 g baby new potatoes
1 kg fresh broad beans or 300 g
frozen baby broad beans
1 teaspoon sugar
1 teaspoon English mustard
1 teaspoon cider vinegar
3 tablespoons olive oil
3 large sprigs thyme
100 g beetroot leaves or mixed
salad leaves
4 tablespoons snipped fresh chives

ALTERNATIVE INGREDIENTS
• Freshly cooked baby beetroot work well in this salad with the broad beans. Trim off the leaves but keep the roots and stalks in place. Wash and boil 300 g beetroot for 20 minutes until tender. Drain and place in cold water until cool enough to handle, then rub off the skins under water. Cook the broad beans separately. Add the hot beetroot to the dressing and then the broad beans.

1 Put the potatoes in a large saucepan and pour in boiling water to cover. Bring back to the boil, reduce the heat, cover and cook for 10 minutes. Meanwhile, shell the broad beans, if using fresh ones. Soak the shelled beans in a bowl of hot water for 3–4 minutes before peeling off the pale green outer skins. Add the beans to the potatoes, bring back to the boil, cover and cook for 4 minutes until tender.

2 Make a vinaigrette by whisking the sugar, mustard and vinegar in a large bowl until the sugar has dissolved. Whisk in the oil and rub the thyme leaves off the stalks and into the bowl. Season to taste.

3 Make a bed of salad leaves on four plates. Drain the potatoes and beans and stir them into the vinaigrette. Sprinkle with chives and mix again. Top the leaves with the potato and bean salad.

COOK'S TIPS
● Sugar does not dissolve in oil, so to avoid a grainy vinaigrette combine the sugar with the mustard and vinegar before adding the olive oil.
● Some salad leaves have a slightly bitter taste that is pleasant in young leaves but can be a little too strong in older ones. Choose small, young leaves, or if only older ones are available, reduce their quantity by half and mix them with 'sweeter' leaves, such as lamb's lettuce (mâche), oakleaf or mignonette lettuce or finely shredded Chinese cabbage.

SUPER FOOD

BROAD BEANS
Part of the legume family, broad beans are a good source of both soluble and insoluble fibre to keep the digestive system in good order. They also contain energy-releasing B vitamins, including folate, which helps to maintain healthy blood and circulation.

WITLOF AND APPLE SALAD

Apples and dates add sweetness to the subtle flavours of celeriac and crisp witlof to conjure a fresh, light salad or accompaniment for grilled poultry or pork.

Serves 4
Preparation 15 minutes

1 tablespoon cider vinegar
2 tablespoons olive oil,
    plus 1 tablespoon for serving
250 g celeriac, about ¼ large
    celeriac
2–3 apples, about 250 g
50 g pistachios
150 g medjool dates
3–4 heads witlof

Each serving provides
• 1397 kJ • 334 kcal • 5 g protein
• 20 g fat of which 3 g saturates
• 37 g carbohydrates of which
35 g sugars • 7 g fibre

ALTERNATIVE INGREDIENTS
• Try 50 g walnuts or pecans instead
of the pistachios.
• Any fresh dates are fine if you cannot
find medjool dates.
• Dried apricots or dried cranberries
make good alternatives to the dates.
• For a more substantial meal, top
the salad with 100 g crumbled fetta.
For a meat option stir-fry 100 g sliced
chorizo or other cured sausage for
1 minute before adding to the salad.
• This salad is great served in wraps.
Spread wheat tortillas with low-fat
ricotta or low-fat cream cheese
flavoured with garlic and herbs. Top
with the salad, omitting the witlof,
and roll up.

1 Whisk the vinegar and 2 tablespoons of oil together in a large bowl to make a dressing. Peel and coarsely grate the celeriac, add it to the dressing and mix thoroughly.

2 Cut the apples into quarters, remove the cores, then cut each quarter into two wedges. Slice the wedges across widthwise and mix with the celeriac. Shell and roughly chop the pistachios. Halve, pit and chop the dates. Stir the nuts and dates into the celeriac mixture.

3 Separate the individual witlof leaves and arrange them on a serving plate. Drizzle with the remaining oil. Pile the salad onto the plate and use the witlof leaves to scoop up the salad.

COOK'S TIPS
● The coarsest disc on a food processor is ideal for grating celeriac. Alternatively, use the coarse blade on a hand-held grater and press firmly to remove good-sized shreds.
● Prepare the salad up to 2 hours in advance of serving. Cover the serving plate with plastic wrap and store in the fridge until needed.

SUPER FOOD

WITLOF
A mildly bitter salad leaf, witlof (also called Belgian endive) is high in fibre, vitamin C and a variety of minerals. The red variety provides good amounts of beneficial anti-oxidants.

APPLES

Easily available, apples offer many nutritional benefits and may even help to sharpen mental alertness. They also contain plenty of soluble fibre that can help to lower blood cholesterol, and, with an average content of only 273 kJ (65 kcal), an apple is the perfect healthy snack.

BAKED OATY APPLES

Serves 4
Preparation 10 minutes, plus 15 minutes standing
Cooking 40 minutes

Each serving provides • 1042 kJ • 249 kcal
• 2 g protein • 7 g fat of which 4 g saturates
• 48 g carbohydrates of which 43 g sugars • 5 g fibre

Preheat the oven to 180°C (160°C fan-forced). Put **100 g sultanas** in a heatproof bowl and cover with hot water. Leave them to plump up for 15 minutes. Meanwhile, warm **2 tablespoons runny honey** in a small saucepan with **2 tablespoons rolled oats** and **½ teaspoon ground mixed spice**. Drain the sultanas and stir them into the oats. Core **4 cooking apples** and score them horizontally with a sharp knife to penetrate the skin. Place the apples in an ovenproof dish and fill each cavity with the sultanas and oats. Place **1 small knob of butter** on the top of each apple. Pour **200 ml water** around the apples in the dish. Bake for 40 minutes, or until the apples are soft. Baste the apples with the juices halfway through cooking to keep them moist.

COOK'S TIPS

● Try to use unblemished apples, as bruises may spoil the appearance of your dessert and may affect the dish's nutritional content. Choose from a variety of cooking apples, such as granny smith or golden delicious.
● Piping-hot custard makes a tasty accompaniment to stuffed apples.
● Vary the sweet filling by using chopped dried apricots instead of sultanas and replace the oats with chopped or flaked almonds.

WALNUT AND APPLE STUFFING

Serves 4
Preparation 10 minutes Cooking 40 minutes

Each serving provides • 619 kJ • 148 kcal
• 4 g protein • 5 g fat of which 1 g saturates
• 24 g carbohydrates of which 11 g sugars • 4 g fibre

Preheat the oven to 180°C (160°C fan-forced). Heat **1 tablespoon olive oil** in a frying pan and cook **1 large finely chopped onion** over a medium-low heat for 5 minutes, or until softened. Meanwhile, put **125 g stale wholemeal bread** in a food processor and turn it into breadcrumbs. Finely chop **2 red apples**, leaving on the nutritious skins, and add them to the pan. Stir for

2 minutes, take off the heat and add the wholemeal breadcrumbs, **3 tablespoons chopped fresh parsley, 1 tablespoon chopped fresh sage, 2 tablespoons chopped walnuts** and **2 tablespoons dried cranberries**. Mix and leave to cool for 1 minute before stirring in **1 beaten egg yolk**. Season to taste then spoon the mixture into a shallow ovenproof dish. Dissolve **1 vegetable stock cube** in **100 ml boiling water** and pour it over the stuffing. Bake in the oven for 25 minutes, or until golden.

COOK'S TIP

● If you do not have a food processor, use a blender to make the breadcrumbs, or rub the stale bread against the coarse side of a grater until it crumbles.

APPLE AND GINGER SMOOTHIE

Serves 4
Preparation 10 minutes

Each serving provides • 1305 kJ • 312 kcal • 9 g protein • 3 g fat of which 2 g saturates • 64 g carbohydrates of which 63 g sugars • 2 g fibre

Roughly chop **4 apples**. Place them in a blender, or in a bowl if you have a stick blender. Add **200 ml apple juice** and **20 g finely grated fresh ginger**. Blend until smooth then add **500 ml frozen vanilla low-fat yogurt** and an additional **300 ml apple juice**. Blend again until smooth and pour the smoothie into four tall glasses.

COOK'S TIPS

● This smoothie works well with any type of apple, but the flavour is best with slightly sharp green apples, such as granny smith.
● Try 1 teaspoon ground ginger or 20 g finely chopped glacé ginger instead of the fresh ginger.

CARROT, APPLE AND BEETROOT SALAD

Serves 4
Preparation 15 minutes Marinating 30 minutes

Each serving provides • 548 kJ • 131 kcal • 1 g protein • 11 g fat of which 2 g saturates • 6 g carbohydrates of which 6 g sugars • 2 g fibre

Grate **2 carrots** and **1 small cooked beetroot** into a large serving bowl. Make the French dressing by mixing **3 tablespoons olive oil, ½ tablespoon white wine vinegar, ½ tablespoon balsamic vinegar, ½ teaspoon**

French mustard, a pinch of sugar and a little salt and pepper. Add **3 tablespoons raisins, 2 tablespoons cashew nuts** and **4 tablespoons French dressing** to the serving bowl. Finely chop **2 red apples**, leaving on the skins. Stir the apples into the salad, making sure that they are coated with the dressing to prevent them from discolouring. Marinate the salad for 30 minutes before serving.

COOK'S TIP

● To cook raw beetroot, place a small whole beetroot in a fine-meshed sieve over a pan of boiling water and steam for 15 minutes, or until cooked but still firm. Drain the beetroot and run it under cold water, then peel off the skin. Leave it to cool before grating. Do not over-cook the beetroot because it will not grate easily when soft and the crunchy texture of the salad will be lost.

FIG, APPLE AND CINNAMON COMPOTE

Serves 4
Preparation 5 minutes Cooking 22 minutes

Each serving provides • 598 kJ • 143 kcal • 2 g protein • 6 g fat (no saturates) • 22 g carbohydrates of which 22 g sugars • 4 g fibre

Slice **2 sweet apples** and **1 cooking apple** (such as granny smith). Put them in a saucepan with **125 ml orange juice, 4 chopped dried figs** and **1 level teaspoon ground cinnamon**. Bring to the boil, then turn down the heat and simmer, uncovered, for 20 minutes, or until the apples are tender when gently pressed with the back of a spoon. Sprinkle over **2 tablespoons toasted pine nuts** before dividing among four bowls to serve.

COOK'S TIPS

● Cinnamon is a sweet spice and using it in this fruity dish means that there is no need for added sweeteners, such as sugar. Add half a cinnamon stick to the compote instead of ground cinnamon, but remember to remove it before serving.
● Vanilla or butterscotch ice cream, or a spoonful of crème fraîche, tastes great with the compote.

LIGHTLY SPICED **VEGETABLE** MEDLEY

An imaginative combination of flavours that will really lift a simple fish, meat or poultry dish. The warm and aromatic cardamom seeds add a delicate hint of spice to the tender vegetables.

Serves 4
Preparation 20 minutes
Cooking 25 minutes

Each serving provides
- 1197 kJ • 286 kcal • 13 g protein
- 13 g fat of which 3 g saturates
- 36 g carbohydrates of which
15 g sugars • 7 g fibre

1 onion
2 sticks celery
1 large carrot
1 eggplant
450 g potatoes
250 g cauliflower florets
10 green cardamom pods
2 tablespoons olive oil or canola oil
4 cloves garlic, crushed
2 tablespoons ground coriander
250 g spinach
20 g chopped fresh coriander
finely grated zest of 1 lemon
300 g natural yogurt

ALTERNATIVE INGREDIENTS
- Try sweet potatoes instead of regular potatoes.
- Leave out the eggplant and add 2 chopped parsnips at the same time as the cauliflower.
- For a different take on spiced vegetables, add 1 finely chopped fresh green chilli to the onion mixture in step 2, then add a 400 g can of chopped tomatoes in step 3 and reduce the water to 100 ml.

1 Thinly slice the onion and celery. Halve and slice the carrot. Chop the eggplant into small chunks. Dice the potatoes. Break any larger cauliflower florets in half or into quarters. Scrape out the seeds from the cardamom pods.

2 Heat the oil in a large pan over a medium–high heat. Add the onion, celery, carrot, garlic and cardamom seeds. Stir, cover and cook for 3 minutes. Stir in the eggplant and sprinkle in the ground coriander without stirring. Cover and cook for a further 3 minutes.

3 Add the potatoes. Stir in 200 ml of boiling water, cover and bring back to the boil. Reduce the heat so that the mixture simmers steadily, then cook for 10 minutes. Stir in the cauliflower and cook for a further 8 minutes, or until all the vegetables are tender.

4 Shred the spinach and stir it thoroughly into the vegetable mixture. Cook, stirring, for 1 minute, or until the spinach has wilted. Stir in the fresh coriander and lemon zest. Divide the vegetables among four plates or bowls and serve with natural yogurt.

COOK'S TIP
● To remove the small seeds from cardamom pods, slit the papery pods with the point of a knife and scrape out the small black or beige seeds with the blade.

SUPER FOOD

SPINACH
A superstar among green vegetables, spinach is bursting with the colourful carotenoids named lutein, zeaxanthin and beta-carotene. These natural chemicals are great for eye health and cancer protection. Rich in folate, spinach is also good for the heart.

WILTED **GREENS**, CRISP **BACON** AND **PINE NUTS** ON **POLENTA**

Savour tender, iron-rich spinach and cabbage with crisp bacon on a bed of golden polenta. Garlic, fennel seeds, juicy sultanas and pine nuts provide colour and texture.

Serves 4
Preparation 10 minutes
Cooking 15 minutes

100 g smoked bacon or pancetta
300 g cabbage
3 tablespoons olive oil
2 cloves garlic, crushed
1 teaspoon fennel seeds
50 g sultanas
⅓ cup (50 g) pine nuts
200 g baby spinach
500 g ready-made polenta
  (see Cook's Tip)

Each serving provides
• 1686 kJ • 403 kcal • 1 g protein
• 26 g fat of which 4 g saturates
• 32 g carbohydrates of which
13 g sugars • 4 g fibre

ALTERNATIVE INGREDIENTS
• Cavolo nero, a dark-leafed Italian cabbage, is ideal for this recipe, but any green cabbage, such as savoy, works well.

1 Preheat the grill to the hottest setting and cover the grill pan with foil. Dice the bacon. Finely shred the cabbage. Heat 2 tablespoons of the oil in a large frying pan over a high heat. Add the smoked bacon or pancetta to the pan with the garlic and fennel seeds. Reduce the heat to medium and cook for 3 minutes, or until the bacon begins to crisp.

2 Add the sultanas, pine nuts and cabbage to the frying pan. Mix well, cover and cook for 3 minutes, or until the cabbage has softened slightly. Stir in the spinach. Cover and cook for a further 2 minutes, or until the spinach has wilted and the cabbage is tender.

3 Meanwhile, cut the polenta into 1 cm slices and position them on the grill pan. Brush with ½ tablespoon of the remaining oil and grill for 5 minutes, or until golden. Turn over, brush with the remaining oil and grill for a further 5 minutes. Allow 2–3 slices of polenta per portion and spoon the cabbage and spinach mixture over the top.

COOK'S TIP
● To cook your own polenta, pour 6 cups (1.5 litres) of water into a saucepan and bring to the boil. Gradually stir in 350 g polenta. Bring back to the boil, reduce the heat and simmer for 35–40 minutes, stirring continuously, until the polenta is thick and smooth. Brush a baking sheet with olive oil and turn the polenta out onto it. Spread evenly with a palette knife and leave to set. When cold, use a sharp, wet knife to cut the polenta into blocks or slices.

SUPER FOOD

PINE NUTS
Like most nuts, pine nuts are a good source of both polyunsaturated and monounsaturated fats, which help to lower harmful cholesterol in the blood. Pine nuts also contain vitamin E and folate, which help to protect the heart.

SWEET POTATO MEDALLIONS WITH MINTED PEA PURÉE

Colourful baby peas puréed with mint make a creamy topping for roasted sweet potato slices. Brimming with carotenoids and other anti-oxidants, this dish is a powerhouse of goodness.

Serves 4
Preparation 10 minutes
Cooking 32 minutes

2 tablespoons olive oil or canola oil
1 large sweet potato
250 g frozen baby peas
100 g low-fat ricotta or low-fat
   cream cheese
8 large shredded fresh mint leaves
2 tablespoons snipped fresh chives
4 sprigs marjoram

Each serving provides
• 881 kJ • 211 kcal • 8 g protein
• 12 g fat of which 3 g saturates
• 17 g carbohydrates of which
7 g sugars • 2 g fibre

ALTERNATIVE INGREDIENTS
• Use ordinary potatoes instead of sweet potatoes.
• Try slices of celeriac instead of sweet potato. Omit the mint from the pea purée.
• For a tasty lunch dish, top the potatoes with sliced mozzarella or thin slices of goat's cheese for the final 3 minutes of cooking. Add the pea purée and heat for 1–2 minutes.

1 Preheat the oven to 200°C (180°C fan-forced). Brush a baking tray with a little of the oil or line it with a sheet of baking paper. Peel the potato, cut it into slices 1 cm thick, and place them on the baking tray. Carefully brush the potato slices with oil, season to taste and bake for 30 minutes, or until beginning to brown.

2 Meanwhile, put the baby peas in a saucepan. Pour over boiling water, bring back to the boil, cover and cook for 2 minutes. Drain and purée in a blender or food processor. Mix the peas with the ricotta or cream cheese, mint and chives. Season to taste.

3 Remove the roasted potato circles from the oven. Strip the leaves from the marjoram, sprinkle them over the potatoes and top with the pea purée. Warm through in the oven for 2 minutes, then grind a little black pepper over each medallion before serving.

COOK'S TIPS
● Baby peas are better than ordinary peas for this recipe because they have tender skins. Standard frozen peas or mature fresh peas do not produce a fine purée.
● If you do not have a blender or food processor, mash the baby peas with a potato masher.

SUPER FOOD

SWEET POTATOES
Anti-oxidant carotenes give nutrient-packed sweet potatoes their orange colour. The potatoes also contain vitamin E, which helps to protect against heart disease, and are a good source of fibre, especially if you eat the skins.

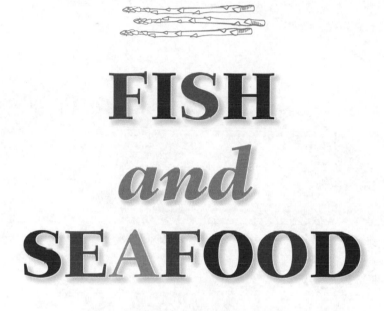

FISH *and* SEAFOOD

ONE-POT **FISH** CASSEROLE WITH SPICY **YOGURT**

This chunky vegetable-laden fish casserole has toasty croutons spread with a piquant yogurt topping to give a tangy crunch with every scrumptious mouthful.

Serves 4
Preparation 15 minutes
Cooking 20 minutes

1 leek
2 sticks celery
1 carrot
700 g potatoes
2 tablespoons olive oil
100 g button mushrooms
600 ml hot fish stock
250 g skinless white fish fillet
250 g skinless salmon fillet
1 tablespoon chopped fresh tarragon
2 tablespoons chopped fresh parsley

Spicy yogurt
40 g mayonnaise
40 g natural yogurt
1 clove garlic, crushed
½ teaspoon paprika
pinch of chilli powder
1 baguette

Each serving provides
• 2364 kJ • 565 kcal • 34 g protein
• 24 g fat of which 4 g saturates
• 26 g carbohydrates of which
6 g sugars • 6 g fibre

ALTERNATIVE INGREDIENTS
• Make this casserole with mixed fresh or frozen seafood instead of, or in addition to, the fish.
• Try fresh sardine or mackerel fillets instead of the salmon.

1 Preheat the grill to the hottest setting. Slice and rinse the leek. Slice the celery, dice the carrot and cut the potatoes into 4 cm chunks. Heat the oil in a large saucepan over a high heat. Add the leek, celery and carrot, reduce the heat to medium, cover and cook for 3 minutes.

2 Add the potatoes and mushrooms to the pan and stir in the hot stock. Bring to the boil, cover and simmer for 10 minutes, or until the potatoes are tender. Cut the white fish and salmon into 3 cm pieces and stir them into the casserole. Bring back to simmering point, re-cover the pan and cook for a further 5 minutes, or until the fish is cooked.

3 Meanwhile, mix the mayonnaise, yogurt, garlic, paprika and chilli powder. Slice the baguette and grill both sides for 2–3 minutes, or until golden. Stir the tarragon and parsley into the casserole before transferring it to four large bowls. Serve with the spicy yogurt and toasted baguette slices.

COOK'S TIP
● Select boiling potatoes rather than baking potatoes, as the pieces will hold their shape within the casserole rather than breaking down.

SUPER FOOD

YOGURT
With an ideal combination of protein and carbohydrate, low-fat natural yogurt can help to fight fatigue and keep hunger at bay – good news for weight control. Yogurt is also a good source of calcium – important to help prevent osteoporosis. One 200 g tub provides almost one-third of your daily calcium needs.

SEARED **TUNA STEAKS** IN A WARM **HERB** DRESSING

A punchy dill and horseradish sauce adds bite to the delicate combination of fresh vegetables and lightly seared tuna. It is a great way to raise energy levels and safeguard your heart.

Serves 4
Preparation 10 minutes
Cooking 8 minutes

Each serving provides
- 1515 kJ • 362 kcal • 42 g protein
- 19 g fat of which 5 g saturates
- 5 g carbohydrates of which
3 g sugars • 3 g fibre

160 g oyster mushrooms
250 g baby corn
250 g sugarsnap peas
2 tablespoons olive oil or canola oil
4 fresh tuna steaks, about 150 g each
2 tablespoons horseradish sauce
⅓ cup (90 g) low-fat natural yogurt
4 tablespoons snipped fresh chives
2 tablespoons chopped fresh dill

ALTERNATIVE INGREDIENTS
• Try enoki or other mushrooms instead of oyster, stir frying them over a high heat for 1 minute until softened.
• Fresh sardine or mackerel fillets taste terrific as an alternative to tuna when flash-fried. Use 4 sardine or mackerel fillets and cook them skin side up for 1 minute, then turn them over and cook for a further 2 minutes, or until the skin is crisp.

1 Slice the mushrooms. Put the baby corn in a saucepan and cover with boiling water. Bring back to the boil over a high heat, cover and cook for 1 minute. Add the sugarsnap peas, cover, bring back to the boil then drain immediately.

2 Heat a large frying pan and swirl 1 tablespoon of the oil around the pan. Add the tuna steaks and cook over a high heat for 2 minutes on each side, or until just firm and browned. The fish should feel slightly springy, not hard, and still be pink in the middle. Transfer the tuna to a dish, cover and keep warm.

3 Add the remaining 1 tablespoon of oil to the frying pan and stir-fry the corn and sugarsnap peas for 1 minute. Divide the vegetables among four warmed plates. Add the mushrooms to the pan and stir-fry over a high heat for 30 seconds. Transfer to the plates.

4 Add the horseradish, yogurt, chives and dill to the pan. Stir to combine then instantly take off the heat. Slice the tuna steaks and put them on the plates. Add a spoonful of sauce and serve.

COOK'S TIP
● Tuna is an oily fish that quickly goes past its best. When buying tuna, choose steaks that have been neatly trimmed, with firm, dense red flesh. Avoid steaks with a strong meaty smell or ones that look a dull brown.

SUPER FOOD

TUNA
Fresh tuna is packed with essential omega-3 oils. Proven to help to protect against heart disease, these oils are also good for joint and brain health. Tuna contains iodine, needed for a healthy metabolism, plus vitamins D and B$_{12}$ to help to fight fatigue.

TROUT WITH ALMONDS AND CAPSICUM

Tuck into succulent grilled trout fillets, combined with vitamin-packed sweet capsicums and toasted almonds, and savour the anti-ageing benefits of this dish. Serve with a green salad.

Serves 4
Preparation 5 minutes
Cooking 6 minutes

1½ tablespoons olive oil or canola oil
4 trout fillets, about 175 g each
2 large capsicums (1 red, 1 yellow)
50 g flaked almonds
4 lemon wedges, to garnish

Each serving provides
- 1544 kJ • 369 kcal • 38 g protein
- 22 g fat of which 3 g saturates
- 6 g carbohydrates of which
5 g sugars • 4 g fibre

ALTERNATIVE INGREDIENTS
- Add a chopped mild or medium-hot fresh green chilli to the capsicums and garnish the dish with a lime instead of the lemon.
- Green capsicums work just as well as yellow capsicums. Sprinkle with plenty of chopped fresh parsley before serving.
- Fresh sardine or mackerel fillets are a good alternative to the trout.

1 Preheat the grill to the hottest setting. Line a grill pan with a layer of foil and brush with a little of the oil. Lay the trout fillets in the middle of the pan, skin side down. Cut the capsicums into 1 cm slices and arrange them around the edges of the fish.

2 Brush the trout and capsicum with a little more oil and then grill for 2–3 minutes, or until the fish is firm and opaque on top. Turn the fish fillets over and brush the skin with the remaining oil. Grill for a further 2 minutes, or until the skin is bubbling and beginning to crisp.

3 Sprinkle the almonds over the fish and grill for 30–60 seconds until browned. Transfer to plates and serve the fish skin side up, so the skin can be savoured or discarded, and garnish with lemon wedges.

COOK'S TIP
- Watch the flaked almonds closely as they cook – they brown quickly and will then taste bitter. Take the fish from under the grill as soon as the almonds are golden.

SUPER FOOD

TROUT
The freshwater trout is a good source of high-quality protein and vitamins A and D. As with other oil-rich fish, it is an excellent source of omega-3 oils, which help to lower the risk of heart disease and stroke. These oils can also help to alleviate symptoms of rheumatoid arthritis and help to maintain mental alertness.

CRISP CORIANDER **FISH** WITH ZESTY **BEANS**

Lemon and rosemary transform a dish of creamy butterbeans into the perfect foil for robustly flavoured grilled fish. Ready in under half an hour, this brain-power booster is the smart choice for a quick, tasty meal.

Serves 4
Preparation 10 minutes
Cooking 10 minutes

Each serving provides
• 1648 kJ • 394 kcal • 29 g protein
• 25 g fat of which 5 g saturates
• 15 g carbohydrates of which
2 g sugars • 5 g fibre

1 leek
1 tablespoon olive oil
2 sprigs rosemary, finely chopped
400 g can butterbeans, drained
finely grated zest of 1 lemon
4 large or 8 small sardine or
  mackerel fillets, about 500 g
  (see Cook's Tips)
1 tablespoon olive oil or canola oil
1 tablespoon crushed coriander
  seeds (see Cook's Tips)
8 lemon wedges, to garnish

ALTERNATIVE INGREDIENTS
• Other white beans, such as cannellini beans, make an excellent substitute for butterbeans.
• To serve the bean and leek mixture as a base for grilled sausages, steaks or burgers, use canned mixed beans instead of butterbeans.

1 Preheat the grill to the hottest setting and line the grill pan with foil. Slice the leek. Heat the olive oil in a large frying pan over a high heat. Add the rosemary and leek to the pan, reduce the heat and cook for 5 minutes, or until the leek is tender. Stir in the butterbeans and lemon zest. Set aside and keep warm.

2 Place the fish fillets, skin side down, on the grill pan then brush each one with a little olive oil or canola oil. Sprinkle with ½ tablespoon crushed coriander seeds and grill for 2 minutes, or until just firm.

3 Turn the fish over and brush the skin with the rest of the oil. Grill for 1 minute and sprinkle with the remaining ½ tablespoon crushed coriander seeds. Cook for a further 2 minutes to crisp the skin.

4 Transfer the butterbean and leek mixture to a serving plate. Top with the fish fillets and pour over the juices from the foil. Garnish with lemon wedges and serve.

SUPER FOOD

OILY FISH
The omega-3 oils found in oil-rich fish such as sardines, mackerel and blue-eye trevalla have many health benefits beyond keeping the heart healthy. Evidence is emerging about their role in maintaining mental alertness and helping to prevent the onset of dementia.

COOK'S TIPS
● Use a mortar and pestle to crush the coriander seeds. Put the mortar in a plastic bag, gather the edges around the pestle to prevent the seeds from escaping and pound the seeds. If you do not have a mortar and pestle, put the coriander seeds into a bowl and crush them with the end of a rolling pin.
● Buy gutted and cleaned fish and open them out flat for grilling.

PAN-FRIED **SALMON** ON A BED OF BABY **SPINACH**

The heat from the cooked salmon is all that it takes to soften fresh spinach leaves and enhance their flavour. Serve with tagliatelle for a warm, vitamin-rich, multi-textured salad.

Serves 4
Preparation 10 minutes
Cooking 5 minutes

Each serving provides
• 2228 kJ • 532 kcal • 34 g protein
• 20 g fat of which 3 g saturates
• 54 g carbohydrates of which
2 g sugars • 5 g fibre

300 g tagliatelle
500 g skinless salmon fillet
40 g green pimento-stuffed olives
2 spring onions
200 g cherry tomatoes
100 g baby spinach
20 fresh basil leaves
2 tablespoons olive oil
grated zest and juice of 1 lemon

1 Cook the tagliatelle in a large saucepan of salted boiling water until tender but not soft.

2 Meanwhile, cut the salmon fillet into 4 cm square chunks. Slice the stuffed olives in half, finely chop the spring onions and cut the cherry tomatoes in half. Divide the spinach among four plates and sprinkle each portion with 5 basil leaves.

3 Heat the oil in a large frying pan over a high heat. Add the salmon chunks and cook for 4 minutes, turning occasionally, until they are opaque but soft. Add the olives, lemon zest and juice, and spring onions to the pan. Leave to bubble for a few seconds, then spoon the salmon and its juices over each bed of spinach and basil.

4 Add the tomatoes to the pan and stir them around for 30 seconds to warm through and to pick up any cooking sediments from the pan. Spoon the tomatoes over the salmon and serve.

COOK'S TIP
● If baby spinach leaves are not available, choose small regular spinach leaves for maximum flavour. Avoid mature spinach leaves as these are too large and firm to eat raw as a salad.

ALTERNATIVE INGREDIENTS
• Use a mixed leaf base instead of spinach – try rocket, lamb's lettuce (mâche), mizuna or watercress.
• Use scallops and pancetta instead of the salmon. Dry-fry 100 g diced smoked bacon or pancetta before adding the oil and cooking 300 g small scallops, without the roes, for about 1 minute, or until opaque.
• Cook 450–500 g squid rings instead of salmon. You can buy squid from the fishmonger's counter and ask to have it sliced into rings. Cook as for the salmon in step 2.

SUPER FOOD

SALMON
A rich source of protein, salmon is also high in vitamin A (great for healthy eyes and skin) and vitamin D (needed to make bones strong and guard against osteoporosis). Salmon is a beneficial source of selenium, too, which helps to boost the immune system and regulate the thyroid gland.

SALMON

Brimming with omega-3, a type of oil beneficial for your heart, brain and joints, salmon is one of the healthiest fish you can buy. High in protein and an excellent source of heart-protective vitamin E, salmon is also one of the few dietary sources of vitamin D, a crucial nutrient for keeping your bones strong.

SALMON NIÇOISE

Serves 4
Preparation 10 minutes Cooking 6 minutes

Each serving provides • 1364 kJ • 326 kcal
• 28 g protein • 21 g fat of which 4 g saturates
• 6 g carbohydrates of which 5 g sugars • 2 g fibre

Cook **3 eggs** in a pan of boiling water for 6 minutes, or until hard boiled. Meanwhile, steam **400 g skinless salmon tail** and **75 g green beans** for 5 minutes, or until the salmon is just cooked but still moist and the green beans are tender. Leave to cool. Drain the eggs, remove the shells and cut into quarters. Cut **8 pitted black olives** in half and halve **4 drained anchovy fillets**. Wash the outer leaves from **1 cos or little gem lettuce** and place them in a large salad bowl. Cut the lettuce heart into 8 segments and add to the bowl. Add **3 roughly chopped tomatoes, 6 finely chopped spring onions** and the green beans. Make a French dressing by mixing **4 tablespoons virgin olive oil, 1 tablespoon red wine vinegar, ½ teaspoon French mustard, ½ teaspoon caster sugar** and **1 crushed clove garlic**. Season to taste and pour over the salad. Divide the salmon tail into 12 large pieces and place them on the salad. Add the olives and anchovy fillets. Arrange the eggs on top of the salad before serving.

COOK'S TIP

● If you do not have a steamer, microwave the salmon and beans in a microwave-proof dish with a tight-fitting lid. Pour in 2 tablespoons of water, cover with the lid and cook on high for 3–4 minutes, or until the fish is opaque and the beans are cooked but still crunchy.

SALMON AND BROCCOLI RISOTTO

Serves 4
Preparation 10 minutes Cooking 35 minutes

Each serving provides • 2368 kJ • 566 kcal
• 26 g protein • 25 g fat of which 5 g saturates
• 64 g carbohydrates of which 3 g sugars • 3 g fibre

Heat **3 tablespoons olive oil** in a large frying pan. Add **1 finely chopped onion** and fry over a medium–low heat for 5 minutes, or until softened. Add **3 crushed cloves garlic** and **275 g risotto rice**. Stir for 1 minute and add **1.3 litres fish stock** in 200 ml amounts, stirring regularly. Allow each ladleful of stock to be absorbed by the rice before adding the next one. This will take about 25 minutes. Meanwhile, cut **300 g skinless salmon fillet** into bite-sized pieces. Stir the salmon into the rice after 12 minutes of cooking time.

Continue to cook the risotto for 6 minutes, then stir in **250 g broccoli florets**, cut in half if large. Cook for 5 minutes, or until the salmon and broccoli are cooked through and the rice is creamy but still slightly nutty in the centres. Stir in **2 tablespoons grated parmesan** and transfer to four plates. Garnish with **1 tablespoon chopped fresh parsley** before serving.

COOK'S TIP

● For a change, replace the broccoli with cooked peas or asparagus tips.

CRUNCHY BAKED SALMON

Serves 4
Preparation 10 minutes Cooking 15 minutes

Each serving provides • 1736 kJ • 415 kcal
• 28 g protein • 30 g fat of which 4 g saturates
• 8 g carbohydrates of which 1 g sugars • 1 g fibre

Preheat the oven to 180°C (160°C fan-forced). Put **3 crushed cloves garlic, 2 tablespoons pine nuts** and the leaves from **4–5 sprigs fresh basil** in a bowl and pound them together to release the aroma of the basil. Stir in **3 tablespoons olive oil** and **60 g fresh breadcrumbs**. Season to taste. Place **4 salmon fillets, about 125 g each**, skin side down, on a baking tray and cover each one with a quarter of the topping, spreading it evenly over the fish. Bake for 15 minutes, or until the fish is cooked through and the topping is slightly browned and crisp.

COOK'S TIP

● Serve with a mixed leaf and avocado salad, or cherry tomatoes on the vine baked in the oven at the same time as the fish.

GINGER SALMON KEBABS

Serves 4
Preparation 10 minutes Marinating 30 minutes
Cooking 5 minutes

Each serving provides • 1138 kJ • 272 kcal
• 21 g protein • 19 g fat of which 3 g saturates
• 5 g carbohydrates of which 4 g sugars • 2 g fibre

Preheat the grill to hot. Cut **400 g skinless salmon fillets** into bite-sized cubes and put them in a non-metallic shallow dish. Cut **2 yellow capsicums** into squares and add them to the dish. In a bowl, combine **2 tablespoons olive oil, 3 teaspoons finely grated fresh ginger, 2 crushed cloves garlic, 1 finely chopped green chilli (optional)** and the **juice of ½ lemon**. Gradually

spoon the marinade over the salmon and capsicum then turn to coat. Cover and marinate for 30 minutes. Thread the marinated salmon and capsicum pieces alternately onto four skewers. Grill the kebabs for about 3 minutes, and then turn, brush with the remaining marinade and grill for a further 2 minutes. Garnish with **2 tablespoons chopped fresh coriander** and serve.

COOK'S TIP

● Make this dish as hot or mild as you prefer. Choose the chilli according to its strength – mild, medium or very hot – or omit the chilli altogether for a non-spicy meal.

TROPICAL MANGO AND SALMON SALAD

Serves 4
Preparation 10 minutes Marinating 30 minutes
Cooking 5 minutes

Each serving provides • 1134 kJ • 271 kcal
• 23 g protein • 12 g fat of which 2 g saturates
• 20 g carbohydrates of which 8 g sugars • 2 g fibre

Preheat the grill to high. Place **400 g skinless salmon fillets**, cut into 50 g pieces, in a non-metallic dish. Make a marinade by combining **4 tablespoons light coconut milk, 2 teaspoons fish sauce, 1 finely chopped red chilli** and **1 teaspoon ground coriander seeds**. Pour the marinade over the salmon and gently turn to coat. Cover and marinate for 30 minutes. Meanwhile, slice **½ cucumber** and **1 fresh ripe mango**. Arrange **100 g mixed green salad** on four plates and add the cucumber slices. In a bowl, make a dressing by mixing **4 tablespoons light coconut milk, 1 tablespoon fish sauce**, the **juice of ½ lime, 1 crushed clove garlic, 1 teaspoon Thai chilli sauce** and **½ teaspoon caster sugar**. Remove the salmon from the marinade and grill for 5 minutes, or until cooked through in the centre. Arrange the salmon on the salad, drizzle with dressing and garnish each plate with **2 fresh basil leaves**.

COOK'S TIP

● Marinate the salmon for up to an hour if you have time, but avoid leaving it for any longer as the fish will begin to 'cook' in the marinade.

SALMON WITH POMEGRANATE GLAZE

Jewel-like pomegranate seeds add colour and zing to salmon fillets soaked in a mouthwatering fruity marinade. A quick dish to prepare and one that is guaranteed to impress.

Serves 4
Preparation 10 minutes
Marinating 15 minutes
Cooking 12 minutes

Each serving provides
• 1482 kJ • 354 kcal • 31 g protein
• 24 g fat of which 4 g saturates
• 4 g carbohydrates of which
4 g sugars • no fibre

100 ml pomegranate juice drink
2 tablespoons soy sauce
1 clove garlic, sliced
4 salmon fillets, about 150 g each
2 tablespoons olive oil or canola oil
seeds from ½ pomegranate
  (see Cook's Tips)

ALTERNATIVE INGREDIENTS
• Use tuna steaks instead of salmon, allowing about 100 g per portion.
• If you have a juicer, use it to make fresh pomegranate juice for the marinade. Juice the seeds from 1–2 fresh pomegranates to get 100 ml juice.

1 To make the marinade, pour the pomegranate juice drink and soy sauce into a large, shallow non-metallic dish. Stir the garlic into the juice. Place the salmon in the marinade and turn to coat. Cover and set aside to marinate for 15 minutes.

2 Preheat the grill to the hottest setting. Line the grill pan with foil and brush with a little of the oil. Drain the salmon, place on the foil, skin side down, and brush with oil. Pour the marinade into a small saucepan over a high heat and boil for 2–3 minutes, or until thick and syrupy.

3 Spoon a little of the reduced marinade over the salmon portions and grill for 3 minutes. Turn, baste with more marinade and grill for a further 4–6 minutes, basting once more, until glazed and cooked through. Transfer the salmon to four plates, pour any glaze from the grill pan over the fish and sprinkle with pomegranate seeds before serving.

COOK'S TIPS
● To prepare a pomegranate, use a sharp knife to score the skin into quarters, top to bottom, without piercing deeply into the fruit. Hold the pomegranate over a large bowl and pull it apart. The membranes and seeds will separate into uneven sections. Remove the seeds from the sections with your fingers, taking care to remove all the membrane and any pith, which both taste bitter.
● Serve the salmon with 100 g mixed salad leaves divided among the four portions.

SUPER FOOD

POMEGRANATES
There is some evidence that links pomegranate juice with slowing down the effects of ageing. The natural phytochemicals found in pomegranates may have anti-inflammatory properties that can help to relieve some of the symptoms of rheumatoid arthritis.

OAT-CRUNCH **FISH** WITH **AVOCADO** SALSA

Wholegrain rolled oats make a fibre-rich, crisp golden coating for melt-in-the-mouth pan-fried fish. They're served with a tomato and avocado salsa for just the right amount of palate-cleansing bite.

Serves 4
Preparation 10 minutes
Cooking 12 minutes

Each serving provides
• 1707 kJ • 408 kcal • 35 g protein
• 24 g fat of which 5 g saturates
• 12 g carbohydrates of which
3 g sugars • 3 g fibre

1 large ripe tomato
1 small green capsicum
1 spring onion
1 clove garlic, crushed
dash of hot chilli sauce
    such as Tabasco
1 ripe avocado
4 tablespoons low-fat milk
½ cup (60 g) rolled oats
4 skinless white fish fillets,
    such as bream, snapper or hoki
2 tablespoons olive oil
lemon wedges, to garnish

ALTERNATIVE INGREDIENTS
• Try thick pieces of skinned flounder or other skinned flatfish fillets. Trout and sardines are also delicious served in this way.
• Use a pinch of dried chilli flakes or 1 finely chopped fresh chilli instead of hot chilli sauce.
• For a Mediterranean slant on the salsa, add 4–6 shredded basil leaves in step 1, plus the finely grated zest of 1 lime.

1 Dice the tomato and capsicum and finely chop the spring onion. Mix them with the garlic in a small bowl. Stir in the hot chilli sauce. Dice the avocado and gently mix it with the other salsa ingredients.

2 Place the milk in a large shallow dish and spread half the oats over a large plate. Place the fish fillets in the milk and turn to coat them thoroughly. Transfer one fish fillet from the milk to the oats. Sprinkle 1 tablespoon of oats on top of the fillet and press them on gently to form a crust on both sides.

3 Heat a large frying pan over a medium–high heat. Add 1 tablespoon oil then transfer the oat-coated fillet to the pan. Coat a second fillet and add it to the pan. Cook the fish for 3 minutes, or until the underside is crisp. Turn the fillets and cook the second side for a further 3 minutes, or until crisp and golden.

4 Transfer the cooked fillets to a plate and keep them warm. Cook the remaining two fillets in the same way. Put the fish on four plates, add the salsa and garnish with lemon wedges.

COOK'S TIPS
● Use a large spatula and fork to turn the fillets. Be gentle but firm, sliding the spatula under each fillet in one movement to avoid breaking the fish.
● Rolled oats, or porridge oats, are the most successful variety for the oat crunch because they are slightly flaky and broken, which helps them to coat the fish.

SUPER FOOD

OATS
With a low glycaemic index (GI) value, oats provide sustained energy, helping to regulate blood glucose levels. Rolled oats and oatmeal are wholegrain foods that are packed with fibre for heart and digestive health. Oats are also plentiful in B vitamins, which are vital for maintaining a healthy metabolism.

CITRUS **FISH** WITH SAUTÉED **LEEKS** AND **ZUCCHINI**

Spoon a piquant orange sauce over moist white fish resting on a bed of vegetables gently infused with garlic – and enjoy. Wholesome fish has never been more delectable.

Serves 4
Preparation 15 minutes
Cooking 15 minutes

2 leeks
2 sticks celery
4 zucchini
450 g thick skinless white fish fillets, such as bream, snapper or hoki
3 tablespoons olive oil
2 cloves garlic, sliced
finely pared zest and juice of 1 orange

Each serving provides
- 1013 kJ • 242 kcal • 24 g protein
- 13 g fat of which 2 g saturates
- 7 g carbohydrates of which 6 g sugars • 4 g fibre

ALTERNATIVE INGREDIENTS
- Use 200 g mixed stir-fry vegetables (fresh or frozen) instead of the zucchini.
- Try salmon fillets with lemon zest and juice instead of white fish with orange zest and juice.
- Serve firm tofu instead of fish. Cook 350 g plain or smoked tofu in the same way as the fish in step 3. Turn over once to brown both sides, then slice the tofu and serve it with the vegetables.

1 Thinly slice the leeks and rinse them in a colander. Slice the celery and zucchini. Cut the fish into 4 cm chunks. Heat a large frying pan over a high heat and pour in 2 tablespoons oil. Add the leeks, celery and garlic. Reduce the heat to medium and cook, stirring, for 4 minutes, or until the leeks are softened.

2 Stir in the zucchini and cook for a further 3 minutes, or until the zucchini begin to soften. Do not overcook them as they will soften further when removed from the heat. Divide the vegetables among four warmed plates, set aside and keep warm.

3 Heat the remaining 1 tablespoon oil in the frying pan over a high heat. Add the fish and orange zest. Reduce the heat to medium and cook for 3 minutes. Pour in the orange juice and simmer for a further 3 minutes, or until the chunks of fish are firm and opaque.

4 Use a slotted spoon to transfer the fish to the plates. Boil the pan juices over a high heat for about 30 seconds, season to taste and spoon them over the fish before serving.

COOK'S TIPS
- If you do not have a parer, peel the orange zest using a potato peeler, then cut the zest into fine strips using a small, sharp knife.
- Serve the dish with a jacket potato baked in the oven for 1 hour at 190°C (170°C fan-forced).

SUPER FOOD

ORANGES
Rich in vitamin C, oranges also contain more than 170 different beneficial plant compounds. The nutrients and natural chemicals in oranges are thought to help to boost the immune system, regulate blood pressure and promote healthy skin.

HERB AND WALNUT CRUSTED FISH FILLETS

Chopped walnuts, herbs and breadcrumbs make a satisfying topping for lightly baked fish. Serve with simple buttered vegetables – these elegant fillets should be the star of the show.

Serves 4
Preparation 10 minutes
Cooking 20 minutes

Each serving provides
- 1381 kJ • 330 kcal • 27 g protein
- 21 g fat of which 3 g saturates
- 8 g carbohydrates of which
1 g sugars • 2 g fibre

2 tablespoons olive oil, plus
    1 teaspoon for greasing
4 thick portions skinless white fish
    fillets, about 125 g each
50 g walnuts
75 g fresh wholemeal breadcrumbs
4 tablespoons chopped fresh parsley
2 tablespoons snipped fresh chives
4 lemon wedges, to garnish

ALTERNATIVE INGREDIENTS
- Use swordfish or tuna steaks instead of white fish. Top each portion with 1–2 thick slices of tomato before adding the breadcrumb topping. Sprinkle 1 chopped garlic clove over the tomatoes for a punchy flavour.

- Try cashew nuts instead of walnuts and 1 tablespoon chopped fresh tarragon instead of parsley.
- Add the grated zest of 1 lemon and 1 finely chopped fresh green chilli to the breadcrumb mix for a citrus topping with a hint of heat.

1 Preheat the oven to 190°C (170°C fan-forced). Grease a large ovenproof dish with oil and place the fish fillets in it.

2 Chop the walnuts and add them to a bowl with the breadcrumbs, parsley and chives. Stir in 2 tablespoons oil, then scatter the breadcrumb topping over each portion of fish, gently pressing it down.

3 Bake in the oven for 20 minutes, or until the topping is browned and the fish is cooked through. Serve garnished with lemon wedges.

COOK'S TIPS
● If the fish fillets are thin, or have thin tail ends, fold them in half and tuck the tail ends underneath to make a thick, neat portion.
● To make 75 g fresh breadcrumbs, whizz 2 medium slices wholemeal bread in a food processor or blender. Alternatively, use a 75 g chunk of stale bread and rub it over the coarse blade of a grater into a large bowl. Fresh breadcrumbs freeze well, so make a large batch if you want extra for another time. The crumbs can be used from frozen.

SUPER FOOD

WALNUTS
Nuts are high in fat, but most of this is the monounsaturated kind that helps to guard against heart disease and lowers blood cholesterol. Walnuts also contain health-promoting omega-3 oils, as well as copper and magnesium to help to maintain strong bones, and nerve and muscle function.

FISH WRAPS WITH GRAPES AND SAVOURY WHITE SAUCE

Try this more substantial variation of a French classic, sole véronique. The generous sprinkling of green grapes melds perfectly with mild fish and a light, creamy sauce.

Serves 4
Preparation 10 minutes
Cooking 18 minutes

40 g lean rindless bacon
1 stick celery
1 small leek
1 tablespoon olive oil
400 ml dry white wine
8 skinless fish fillets such as dory,
    sole or flounder, about 65 g each
    (see Cook's Tips)
2 teaspoons cornflour
200 g seedless green grapes
120 g low-fat cream cheese or
    ½ cup (50 g) grated low-fat
    cheddar or tasty-style cheese

Each serving provides
• 1280 kJ • 306 kcal • 31 g protein
• 8 g fat of which 2 g saturates
• 12 g carbohydrates of which
10 g sugars • 1 g fibre

ALTERNATIVE INGREDIENTS
• For a non-alcoholic meal, use 400 ml grape juice instead of wine.
• Make a fennel sauce to serve with the fish. Trim and chop 1 small bulb fennel and add it to the sauce instead of the celery.
• Parsley, thyme and lemon make a good combination of ingredients for flavouring white sauce. For a herb-flavoured fish recipe, add 2 fresh thyme sprigs and the grated zest of ½ lemon with the wine in step 2. Stir in 2 tablespoons chopped fresh parsley just before serving.

1 Dice the bacon and celery and then chop the leek. Heat the oil in a large frying pan over a high heat. Add the bacon to the pan, reduce the heat to medium and cook for 1 minute. Add the celery and leek and cook for 2 minutes, or until the leek is softened.

2 Pour the wine into the pan, turn up the heat and bring to the boil. Reduce the heat to low, cover and simmer for 3 minutes. Roll up the fish fillets, from head to tail end, and secure with wooden cocktail sticks.

3 Mix the cornflour to a smooth paste with 1 tablespoon cold water, then stir this into the pan. Continue to stir the sauce until it begins to thicken. Add the fish rolls to the pan, bring back to the boil, reduce the heat, cover and simmer for 10 minutes, or until the fish is cooked through. Stir once or twice during cooking.

4 Slice the grapes in half and place half of them on a serving plate. Add the fish rolls and remove the cocktail sticks. Whisk the cheese into the sauce and cook until just beginning to boil. Season to taste and spoon over the fish. Top with the remaining grape halves and a sprinkling of black pepper before serving.

COOK'S TIPS
● Select a white wine for cooking that you would be happy to drink with the meal, otherwise your sauce may taste acidic.
● Look for firm, creamy-coloured fish fillets that are thin enough to be rolled. Avoid any that look old, grey or slightly discoloured. Ask the fishmonger to skin the fish.

SUPER FOOD

GRAPES
The skins of grapes contain large quantities of flavonoids (the pigments that give grapes their colour), which have beneficial anti-oxidant properties. Despite being higher in natural sugars than many other fruit, grapes have a low glycaemic index (GI) rating and so can help with appetite control.

MEDITERRANEAN **SEAFOOD** PIE

For low-fuss healthy eating, it's hard to beat a luscious mix of prawns, squid and mussels. Here, oregano, tomatoes and leeks mix temptingly with the seafood under a cheesy potato crust.

Serves 4
Preparation 10 minutes
Cooking 25 minutes

1 kg potatoes
1 large leek
1 tablespoon olive oil
1 clove garlic, crushed
400 g can chopped tomatoes
¼ teaspoon dried oregano
350 g frozen cooked mixed
   seafood, including mussels,
   prawns and squid
25 g grated parmesan

Each serving provides
• 1582 kJ • 378 kcal • 29 g protein
• 8 g fat of which 2 g saturates
• 50 g carbohydrates of which
6 g sugars • 6 g fibre

ALTERNATIVE INGREDIENTS
• Add 50 g sliced pitted black olives to the seafood mixture and the grated zest of 1 lemon to the potatoes.
• For a 'meatier' dish, include 200 g white fish, cut into chunks, and only half the seafood. Cook for 2–3 minutes at step 3 before adding the seafood.
• Mussels and boiled eggs are a good alternative to mixed seafood. Use 350 g cooked mussels and 4 hard-boiled eggs. Shell the eggs then cut into quarters. Arrange in the dish before pouring in the mussel mixture.

1 Peel the potatoes and cut into 3–5 cm chunks. Transfer them to a large saucepan. Add boiling water, cover and bring back to the boil. Simmer for 10 minutes, or until they are tender.

2 Meanwhile, preheat the grill to the hottest setting. Slice the leek. Heat the oil in a saucepan and cook the leek and garlic over a high heat for 2–3 minutes, stirring regularly, until the leek has softened. Stir in the tomatoes, rinsing out the can with 1 tablespoon of water. Add the oregano and bring to the boil. Reduce the heat, cover and simmer for 2 minutes.

3 Add the frozen cooked seafood to the pan with the tomatoes and bring back to the boil. Stir, then re-cover the pan and simmer for a further 2 minutes, or until the seafood is thoroughly heated through. Season to taste. Pour into a 1.4 litre, or 25 cm diameter, ovenproof dish.

4 Drain the potatoes and mash them. Spoon the potatoes evenly over the seafood, forking them up to the edge of the dish. Sprinkle with the parmesan and grill for 12–13 minutes, or until the topping is golden.

COOK'S TIPS
● Cutting root vegetables into chunks and using boiling water from a kettle reduces cooking time and saves energy. Pour in just enough water to cover the vegetables and use a large pan that covers the stove ring.
● The green parts of leeks add colour, flavour and nutritional value. Thinly slice the leek and separate into rings so that any grit can be washed away when rinsed in a colander under cold running water.
● Baking potatoes are ideal for this recipe as they tend to break down quickly when boiled, making them easy to mash.

SUPER FOOD

SEAFOOD
Low in fat, especially saturated fat, seafood is a good source of high-quality protein. It is also full of vital minerals and trace elements, including iron, zinc and selenium, important for maintaining a healthy immune system.

CHILLI PRAWN
AND PEA STIR-FRY

Rustle up a health-boosting meal in no time using prawns and frozen peas, which are often higher in nutrients than some shop-bought 'fresh' ones. Noodles make a satisfying accompaniment.

Serves 4
Preparation 10 minutes
Cooking 6 minutes

25 g fresh ginger
1 fresh red chilli
300 g white cabbage
1 tablespoon olive oil or canola oil
1 teaspoon sesame oil
300 g frozen peas
350 g peeled cooked large prawns
4 tablespoons chopped fresh
  coriander

Each serving provides
• 745 kJ • 178 kcal • 19 g protein
• 6 g fat of which 1 g saturates
• 11 g carbohydrates of which
6 g sugars • 6 g fibre

ALTERNATIVE INGREDIENTS
• If fresh prawns are not available, use frozen ones instead. Cook them from frozen, adding them to the pan at the end of step 1 and allowing an additional 1–2 minutes cooking time for them to thaw and heat through.
• Substitute small fresh scallops for the prawns. Use them whole or slice larger ones. Other cooked shellfish, such as cockles, baby clams or squid rings, work well in this dish.

1 Peel and finely grate the ginger. Chop the chilli into thin slivers (see Cook's Tips), discarding the seeds. Slice the cabbage into thin strips, 2–3 mm wide.

2 Heat the two oils in a large frying pan over a high heat. Stir-fry the ginger and chilli for a few seconds, then add the peas and stir-fry for 2 minutes, or until they turn bright green and are completely thawed.

3 Add the cabbage to the pan. Stir-fry for a further 3 minutes, then add the prawns and cook for a further 1 minute to heat them through. Toss in the coriander and stir, then serve immediately.

COOK'S TIPS
● Select chillies according to how hot you want the dish to taste – their strength is usually stated on the packaging. Mild to medium are good with light ingredients. Remember that starchy accompaniments such as noodles or rice will 'absorb' the heat.
● When you are preparing chillies, be careful to avoid rubbing your eyes by accident. Wash your hands immediately to get rid of the chilli stains, or wear a pair of rubber washing-up gloves for the task.
● Use whichever frozen peas you prefer – baby peas are small and sweet, but this recipe also works well with ordinary peas.

SUPER FOOD

PEAS
Frozen peas are frozen within hours of harvesting, locking in the nutrients, unlike some fresh peas that may have spent days in transit. Peas are an excellent source of fibre, which promotes a healthy digestive system.

PEAS

Rich in a range of vitamins and minerals, peas are an excellent source of vitamin C to boost the immune system, and potassium for healthy muscle and nerve function. Peas are also high in fibre, which is good for digestion and for the heart, and in lutein, a natural plant pigment that helps to protect eyesight.

FRENCH-STYLE PEAS

Serves 4
Preparation 10 minutes Cooking 25 minutes

Each serving provides • 703 kJ • 168 kcal
• 10 g protein • 7 g fat of which 2 g saturates
• 19 g carbohydrates of which 8 g sugars • 12 g fibre

Melt a **small knob of butter** in a saucepan over a medium heat with **1 tablespoon olive oil**. Add **16 small peeled shallots** and cook, stirring occasionally, for 5 minutes, or until lightly golden. Cut **1 soft round-headed lettuce** into eight pieces and add them to the pan with **600 g frozen peas, 200 ml hot vegetable stock** and **1 teaspoon caster sugar**. Bring to the boil, cover and simmer over a low heat for 20 minutes. Season to taste before serving.

COOK'S TIPS

● Use 2 sliced onions if you cannot buy shallots, and substitute fresh peas for frozen ones when in season. Note that shelling the fresh peas will increase your preparation time by 15 minutes.
● Chicken or lamb are ideal served with these peas.
● To add a minty twist, 5 minutes before the end of cooking sprinkle a few fresh mint leaves, or spearmint if available, and a handful of chopped fresh chervil into the pan. Remove the mint leaves before serving.

SPICY PUNJABI PEAS WITH LAMB

Serves 4
Preparation 10 minutes Cooking 30 minutes

Each serving provides • 1472 kJ • 352 kcal
• 29 g protein • 20 g fat of which 6 g saturates
• 15 g carbohydrates of which 8 g sugars • 2 g fibre

Put **1 large chopped onion, a grated 3 cm piece of fresh ginger, 2 finely chopped chillies** and **2 roughly chopped cloves garlic** in a blender, or in a bowl if you have a stick blender, and whizz to a coarse paste. Heat **2 tablespoons olive oil or canola oil** in a large frying pan over a medium heat. Add the paste and stir until the fragrant aromas begin to rise. Add **400 g minced lamb, 1 tablespoon garam masala** and **2 teaspoons turmeric** and cook, stirring, for 5 minutes, or until the meat is lightly browned. Add **250 g chopped peeled tomatoes** and cook, with a lid on the pan, over a medium-low heat for 20 minutes. Add **250 g frozen peas** and continue cooking for a further 5 minutes. Add salt and pepper to taste. Stir a handful of **chopped fresh coriander** into **200 g low-fat natural yogurt** and serve it with the lamb.

COOK'S TIP

● Serve with plain rice or chapatis (Indian flatbread).

LEMON AND PEA SAUCE

Serves 4
Preparation 5 minutes Cooking 4 minutes

Each serving provides • 824 kJ • 197 kcal
• 9 g protein • 13 g fat of which 2 g saturates
• 12 g carbohydrates of which 3 g sugars • 10 g fibre

Put **500 g frozen peas** in a saucepan and pour in boiling water to cover. Bring back to the boil, cover with a lid and simmer over a low heat for 4 minutes, or until tender. Drain and refresh under cold running water. Put the cooked peas in a blender, or in a bowl if you have a stick blender, with **1 large roughly chopped garlic clove, 1 tablespoon tahini, juice of ½ lemon, 1 teaspoon ground cumin, 1 teaspoon ground coriander, 2 tablespoons olive oil** and **1 teaspoon ground black pepper**. Blend for about 20 seconds, or until smooth. Season, spoon into a serving bowl and garnish with **1 tablespoon finely chopped fresh parsley**.

COOK'S TIPS

● Use this pea sauce as a dip, transforming it into a refreshing starter or party dish when served with batons of crunchy raw vegetables.

● Serve as a refreshing accompaniment to grilled meats or fish.

CREAMY ITALIAN SNOW PEAS WITH PASTA

Serves 4
Preparation 5 minutes Cooking 10 minutes

Each serving provides • 1455 kJ • 347 kcal
• 17 g protein • 6 g fat of which 3 g saturates
• 56 g carbohydrates of which 4 g sugars • 4 g fibre

Add **300 g dried pasta shapes** such as penne or fusilli to a saucepan filled with boiling water. Cook the pasta for 10 minutes, or until tender but with some bite. Meanwhile, cook **300 g snow peas** in a pan of boiling water for 3 minutes, or until cooked. Drain and return the snow peas to the pan. Add **200 ml low-fat ricotta, 1 tablespoon snipped chives, 2 teaspoons finely**

chopped **fresh mint** and **4 chopped spring onions** and toss together gently. Drain the pasta and transfer it to the pan with the sauce and snow peas. Mix it together and serve with **2 teaspoons grated parmesan** scattered over each portion.

COOK'S TIP

● For a contrasting flavour, add 100 g broad beans to this dish, cooked with the snow peas.

MINTED PESTO WITH LEEKS AND PEAS

Serves 4
Preparation 5 minutes Cooking 5 minutes

Each serving provides • 699 kJ • 167 kcal
• 5 g protein • 12 g fat of which 2 g saturates
• 10 g carbohydrates of which 4 g sugars • 7 g fibre

First make the pesto by mixing **1 small handful finely chopped fresh mint leaves, 1 tablespoon extra virgin olive oil, 2 teaspoons balsamic vinegar, ½ teaspoon caster sugar** and salt and pepper to taste in a small bowl. Thinly slice **2 small leeks**. Heat **2 tablespoons olive oil** over a medium-low heat and add the leeks. Fry for 5 minutes, or until softened. Meanwhile, simmer **300 g frozen peas** in a pan of boiling water for 4 minutes, or until cooked. Add the cooked peas to the leeks in the pan then stir in the minted pesto.

COOK'S TIPS

● Try this recipe as a side dish with lamb steaks.

● Mix the pesto, leeks and peas with wholewheat pasta and top with grated parmesan for a tasty supper.

POTATO AND ZUCCHINI MEDLEY WITH PICKLED HERRING

Toss hot new potatoes, crunchy zucchini and gherkins in a dill and yogurt dressing, then heap them on a plate with tangy pickled herring. Here is a meal that will help to keep your body in shape.

Serves 4
Preparation 15 minutes
Cooking 15 minutes

420 g new potatoes or waxy
   salad potatoes
4 small zucchini
4 large gherkins
2 tablespoons chopped fresh dill
2 tablespoons snipped fresh chives
1 tablespoon olive oil
⅓ cup (90 g) natural (plain) yogurt
2 tablespoons wholegrain mustard
260 g pickled herrings or
   rollmops, drained
1 large head of red or white witlof

Each serving provides
• 1364 kJ • 326 kcal • 19 g protein
• 15 g fat of which 2 g saturates
• 32 g carbohydrates of which
15 g sugars • 3 g fibre

ALTERNATIVE INGREDIENTS
• Use smoked mackerel, salmon or trout instead of herring.
• Substitute a small mignonette or baby cos lettuce for the witlof. These have a less bitter flavour than witlof, while still providing a crunchy texture.

1 Cut the potatoes in half, place them in a saucepan and cover with boiling water. Bring back to the boil over a high heat, cover and simmer for 15 minutes, or until tender.

2 Trim and slice the zucchini and slice the gherkins. Mix the raw zucchini and gherkins in a large bowl with the dill, chives and oil. Drain the potatoes and add them to the bowl, tossing them to coat in the herbs and oil.

3 Mix the yogurt and mustard to make a dressing. Slice the herrings in half or thirds. Arrange the witlof leaves on four plates. Divide the potato salad among the plates, arrange the herrings on top and spoon over a little dressing.

COOK'S TIPS
● Scissors are ideal for snipping chives. They are also great for finely shredding soft-leaf herbs, such as dill, fennel, mint and sage.
● Pickled herrings are sold canned or in jars, or in tubs in supermarket chiller cabinets. The name 'rollmops' refers to the way the fillets are rolled up and packed in a sweetened vinegar marinade.

SUPER FOOD

HERRING
Oily fish, such as herring, is one of the few foods naturally high in vitamin D, which is great for bone health. Emerging evidence suggests that a lack of vitamin D may be linked to an increase in the risk of developing diabetes, osteoporosis, multiple sclerosis and cancer.

PRAWN GOULASH WITH CAULIFLOWER AND BEANS

Smoky paprika and the aniseed taste of caraway seeds transform juicy prawns in this twist on a Hungarian classic. Cool yogurt and rice perfectly complement the rich spices.

Serves 4
Preparation 5 minutes
Cooking 13 minutes

Each serving provides
- 971 kJ • 232 kcal • 19 g protein
- 13 g fat of which 4 g saturates
- 11 g carbohydrates of which 8 g sugars • 3 g fibre

1 onion
2 tablespoons olive oil
1 clove garlic, crushed
350 g cauliflower
1 tablespoon paprika
1 teaspoon caraway seeds
2 bay leaves
400 g can chopped tomatoes
300 g frozen green beans
300 g peeled cooked large prawns
150 g natural yogurt

ALTERNATIVE INGREDIENTS
• Use frozen cooked prawns if fresh prawns are not available. Bring the sauce to the boil, add the frozen prawns and simmer for 2–3 minutes until they have thawed. Do not boil the prawns or they will toughen.
• Try skinless fresh salmon instead of prawns. Cut 350–400 g salmon fillet into bite-sized chunks and add them to the pan in step 4. Simmer for 3–4 minutes until cooked but still firm.

1 Finely chop the onion. Put the oil, onion and garlic in a large saucepan over a medium–high heat. Cook for 5 minutes, or until the onion is beginning to soften.

2 Break the cauliflower into bite-sized florets and add them to the pan. Stir in the paprika, caraway seeds and bay leaves. Cover and cook for 2 minutes.

3 Stir in the chopped tomatoes and 4 tablespoons of boiling water. Bring back to the boil, reduce the heat slightly, cover and simmer for 3 minutes, or until the cauliflower is just tender.

4 Stir in the frozen beans. Bring back to the boil, re-cover and cook for 2 minutes. Finally, add the prawns and gently heat through for 1 minute. Serve topped with a large spoonful of yogurt.

COOK'S TIPS
● Tender young cauliflower leaves and stalks are mild and sweet, and are just as nutritious as the florets. Although not used in this recipe, reserve leftover leaves and stalks for stir-fries.
● This dish also works well served with potato gnocchi, which are small dumplings sold fresh or in long-life vacuum packs.

SUPER FOOD

CAULIFLOWER
A member of the brassica family of vegetables, along with brussels sprouts, broccoli and cabbage, cauliflower has a range of anti-oxidants that can disarm potentially harmful free radicals and help to protect the body against cancer and heart disease.

SESAME SQUID
WITH CRUNCHY VEGETABLES

Chilli, garlic and sesame seeds lend their tempting aromas to protein-packed squid. A serving of soft noodles makes a great texture contrast to the crisp vegetables.

Serves 4
Preparation 15 minutes
Cooking 6 minutes

Each serving provides
- 1230 kJ • 294 kcal • 22 g protein
- 21 g fat of which 3 g saturates
- 5 g carbohydrates of which
3 g sugars • 4 g fibre

450 g squid tubes
1 red chilli
2 cloves garlic, crushed
grated zest of 1 lemon
1 leek
2 sticks celery
1 large yellow capsicum
1 large zucchini
250 g bok choy
3 tablespoons olive oil or canola oil
4 tablespoons toasted sesame seeds
4 lemon wedges, to garnish

ALTERNATIVE INGREDIENTS
- Instead of toasted sesame seeds, use 4 tablespoons pine nuts.
- For a stronger vegetable flavour, use red instead of yellow capsicum and choy sum (mustard greens) instead of bok choy.

1 Slice the squid tubes into 2 cm wide rings and place them in a bowl. Finely chop the chilli and mix it with the squid. Stir in the garlic and lemon zest. Thinly slice the leek, celery, capsicum and zucchini. Slice the bok choy, discarding the tough base.

2 Heat 2 tablespoons of the oil in a large frying pan over a high heat. Add the leek and celery and stir-fry for 2 minutes. Add the capsicum and zucchini and continue to stir-fry for 1 minute. Add the bok choy and cook for 2 minutes, or until it has wilted.

3 Heat another pan over a high heat. Add the remaining 1 tablespoon of oil. Add the squid and chilli flavouring. Fry for 1 minute, turning once, until the squid is just firm. Divide the vegetables among four plates. Place the squid on top of the vegetables and sprinkle with sesame seeds. Garnish each portion with a lemon wedge and serve.

COOK'S TIPS
- Heat the pan before adding the oil to cook the squid – the pan will retain the heat and the squid will cook quickly. Cook it too slowly and the squid will be chewy.
- Marinating the squid with garlic and chilli at the end of step 1 will intensify the flavour. Use a mild chilli for a hint of heat or a tiny birdseye chilli for a fiery flavour. If marinating the squid, mix 1 tablespoon oil with the seasoning, then cover and chill until needed.
- If you buy sesame seeds that are not already toasted, heat them in a large frying pan over a medium heat for 3–5 minutes, stirring, until they begin to brown. Don't let them burn or they will be bitter.

SUPER FOOD

SESAME SEEDS
Even eaten in small amounts, sesame seeds are still highly nutritious. They are rich in unsaturated fats, particularly polyunsaturated fats, which help to lower harmful cholesterol and so are good for heart health. The seeds also contain fibre to boost digestive health and calcium to protect bones.

POULTRY
and
GAME

AROMATIC **CHICKEN** WITH GRILLED **VEGETABLES**

Cardamom and lemon lend exotic flavour and irresistible Indian fragrance to simple low-fat ingredients. The zucchini are filling yet low in kilojoules, so you can tuck into this tastebud-tingling dish with gusto.

Serves 4
Preparation 10 minutes
Cooking 15 minutes

8 green whole cardamom pods
grated zest of 2 lemons
2 tablespoons olive oil
12 baby zucchini
½ cucumber
4 boneless, skinless chicken breasts,
   about 120 g each
4 shredded fresh mint leaves

Each serving provides
- 1121 kJ • 268 kcal • 34 g protein
- 13 g fat of which 3 g saturates
- 3 g carbohydrates of which
3 g sugars • 2 g fibre

ALTERNATIVE INGREDIENTS
- Use any white meat, such as turkey or pork, instead of chicken.
- The seasonings and vegetables in this recipe work well with fish, too. Grill mackerel, sardine or salmon fillets for 3–5 minutes on each side depending on the thickness of the fish.
- Substitute 2 teaspoons fennel seeds for the cardamom pods.
- Leave out the cardamom and add 1 tablespoon chopped rosemary and 2 finely chopped garlic cloves.

1 Preheat the grill to the hottest setting and line the grill pan with foil. Scrape the small seeds from the cardamom pods into a small dish. Add the zest from 1 lemon and stir in the oil. Cut the zucchini in half lengthwise. Cut the cucumber in half widthwise, then in half lengthwise and into batons about the same size as the zucchini.

2 Place the chicken in the centre of the grill pan and lay the zucchini and cucumber around the edges. Brush the chicken, zucchini and cucumber with the cardamom and lemon oil.

3 Grill everything for 5 minutes, then turn the chicken and vegetables over and grill for a further 10 minutes, or until the chicken is cooked through and the vegetables begin to brown. Divide the chicken among four plates and sprinkle over the mint and remaining lemon zest. Transfer the zucchini and cucumber batons to the plates and pour over any cooking juices.

COOK'S TIPS
- To check that the chicken is cooked, turn one piece over and pierce the thickest part with the tip of a sharp knife. The meat should be white, not pink, and the juices should run clear. If necessary cook for a few minutes longer. Turn the fillet over to conceal the slit when serving.
- Serve the chicken and vegetables with brown rice or new potatoes.

SUPER FOOD

ZUCCHINI
A water content of over 90 per cent makes the zucchini a low-energy (or low-kilojoule) food. With potassium to help to regulate blood pressure, folate for heart health and carotenes with anti-oxidant benefits, zucchini add plenty of health boosters to a balanced diet.

CHICKEN STIR-FRY WITH MUSHROOMS AND CASHEWS

Mildly sweet and crunchy, cashews are crammed with fibre, anti-oxidants, vitamins and minerals. Even better, tossed in with chicken and vegetables, they make an easy, appetising stir-fry.

Serves 4
Preparation 20 minutes
Cooking 10 minutes

2 teaspoons cornflour
100 ml dry sherry
2 tablespoons soy sauce
2 teaspoons sesame oil
180 g snow peas
1 onion
4 sticks celery
100 g shiitake mushrooms
2 carrots
100 g unsalted cashews
2 tablespoons olive oil or canola oil
300 g stir-fry chicken strips
1 clove garlic, crushed
200 g bean sprouts

Each serving provides
- 1075 kJ • 257 kcal • 23 g protein
- 11 g fat of which 2 g saturates
- 17 g carbohydrates of which
9 g sugars • 4 g fibre

ALTERNATIVE INGREDIENTS
- Try beef stir-fry strips (or frying steak cut into 2 cm strips) instead of the chicken. Use 300 g shiitake mushrooms and omit the bean sprouts.
- This is a good recipe for using 500 g ready-prepared mixed stir-fry vegetables. Add them in step 3 and stir-fry together instead of adding them in stages.
- Use oyster or Swiss brown mushrooms instead of the shiitakes.

1 In a small bowl, mix the cornflour with 1 tablespoon of cold water to form a smooth paste. Stir in the sherry, soy sauce and sesame oil. Put the snow peas in a large saucepan. Add just enough boiling water to cover, bring back to the boil then immediately drain and set aside. Thinly slice the onion, celery and mushrooms. Cut the carrots into 5 mm sticks.

2 Dry-fry the cashew nuts in a large frying pan over a medium–high heat for 2 minutes, shaking the pan until they begin to brown. Transfer to a plate. Add the oil and chicken strips to the pan. Stir-fry for 1 minute, increasing the heat to high, if necessary, so the chicken begins to brown. Add the onion, celery, carrots and garlic and stir-fry for 2 minutes.

3 Return the cashew nuts to the pan, add the mushrooms and stir-fry for 2 minutes. Pour in 120 ml of boiling water and stir in the cornflour paste. Bring to the boil and add the snow peas and bean sprouts. Simmer for 2 minutes, stirring, until the sauce thickens and the bean sprouts are thoroughly cooked. Season to taste and serve with rice or noodles.

COOK'S TIP
● There are many kinds of soy sauce, but the choice in supermarkets will usually be between dark and light varieties. Dark soy sauce is richer and thicker than light, with a lower salt content. If the amount of salt is a concern, look out for bottles of salt-reduced soy.

SUPER FOOD

CASHEWS
High in nutritional value, cashews are a good source of fibre, vitamin E, B vitamins and folate. Like other nuts, they satisfy hunger more readily than many other foods. Studies suggest nuts can help with weight management when eaten as part of a balanced diet.

TARRAGON **CHICKEN** WITH **APRICOT** SAUCE

An energising dish, in which dried fruit, pine nuts and fresh orange juice complement the more traditional tarragon seasoning. It is perfect with green beans and crushed new potatoes.

Serves 4
Preparation 5 minutes
Cooking 20 minutes

4 boneless, skinless chicken breasts, about 120 g each
4 tablespoons dijon mustard
1 tablespoon olive oil or canola oil
120 g dried apricots
6 sprigs fresh tarragon
juice of 2 oranges
4 tablespoons pine nuts

Each serving provides
• 1464 kJ • 350 kcal • 34 g protein
• 17 g fat of which 2 g saturates
• 16 g carbohydrates of which
16 g sugars • 2 g fibre

ALTERNATIVE INGREDIENTS
• Use 1–2 sprigs rosemary instead of the tarragon, or try 1 teaspoon dried tarragon if fresh is not available.
• Substitute chopped walnuts or pecans for the pine nuts.
• Try pork chops or steaks instead of the chicken breasts.

1 Preheat the grill to the hottest setting. Spread 2 tablespoons of the mustard over one side of the chicken breasts. Turn and spread with the remaining 2 tablespoons of mustard. Place the chicken, skin side down, in a flameproof casserole dish and drizzle with the oil. Grill on one side for 10 minutes.

2 Slice the dried apricots. Turn the chicken over and grill for a further 5 minutes. Sprinkle with the apricots and tarragon. Pour over the orange juice and grill for a further 5 minutes, or until the chicken is browned and cooked through.

3 Sprinkle the pine nuts over the chicken and grill for 30 seconds to warm through. Serve the chicken with the apricots, pine nuts and juices spooned over.

COOK'S TIPS
● Salt and pepper are not included in this recipe because the mustard sufficiently seasons the chicken. The apricot and orange bring a sweet-tangy balance that would be spoilt by additional saltiness.
● As an alternative to crushed potatoes, serve the chicken with grilled polenta slices. Buy ready-made polenta and follow the packet instructions, or make your own (see page 95).

SUPER FOOD

DRIED APRICOTS
As a concentrated source of energy-boosting carbohydrate, dried apricots make great snacks. They are also rich in the anti-oxidant beta-carotene, and just a handful of apricots provides up to one-sixth of your daily vitamin A needs – good news for eye health.

HERBED **CHICKEN** WITH **CRANBERRY** COLESLAW

Dried cranberries lend a rich intensity to a yogurty coleslaw, turning it into a light but distinctive accompaniment for thyme and sage-flavoured chicken. Team it with golden roast potatoes.

Serves 4
Preparation 15 minutes
Cooking 12 minutes

Each serving provides
- 1403 kJ • 335 kcal • 27 g protein
- 16 g fat of which 3 g saturates
- 21 g carbohydrates of which
12 g sugars • 7 g fibre

8 sprigs fresh thyme
6 large fresh sage leaves
2 tablespoons olive oil or canola oil
450 g boneless, skinless
   chicken breasts
300 g white cabbage
1 carrot
1 onion
4 tablespoons low-fat mayonnaise
4 tablespoons low-fat natural yogurt
50 g dried cranberries

ALTERNATIVE INGREDIENTS
• This recipe is great for using up leftovers from a roast chicken. Remove the meat from the bones and sprinkle with 2 tablespoons fresh thyme before serving with the coleslaw.
• Try raisins, diced dried apricots or chopped apple with its skin still on instead of cranberries.

1 Rub the leaves off the thyme sprigs into a large, shallow dish. Shred the sage leaves and add them to the dish with 1 tablespoon oil. Add the chicken breasts and turn them in the herb mixture to coat.

2 Shred the cabbage, coarsely grate the carrot and finely chop the onion, then mix them together in a large bowl. Blend the mayonnaise and yogurt and stir them into the vegetables. Season to taste and stir in the cranberries.

3 Heat a frying pan over a high heat. Add the remaining 1 tablespoon oil and add the chicken, including any herb mixture from the dish. Reduce the heat to medium and cook for 2 minutes on each side, or until browned. Reduce the heat to low and cook for 8 minutes, turning once or twice, until the chicken is cooked through (see Cook's Tip).

4 Divide the cranberry coleslaw among four plates. Slice the chicken and divide the pieces evenly over the salad.

COOK'S TIP
● Chicken breast sizes vary and the cooking time will depend on how large and thick they are. Make a small slit in the side of one of the chicken breasts using a sharp knife to see if the centre is cooked. If the meat is slightly pink, then continue to cook for a few more minutes.

SUPER FOOD

CRANBERRIES
Dried cranberries, like other dried fruit, have more concentrated nutritional goodness than the fresh variety. There is some evidence that cranberries can reduce the risk of developing recurrent urinary tract infections.

SPANISH **CHICKEN** WITH **CAPSICUM** AND **OLIVES**

Here is a complete meal-in-a-pan that makes the most of the flavour-drenched ingredients that give Mediterranean cooking its healthy reputation. For contrasting texture, serve with a crisp salad.

Serves 4
Preparation 15 minutes
Cooking 23 minutes

4 boneless, skinless chicken breasts,
    about 120 g each
1 large onion
3 capsicums (2 red, 1 green)
2 tablespoons olive oil
2 large cloves garlic, crushed
225 g long-grain rice
600 ml hot chicken stock
400 g can chopped tomatoes
½ cup (60 g) pitted black olives
1 tablespoon chopped fresh parsley

Each serving provides
• 1950 kJ • 466 kcal • 35 g protein
• 12 g fat of which 2 g saturates
• 59 g carbohydrates of which
8 g sugars • 3 g fibre

ALTERNATIVE INGREDIENTS
• Use stir-fry strips of lamb or beef as a change from chicken. Allow 400–450 g of meat for four people and stir-fry it for just 1 minute in step 1.
• When you have slightly more time to spare, use brown rice instead of white. Cook the rice for an extra 10 minutes in step 2.

1 Cut each piece of chicken lengthwise into three thick strips. Chop the onion and dice the capsicums. Heat the oil in a large lidded frying pan and cook the chicken for 3 minutes over a medium heat or until browned and partly cooked. Transfer the chicken to a plate.

2 Fry the onion, capsicum and garlic for 5 minutes over a medium heat, stirring until slightly softened. Return the chicken to the pan with any juices and sprinkle in the rice. Add the hot stock, then pour in the tomatoes. Bring back to the boil over a high heat. Stir, cover and simmer for 15 minutes, or until the rice is tender. Stir once again to prevent the rice from sticking to the base of the pan.

3 Roughly chop the olives and sprinkle them over the dish together with the parsley. Remove the pan from the heat, season to taste, re-cover and leave to stand for 1–2 minutes before serving.

COOK'S TIP
● If pitted olives are not available, buy olives with their stones still in place and use a cherry pitter to remove the stones quickly and efficiently before chopping.

SUPER FOOD

CHICKEN
Lean chicken is a good source of the amino acid tyrosine, which can help to promote mental alertness. It also contains the energy-releasing B vitamin niacin, which can help to boost energy levels, especially when you eat chicken with starchy foods such as rice.

SUPER FOOD

CHICKEN

High in protein and low in cholesterol-raising saturated fat, succulent chicken is a good meat to eat regularly. It contains all the essential amino acids, including tryptophan, which boosts levels of serotonin in the body, helping to combat emotional fatigue.

CHICKEN AND TOMATO SALAD

Serves 4
Preparation 35 minutes Marinating 30 minutes
Cooking 15 minutes

Each serving provides • 1393 kJ • 333 kcal
• 25 g protein • 22 g fat of which 3 g saturates
• 8 g carbohydrates of which 6 g sugars • 1 g fibre

Preheat the grill to medium–high. In a large bowl, mix **3 tablespoons olive oil, juice of ½ lemon, 2 crushed cloves garlic** and salt and pepper to taste. Cut **3 boneless, skinless chicken breasts**, about 120 g each, into three diagonal slices each and add them to the bowl. Turn the chicken in the oil mixture and leave to marinate for about 30 minutes. Meanwhile, make a dressing by mixing **2 tablespoons olive oil, 1 tablespoon balsamic vinegar, 1 tablespoon oil from a jar of sun-dried tomatoes, pinch of caster sugar** and **ground black pepper**. Transfer the chicken pieces to a non-stick baking tray and grill for 8 minutes. Turn, baste with the marinade and cook for 7 minutes, or until the juices run clear when the chicken is pierced with the tip of a sharp knife. In another large bowl, mix **80 g watercress, 40 g rocket leaves, 10 halved cherry tomatoes, 6 chopped sun-dried tomatoes** and ¼ **sliced cucumber**. Divide the salad among four plates and arrange the grilled chicken on top. Drizzle with the dressing and scatter **1 teaspoon finely chopped sun-dried tomatoes** over each serving.

COOK'S TIP

● Serve with warmed focaccia or olive bread.

LAZY DAYS BAKE

Serves 4
Preparation 10 minutes Cooking 45 minutes

Each serving provides • 1502 kJ • 359 kcal
• 22 g protein • 15 g fat of which 2 g saturates
• 37 g carbohydrates of which 14 g sugars • 5 g fibre

Preheat the oven to 180°C (160°C fan-forced). Heat **1 tablespoon olive oil** in a frying pan over a medium heat. Add **8 boneless, skinless chicken thighs** and fry for 10 minutes to brown all over. Cut **500 g sweet potatoes** into 1.5 cm slices and put them in a large bowl. Add **3 large red onions**, cut into quarters, and **2 tablespoons olive oil**. Coat the vegetables with oil, then transfer to a large roasting tin. Place the browned chicken in the roasting tin then add **8 unpeeled whole cloves garlic, 1 tablespoon finely chopped fresh thyme, 1 teaspoon finely chopped fresh rosemary** and salt and pepper to taste. Roast for 15 minutes, then turn and sprinkle with the **juice of 1 lemon** and **200 ml hot chicken stock**. Roast for a further 20 minutes, or until the chicken is cooked through and the vegetables are tender. Serve with the pan juices poured over.

COOK'S TIPS

● If the pan juices in the roasting tin begin to look dry near the end of cooking, pour in 4 tablespoons hot chicken stock or water.

● Steamed kale or spring greens add bite and plenty of beneficial iron when served as a side vegetable with this dish.

TEX-MEX CHICKEN WRAPS

Serves 4
Preparation 10 minutes Cooking 8 minutes

Each serving provides • 2401 kJ • 574 kcal
• 35 g protein • 17 g fat of which 3 g saturates
• 75 g carbohydrates of which 3 g sugars • 5 g fibre

Cook **130 g frozen sweetcorn** in a saucepan of boiling water for 3 minutes, then drain and set aside. Slice **4 boneless, skinless chicken breasts**, about 120 g each, into 1 cm strips. Heat **1 tablespoon olive oil** in a frying pan over a medium heat. Add the chicken fillets, **1 crushed clove garlic, 1 teaspoon paprika** and salt and pepper to taste. Stir-fry for 5 minutes, or until the chicken is cooked through. In a bowl, mash **1 sliced large ripe avocado** with **4 tablespoons shop-bought tomato salsa**. Stir in the corn and chicken, divide the mixture among **8 warmed wholemeal flour tortillas** (see Cook's Tip) and top with **1 heaped teaspoon reduced-fat crème fraîche**. Fold each tortilla up at the bottom and in at each side to make a handy parcel.

COOK'S TIP

● Warm the tortillas in a microwave or oven, according to the packet instructions.

CHICKEN PASTA SALAD

Serves 4
Preparation 5 minutes Cooking 13 minutes

Each serving provides • 1519 kJ • 363 kcal
• 30 g protein • 6 g fat of which 1 g saturates
• 50 g carbohydrates of which 18 g sugars • 2 g fibre

Cook **175 g wholewheat pasta spirals** in a saucepan of boiling water for 10 minutes, or according to the packet instructions. In a small bowl, make the

dressing by combining **75 g natural yogurt, 1 tablespoon lemon juice, ½ teaspoon French mustard, a pinch of caster sugar** and salt and pepper to taste. Add **250 g small broccoli florets** to the pasta, cook for 3 minutes then drain and leave to cool for 5 minutes. Transfer the pasta and broccoli to a serving bowl, add 4 tablespoons of the dressing and toss to coat. Cut **300 g cooked boneless, skinless chicken breasts** into 2–3 cm chunks and add them to the pasta with **1 chopped green capsicum, 1 chopped red apple** with the skin left on, **3 tablespoons sultanas** and **2 tablespoons walnut pieces**. Mix the salad together and serve.

COOK'S TIPS

● Replace the broccoli with green beans – cook them for 3 minutes, or until tender but still with some bite.

● Add flaked almonds instead of walnut pieces for a slightly sweeter, more delicate flavour.

WINTER BARLEY SOUP

Serves 4
Preparation 10 minutes Cooking 43 minutes

Each serving provides • 1343 kJ • 321 kcal
• 26 g protein • 12 g fat of which 1 g saturates
• 31 g carbohydrates of which 7 g sugars • 6 g fibre

Heat **2 tablespoons olive oil or canola oil** in a large saucepan over a medium–low heat. Add **1 large chopped onion, 2 sliced celery sticks** and **2 sliced carrots**. Cook for 10 minutes, stirring occasionally. Slice **150 g mushrooms** and add them to the pan with **2 crushed cloves garlic**, then stir-fry for 1 minute. Slice **350 g boneless, skinless chicken breasts** into 1 cm strips and add them to the pan with **100 g pearl barley**. Pour in **4 cups (1 litre) hot chicken stock**, cover and bring to the boil. Reduce the heat to low and simmer for 30 minutes, or until the barley is tender. Season to taste. Just before serving, toast **4 teaspoons flaked almonds** by dry-frying them over a medium heat for 2 minutes. Ladle the soup into bowls and garnish with **1 teaspoon chopped fresh parsley** and 1 teaspoon of the toasted flaked almonds per portion.

COOK'S TIP

● Use leftover roast chicken instead of raw chicken and reduce the cooking time by 10 minutes.

SHERRY-INFUSED **CHICKEN LIVERS** WITH **MUSHROOMS** AND **BEANS**

Rich chicken livers are invigorated with a splash of sherry and served with soft mushrooms and crisp green beans in this iron-rich dish. Velvety mash makes the perfect accompaniment.

Serves 4
Preparation 10 minutes
Cooking 15 minutes

Each serving provides
- 883 kJ • 211 kcal • 14 g protein
- 14 g fat of which 2 g saturates
- 6 g carbohydrates of which 4 g sugars • 4 g fibre

250 g chicken livers
1 onion
3 tablespoons olive oil
2 cloves garlic, crushed
5 sage leaves, shredded
300 g small mushrooms
300 g frozen green beans
2 tablespoons dry or medium sherry
grated zest of 1 lemon
4 tablespoons chopped fresh parsley
4 lemon wedges, to garnish

ALTERNATIVE INGREDIENTS
• To use fresh green beans instead of frozen, trim the ends and cook in a pan of boiling water for 3–4 minutes, or until tender. Drain and mix into the chicken livers in step 3 just before serving.
• For fans of liver and bacon, add 50 g diced smoked bacon or pancetta to the onion, garlic and sage in step 1.
• For a non-alcoholic meal, substitute white wine vinegar for the sherry.

1 Remove any tough white parts from the chicken livers and cut them into bite-sized pieces. Slice the onion. Heat 1 tablespoon of the oil in a large frying pan over a high heat. Add the onion, garlic and sage, reduce the heat to medium and cook for 5 minutes, or until softened.

2 Cut the mushrooms in half and add them to the frying pan. Cook for 3 minutes then add the frozen beans and cook, stirring, for a further 3 minutes, or until the beans are hot and most of the juice from the mushrooms has evaporated.

3 Push the vegetables to one side of the pan and pour in the remaining 2 tablespoons of oil. Add the chicken livers and cook over a medium heat for 2–3 minutes, turning until they are firm and cooked. Stir in the sherry and lemon zest and simmer for 1 minute. Sprinkle with parsley and garnish with lemon wedges.

COOK'S TIP
● The best way to prepare chicken livers is to place them on a plate and snip away the tough white sinews with a pair of scissors.

SUPER FOOD

CHICKEN LIVER

A rich source of easily absorbed iron and low in fat, chicken livers are packed with vitamin A, needed for healthy skin and to promote good vision. In addition, they contain some zinc and B vitamins, including B_{12}, and heart-protecting folate.

SWEET **CAPSICUM** AND **TURKEY** GRILL WITH GLAZED **MANGO**

The classic combo of turkey, ham and cheese is made lighter and healthier by adding grilled fruit and vegetables. High levels of protein and fibre will satisfy your hunger and help to keep you lean.

Serves 4
Preparation 10 minutes
Cooking 15 minutes

Each serving provides
- 1163 kJ • 278 kcal • 27 g protein
- 13 g fat of which 4 g saturates
- 12 g carbohydrates of which 11 g sugars • 2 g fibre

4 turkey breast steaks, about 100 g each
2 tablespoons olive oil or canola oil
1 ripe mango
2 red capsicums
1 teaspoon sugar
1 tablespoon cider vinegar
4 thin slices cooked ham
4 large fresh sage leaves
50 g grated mature cheddar

ALTERNATIVE INGREDIENTS
- Boneless, skinless chicken breasts or thighs or pork escalopes make good alternatives to turkey.
- Thinly sliced pears work just as well as mango. Use green capsicum strips instead of red and swap blue cheese for the cheddar.

1 Preheat the grill to the hottest setting. Lay the turkey steaks on the grill pan and brush with 1 tablespoon of the oil. Grill for 6 minutes, or until lightly browned. Peel and thinly slice the mango. Cut the capsicums into 1 cm strips.

2 Turn the turkey steaks over. Lay the mango around the turkey, then top the steaks with the capsicum strips and brush with the remaining oil. Grill for a further 6 minutes, or until the turkey is cooked – pierce it with a knife and if the juices run clear, then it is done.

3 Stir the sugar and cider vinegar together until the sugar dissolves, then sprinkle it over the capsicums and mango. Top each turkey steak with a folded ham slice, 1 sage leaf and some cheese. Grill for 3 minutes, or until the cheese has melted to a golden crispness. Serve drizzled with any cooking juices.

COOK'S TIPS
- Reduce the total fat content of this recipe by using reduced-fat cheddar and lean slices of ham with any excess fat trimmed off.
- Serve the turkey grills with couscous or burghul for added fibre and B vitamins, or turn it into a turkey melt sandwich on wholegrain bread.

SUPER FOOD

RED CAPSICUMS
Red capsicums are low in saturated fat and are a good source of fibre. They are rich in anti-oxidants and packed with several essential nutrients including vitamin C and betacarotene.

LIGHT AND SPICY **TURKEY CHILLI**

Cholesterol-lowering turkey guarantees the feel-good factor in this variation on a traditional chilli, while mushrooms and kidney beans add low-fat flavour. Serve with rice and salad for a main meal.

Serves 4
Preparation 10 minutes
Cooking 30 minutes

Each serving provides
- 1922 kJ • 459 kcal • 57 g protein
- 15 g fat of which 4 g saturates
- 24 g carbohydrates of which 11 g sugars • 8 g fibre

ALTERNATIVE INGREDIENTS
- For a vegetarian chilli, replace the turkey with 500 g minced Quorn or tofu.
- An equal quantity of pork or chicken mince makes a tasty alternative.
- Replace the peas with 250 g sliced zucchini and cook for a further 2–3 minutes, or until the zucchini are tender.
- Try cannellini beans or chickpeas instead of red kidney beans, and add frozen sweetcorn instead of peas.
- Okra is a good addition in this recipe. Thickly slice 250 g okra, discarding the stalk ends. Add to the chilli 5 minutes before the end of cooking in step 3.

SUPER FOOD

MUSHROOMS
Low in fat and kilojoules, mushrooms make an ideal addition to any weight-control dietary plan. They provide some B vitamins that encourage energy release from foods and are a useful source of selenium, an important anti-oxidant.

1 tablespoon olive oil or canola oil
500 g turkey mince
2 teaspoons cumin seeds
½–2 teaspoons dried chilli flakes (see Cook's Tips)
1 large onion
1 red capsicum
2 carrots
100 g small mushrooms
2 cloves garlic, crushed
400 g can chopped tomatoes
420 g can red kidney beans, drained
200 g frozen peas

1 Heat the oil in a large saucepan over a medium–high heat for a few seconds. Add the turkey mince, cumin seeds and chilli flakes and cook for 5 minutes, stirring occasionally, until the mince is lightly browned. If necessary, increase the heat to high for the final minute to boil off any excess juices from the turkey.

2 Prepare the vegetables – coarsely chop the onion, seed and dice the capsicum, coarsely dice the carrots and chop the mushrooms into quarters. Add the garlic, onion, capsicum, carrots and mushrooms to the pan. Continue to cook over a medium–high heat for a further 5 minutes, stirring frequently, until the vegetables are softened.

3 Stir in the tomatoes and 100 ml of boiling water. Bring back to the boil, reduce the heat slightly and cover the pan. Cook at a fairly rapid simmer for 15 minutes, stirring once or twice. Stir in the kidney beans and peas. Simmer for 1 minute, or until the beans and peas are heated through.

COOK'S TIPS
- If you cannot buy turkey mince in your local supermarket, make your own by processing 500 g lean turkey meat in a mincer or food processor, in batches, until the turkey has an even consistency.
- Add chilli flakes according to taste – ½ teaspoon will give a slight piquancy, 1 teaspoon will create a medium–hot chilli, while 2 teaspoons will produce a hot result.

TURKEY SOUVLAKI WITH GRILLED VEGETABLES

Take a popular Greek fast food, combine it with sweet red capsicums, punchy garlic and onions, and you have a mouth-watering, easy-to-prepare meal. Serve it with brown rice.

Serves 4
Preparation 10 minutes
Cooking 10 minutes

Each serving provides
- 2071 kJ • 495 kcal • 34 g protein
- 15 g fat of which 2 g saturates
- 61 g carbohydrates of which 12 g sugars • 5 g fibre

225 g quick-cook brown rice
½ teaspoon dried chilli flakes
3 teaspoons dried oregano
½ teaspoon ground mace or nutmeg
4 cloves garlic, crushed
3 tablespoons olive oil or canola oil
4 thin boneless, skinless turkey breasts, about 450 g
3 onions
2 red capsicums
½ cucumber
200 g natural yogurt
8–10 large fresh mint leaves, shredded to garnish
4 lemon wedges, to garnish

ALTERNATIVE INGREDIENTS
- Use chopped fresh green or red chillies instead of dried chilli flakes, selecting the variety according to your taste for fiery food.
- For a meat-free alternative, use 2 large eggplant instead of the turkey. Trim the ends and slice the eggplant lengthwise before grilling.
- Serve a large bowl of mixed salad instead of the cucumber and yogurt. Allow 1 large tomato, 1 spring onion and a wedge of lettuce per portion.

1 Put the rice in a pan of boiling water, cover, bring back to the boil and cook for 10 minutes, or according to the packet instructions. Preheat the grill to the hottest setting.

2 Meanwhile, cover the grill pan with foil. Mix the chilli flakes, oregano, mace or nutmeg, garlic and oil in a large shallow dish. Add the turkey breasts, turning them in the mixture to coat.

3 Cut the onions into wedges then cut the capsicums into thick strips. Transfer the turkey breasts to the foil. Put the onions and capsicums in the shallow dish. Using a spatula, scrape the remaining herb mixture over the vegetables and transfer them to the foil. Grill the turkey and vegetables for 8 minutes, turning to make sure they do not burn.

4 Slice the cucumber and cut each slice in half. Drain the rice when cooked and divide it among four plates. Top with the vegetables and turkey and add a spoonful of yogurt to each portion. Sprinkle with mint and garnish with lemon wedges to serve.

COOK'S TIP
● Thin turkey breast fillets may be labelled as quick-cook turkey breast steaks. Thicker portions, or packs that contain unevenly cut breast meat, are more economical and also suitable for this recipe. To ensure even cooking, slice the turkey into similar thicknesses before grilling.

SUPER FOOD

TURKEY
Lower in fat than red meats, turkey is a healthy choice when watching your weight. Rich in high-quality protein, needed for the growth and repair of body tissues, turkey makes a nutritious contribution to a well-balanced diet.

DUCK WITH CHESTNUTS AND PRUNES

Red wine and prunes bring out the richness of duck, seasoned with robust rosemary and juniper, while chestnuts and a hint of orange add extra flavour. This dish is particularly good served with zucchini batons and mash.

Serves 4
Preparation 10 minutes
Cooking 15 minutes

Each serving provides
- 1414 kJ • 338 kcal • 26 g protein
- 13 g fat of which 3 g saturates
- 32 g carbohydrates of which 20 g sugars • 5 g fibre

1 onion
6 juniper berries
1 tablespoon olive oil or canola oil
4 boneless, skinless duck breasts, about 120 g each
2 sprigs fresh rosemary
16 pitted prunes
150 g peeled cooked chestnuts
pared zest of 1 orange
400 ml red wine
8 orange slices, to garnish

ALTERNATIVE INGREDIENTS
- Try venison leg steaks or pork loin steaks instead of duck.
- Use dried peaches as a change from prunes. Cut the peaches in half and again widthwise to form chunks.
- Substitute cranberry juice or pomegranate juice drink for the red wine. Pomegranate juice drink tends to be very sweet, so mix it with the juice of 1 orange before adding it to the pan.
- Replace the chestnuts with small button mushrooms.

1 Slice the onion and crush the juniper berries. Heat a frying pan over a high heat. Add the oil and the duck breasts and pan-fry for 1 minute on each side, pressing the duck onto the hot pan to brown evenly. Reduce the heat to medium, add the onion and rosemary and cook for 2 minutes. Turn the duck and onions, cover with a lid and cook for a further 2 minutes. Transfer them to a plate.

2 Add the crushed juniper berries, prunes, chestnuts and orange zest to the pan. Pour in the wine and bring to the boil over a high heat. Boil for 3 minutes to reduce the wine a little.

3 Return the duck and onions to the pan with any juices and turn down the heat to low. Cover and simmer for 3 minutes, stirring now and then. Divide the duck, chestnuts and prunes among four plates. Spoon over the sauce and garnish with orange slices.

COOK'S TIPS
- Juniper berries are one of the flavouring ingredients in gin. They are dark purple-black, tender and easily crushed into small pieces with a mortar and pestle. You will find them in the herb and spice aisle in most large supermarkets.
- Cooked chestnuts are usually sold vacuum packed or in cans.

SUPER FOOD

PRUNES

Prunes have the highest anti-oxidant score of all fruit, helping to protect the body against cancer. They also provide a concentrated source of valuable nutrients, including fibre, carbohydrate, vitamins, minerals and phytonutrients (essential nutrients found in plants that help to keep us healthy).

CHINESE **DUCK** WITH **PANCAKES**

A lower-fat version of crisp-skinned duck, this recipe uses skinless duck breasts and balances the richness of the hoisin sauce with green capsicums and a simple ginger marinade.

Serves 4
Preparation 15 minutes
Marinating 30–60 minutes
Cooking 8 minutes

Each serving provides
- 1920 kJ • 459 kcal • 29 g protein
- 18 g fat of which 4 g saturates
- 37 g carbohydrates of which
9 g sugars • 3 g fibre

60 g fresh ginger
1 clove garlic, crushed
1 tablespoon soy sauce
1 tablespoon sesame oil
90 ml dry sherry
4 boneless, skinless duck breasts, about 120 g each
1 green capsicum
½ cucumber
8 spring onions
2 tablespoons olive oil or canola oil
20 Chinese pancakes
4 tablespoons hoisin sauce

ALTERNATIVE INGREDIENTS
- Instead of using whole duck breasts, try more economical stir-fry duck breasts. Stir-fry in hot oil for 3–5 minutes, then pour in the marinade and stir in the hoisin sauce. Bring to the boil, reduce the heat and simmer for 1 minute.
- Pork or lamb steaks make a good alternative to duck.
- As a change from Chinese pancakes, serve 2 large wholemeal tortillas for each portion.

1 Grate the ginger into a large shallow dish. Stir in the garlic, soy sauce, sesame oil and sherry. Add the duck and turn to coat in the marinade. Cover and marinate for 30–60 minutes. Cut the capsicum and cucumber into batons. Trim and slice the spring onions into fine strips. Arrange the vegetables on a serving dish.

2 Heat the oil in a frying pan over a high heat. Transfer the duck to the pan, reserving the marinade. Fry the duck for 1 minute on each side. Reduce the heat to low, cover and cook for 5 minutes, turning twice, until the duck is browned but still pink inside. Warm the pancakes according to the packet instructions.

3 Slice the duck and transfer it to a warmed serving dish. Add the marinade to the pan and boil it with the pan juices for 1 minute to thicken. Scrape the sediment off the base of the pan and stir in the hoisin sauce before removing from the heat. Serve each pancake with the vegetable batons, onion strips, a few slices of duck and the sauce.

COOK'S TIPS
- Marinate the duck breasts in an airtight container in the fridge for up to 24 hours to intensify the garlic flavour.
- To check whether the duck is cooked, pierce one breast with a small knife – if the meat is bloody, it needs further cooking; if it is pink but firm, it is cooked. If you prefer your meat well done, cook the duck for 9–10 minutes until the inside is brown.

SUPER FOOD

GINGER
Some studies have linked ginger to relief from arthritis and joint pain. Compounds in ginger called gingerols may have anti-oxidant properties, helping to protect against heart disease and some cancers.

PAN-FRIED **VENISON** WITH **NECTARINE** CHUTNEY

Venison has about one-third the fat of beef, and is lower in saturated fat and kilojoules, too. Dress it up with a fruity chutney, and accompany with crushed potatoes and watercress for a mouth-watering, guilt-free steak dinner.

Serves 4
Preparation 15 minutes
Cooking 15 minutes

Each serving provides
- 1180 kJ • 282 kcal • 30 g protein
- 11 g fat of which 2 g saturates
- 20 g carbohydrates of which 19 g sugars • 2 g fibre

2 red onions
4 ripe nectarines
2 tablespoons olive oil or canola oil
2 tablespoons soft light brown sugar
2 tablespoons red wine vinegar
¼ teaspoon ground allspice
4 venison steaks, about 125 g each

ALTERNATIVE INGREDIENTS
- Use duck breasts or kangaroo fillets instead of venison. Both taste excellent with this fruit chutney.
- A pinch each of ground cinnamon and mace or nutmeg, instead of allspice, gives warmth to the chutney.
- Try peaches, plums or firm mangoes as a change from nectarines.

1 Thinly slice the onions and cut the nectarines into 1 cm slices. Heat 1 tablespoon of the oil in a saucepan over a medium heat. Add the onions and cook for 5 minutes, or until beginning to brown. Stir in the sugar and vinegar then reduce the heat to low. Stir in the allspice and nectarines. Cook for 3 minutes, or until the onions and nectarines are softened.

2 Meanwhile, use scissors to snip off any membrane around the edge of the venison steaks as this will shrink rapidly during cooking and cause the steaks to curl. Heat a large frying pan over a high heat until very hot. Pour in the remaining 1 tablespoon of oil and add the steaks. Cook for 2 minutes on each side, or until browned. Use a spatula to press them gently onto the pan so that they cook evenly.

3 Reduce the heat to medium–low and cook the steaks for a further 2 minutes, turning once, until the meat is cooked to your liking (see Cook's Tips). Transfer the steaks to four warmed plates, season with freshly ground black pepper and serve with the chutney.

SUPER FOOD

NECTARINES

As a good source of potassium, which lowers blood pressure, nectarines may help to protect against strokes. They also contain some insoluble fibre for keeping the digestive system healthy, plus soluble fibre to help to lower blood cholesterol.

COOK'S TIPS
- Cook the venison for 5 minutes, turning once, for a steak that is pink in the middle, or up to 8 minutes, turning twice, for a steak that is well done and brown throughout.
- Venison steaks vary in thickness, which will affect their cooking times. Lay the steaks well apart on a sheet of baking paper or plastic wrap, cover with a second sheet, then lightly beat the steaks with a rolling pin or meat tenderiser until they are an even thickness. For this recipe, a steak 1.5–2 cm thick is best.

SAUSAGES WITH SWEETCORN RELISH

A honey and vinegar relish full of colourful vegetables makes an eye-catching accompaniment to meaty sausages. Serve with green salad and crisp roast potatoes for a satisfying meal.

Serves 4
Preparation 10 minutes
Cooking 20 minutes

2 capsicums (1 red, 1 orange)
1 carrot
1 onion
8 good-quality sausages
2 tablespoons olive oil or canola oil
1 clove garlic, crushed
150 g frozen sweetcorn
1 teaspoon cornflour
3 tablespoons cider vinegar
3 tablespoons honey
1 tablespoon wholegrain mustard

Each serving provides
• 1983 kJ • 474 kcal • 28 g protein
• 26 g fat of which 7 g saturates
• 34 g carbohydrates of which 24 g sugars • 5 g fibre

ALTERNATIVE INGREDIENTS
• Transform the relish into a cold accompaniment by reducing the vinegar and honey to 1 tablespoon each. Add 100 g frozen broad beans with the sweetcorn. Stir in the vinegar and honey but leave out the cornflour and mustard. Allow the relish to cool before serving.
• Serve the sausages sliced on top of large baked potatoes with the relish. Add a spoonful of crème fraîche or Greek yogurt.
• Try any good-quality sausages, such as venison, kangaroo, bratwurst, pork or Italian style.

1 Preheat the grill to high. Finely dice the capsicums and carrot, and chop the onion. Grill the sausages for 20 minutes, turning, until they are evenly browned.

2 Meanwhile, heat the oil in a saucepan over a high heat. Add the capsicum, carrot, onion and garlic. Mix well, reduce the heat to medium and cook for 5 minutes, stirring occasionally, until the vegetables have softened. Stir in the sweetcorn, cover and cook for 1 minute, or until the corn has thawed.

3 Mix the cornflour with the vinegar to form a paste. Stir the honey, mustard and vinegar paste into the pan. Bring the relish to the boil and simmer for 1 minute. Transfer the cooked sausages to four plates and serve with the relish.

COOK'S TIP
● If your oven is on for the roast potato accompaniment, place the sausages in a shallow ovenproof dish or in a roasting tin. Allow about 30 minutes at 180°C (160°C fan-forced), until the skins are browned and the sausages are cooked. Turn them halfway through cooking.

SUPER FOOD

SWEETCORN
The distinctive yellow colour of corn is due to the pigment lutein, a compound with an important role in eye health. Lutein can help to protect eyes from age-related macular degeneration, which is a common form of blindness in industrialised countries.

MEAT

LAMB MEDALLIONS WITH REDCURRANT JUS

Try a quick, lower-fat version of a slow-roasted country classic that has lost none of its flavour or goodness. Team it with crushed new potatoes for a hearty, sustaining meal.

Serves 4
Preparation 10 minutes
Cooking 15 minutes

Each serving provides
- 1828 kJ • 437 kcal • 26 g protein
- 28 g fat of which 9 g saturates
- 20 g carbohydrates of which 12 g sugars • 2 g fibre

200 g new potatoes
2 leeks
450 g lamb loin fillet
3 tablespoons olive oil
250 g small broccoli florets
400 g can cannellini beans, drained
2 chopped fresh rosemary sprigs
90 ml balsamic vinegar
2 tablespoons redcurrant jelly

SUPER FOOD

CANNELLINI BEANS

As with other beans, cannellini beans score low on the glycaemic index (GI) scale, which makes them a longer-lasting energy source than many other foods. These beans also contain high levels of fibre – good news for heart and digestive health.

ALTERNATIVE INGREDIENTS
- As a less expensive alternative to fillet, slice lean lamb steaks into wide strips at an acute angle across the grain of the meat.
- Sliced pork tenderloin or stir-fry pork strips make good alternatives to lamb.
- Try chickpeas, borlotti beans or flageolet beans instead of cannellini beans.
- Redcurrant jelly has a sharp-sweet flavour. Other suitable fruit preserves include crabapple jelly and orange marmalade.

1 Boil the potatoes in a pan of boiling water for 15 minutes, or until cooked. Meanwhile, slice the leeks, cut each slice in half and rinse in a colander. Cut the lamb fillet into 2 cm thick slices. Heat 2 tablespoons oil in a large frying pan over a high heat. Add the leeks, reduce the heat to medium and cook, stirring, for 3 minutes, or until tender.

2 Add the broccoli and cook, stirring, for a further 3 minutes. Stir in the cannellini beans and heat through for 1 minute. Put the vegetables and beans in a dish, cover and keep warm.

3 Add the remaining 1 tablespoon oil, lamb slices and rosemary to the pan. Cook over a medium–high heat for 2 minutes, pressing the lamb slices onto the pan so that they brown quickly and evenly. Turn the slices and cook for a further 3 minutes, or until browned. Transfer the lamb to the dish with the vegetables and keep warm.

4 Replace the pan over a high heat. Pour in 4 tablespoons of water and the balsamic vinegar. Add the redcurrant jelly, stirring until melted. Boil the redcurrant sauce rapidly, stirring continuously, for 1 minute. Drain the potatoes and gently crush them with a fork. Divide the lamb, beans and potatoes among four plates and spoon over the sauce.

COOK'S TIP
● Fillet of lamb is a lean section of meat cut from the neck or loin of the animal. It is sometimes sold as tenderloin, or ready sliced as medallions. This recipe uses loin fillet as it can be cooked reasonably quickly without becoming tough.

INDIAN **LAMB** WITH **APRICOTS**

Everyone enjoys a no-fuss meal at the weekend, and this korma-style curry is both quick and nutritious. Serve the tender strips of lamb and succulent apricots with warmed naan.

Serves 4
Preparation 15 minutes
Cooking 12 minutes

4 tablespoons flaked almonds
350 g lean lamb
1 onion
100 g dried apricots
1 tablespoon olive oil or canola oil
1 large clove garlic, crushed
4 tablespoons ground almonds
1 tablespoon tandoori spice mix
200 ml plain yogurt
25 g fresh coriander leaves, chopped

Each serving provides
• 1230 kJ • 294 kcal • 23 g protein
• 15 g fat of which 4 g saturates
• 17 g carbohydrates of which
15 g sugars • 7 g fibre

ALTERNATIVE INGREDIENTS
• For a change, use pork or chicken instead of lamb.
• For a full flavoured alternative, kangaroo and ostrich, sometimes found at farmers' markets, are both lean meats that are great for stir-frying.
• If you cannot find tandoori spice mix, good-quality curry powder works well.
• Try pistachios instead of flaked almonds, toasting them very lightly.
• Reduce the apricots to 75 g and add 25 g dried cranberries.

1 Toast the flaked almonds in a large, dry frying pan over a medium heat, shaking the pan occasionally, until they are browned. Remove from the pan and set aside. Cut the lamb into bite-sized strips, halve and thinly slice the onion and slice the dried apricots.

2 Increase the heat to high, add the oil and stir-fry the lamb for about 4 minutes, or until the meat is browned. Add the onion and the garlic to the pan. Stir-fry for 2 minutes, or until the onion begins to soften.

3 Stir the apricots, ground almonds and spice mix into the lamb and continue to fry for 2–3 minutes, reducing the heat slightly if needed to prevent the mixture from burning.

4 Stir in the yogurt, taking care as the hot liquid may split. Let the sauce bubble for 1–2 minutes, turning and stirring, until it is thick and creamy. Stir in the coriander leaves and toasted almonds before serving.

COOK'S TIPS
● Scissors are more effective than a knife for cutting apricots into strips.
● Leg steaks or fillet are the best cuts of lamb for this recipe. Look out for ready-cut stir-fry strips, too.
● Getting the pan hot before adding the meat is important for a tasty result. This way, the meat browns and cooks quickly to become tender and succulent, instead of stewing and toughening in its own juices.

SUPER FOOD

DRIED APRICOTS
Good for eye, heart and digestive health, just three dried apricots count as one of your seven-a-day servings of fruit and vegetables. Unusually for a fruit, dried apricots are a useful source of calcium, which is good for keeping bones strong.

SAUTÉED LAMB AND GREEN BEANS WITH CREAMY CAPER SAUCE

A seemingly self-indulgent dish cleverly deceives your taste buds by using low-fat cream cheese instead of cream. Salty capers work brilliantly with lamb and give a real flavour kick. Serve with boiled new potatoes.

Serves 4
Preparation 10 minutes
Cooking 20 minutes

Each serving provides
• 1056 kJ • 252 kcal • 27 g protein
• 12 g fat of which 3 g saturates
• 6 g carbohydrates of which
4 g sugars • 3 g fibre

1 onion
400 g lamb fillet, trimmed of fat
2 tablespoons capers
1 tablespoon olive oil or canola oil
250 g frozen green beans
1 teaspoon cornflour
2 tablespoons low-fat milk
100 g low-fat cream cheese or
   ½ cup (50 g) grated low-fat
   cheddar or tasty-style cheese
3 tablespoons chopped fresh parsley

ALTERNATIVE INGREDIENTS
• Fresh green beans work just as well as frozen ones. Trim them then cook in boiling water for 2–3 minutes until just tender. Drain and continue as for the frozen beans.
• Use frozen broad beans instead of green beans.
• Try veal or pork escalopes instead of lamb. Cook the meat whole, frying it on either side, or cut it into thin strips and stir-fry it.

1 Slice the onion, then slice the lamb into 1 cm thick pieces. Drain and rinse the capers. Heat the oil in a large frying pan over a high heat. Add the onion, reduce the heat to medium and cook for 5 minutes, or until the onion begins to soften and brown.

2 Push the onion to one side of the pan and add the lamb. Cook for 6 minutes, turning the meat occasionally and pressing the pieces onto the bottom of the hot pan to ensure they brown evenly. Add the green beans and onion and cook, stirring, for a further 2 minutes. In a small dish, stir the cornflour and milk together to form a smooth paste. Use tongs or a slotted spoon to transfer the meat, beans and onion to a dish and keep warm.

3 Add 6 tablespoons of boiling water to the pan and boil over a high heat, stirring with a whisk. Reduce the heat to low, whisk in the milk and cornflour paste and bring back to the boil. Beat the cream cheese lightly with a fork to soften it then gradually whisk it into the sauce until smooth and hot. Stir in the capers and parsley. Transfer the lamb and beans to four plates and spoon a little sauce over each portion.

COOK'S TIP
• When adding the boiling water to the empty pan in step 3, run the whisk over the bottom of the pan to remove any meat and vegetable sediment. This will add extra flavour to the creamy caper sauce.

SUPER FOOD

GREEN BEANS
This versatile vegetable is a good source of both vitamins and minerals, including some calcium and folate. Just 4 tablespoons of green beans count as one of your seven-a-day, and with virtually no fat they are a low-kilojoule bonus to any weight-management program.

DEVILLED **STEAK** WITH **CAPSICUM** BATONS

A hot tomato and mustard coating gives plenty of 'devilish' flavour to lean beef. Then sun-ripened capsicums and onions soak up the delicious pan juices. Serve with oven-baked potato wedges.

Serves 4
Preparation 15 minutes
Cooking 10 minutes

1 tablespoon tomato purée
2 tablespoons wholegrain mustard
4 thin beef escalopes, about
   75 g each
4 tablespoons rolled oats
4 capsicums (2 red, 2 yellow)
2 onions
2 tablespoons olive oil or canola oil

Each serving provides
- 1088 kJ • 260 kcal • 21 g protein
- 13 g fat of which 3 g saturates
- 16 g carbohydrates of which
14 g sugars • 5 g fibre

ALTERNATIVE INGREDIENTS
- When time is short, serve the steaks in hamburger buns with a side salad.
- For a spicier topping, add 1 crushed clove garlic and a pinch of dried chilli flakes to the tomato mixture.
- Use pork, veal, chicken or turkey escalopes instead of beef.
- To make a rich mushroom glaze for this dish, fry 250 g sliced or button mushrooms in the pan after cooking the meat for 2–3 minutes. Add 2 tablespoons brandy and boil rapidly to reduce the alcohol to a thick consistency. Remove from the heat and pour over the steak.

1 Mix the tomato purée and wholegrain mustard. Place the beef escalopes on a board and spread a thin layer of the mixture over them. Sprinkle the escalopes with oats and pat to make a neat coating. Turn and repeat for the other sides. Slice the capsicums and onions into long strips.

2 Heat a large non-stick frying pan over a high heat. Add 1 tablespoon oil, reduce the heat to medium and add the steaks. Press down on the steaks gently but firmly with a spatula for 3 minutes, or until the oat base is crisp and golden. Turn the steaks and cook for 2 minutes, or until browned. Transfer to four plates and keep warm.

3 Replace the pan over a high heat and add the remaining oil, the capsicums and onions. Cook for 2 minutes, stirring up the juices from the pan. Reduce the heat and cook for a further 3 minutes, or until the vegetables slightly soften. Transfer the capsicums and onions to the plates of steak and serve.

COOK'S TIP
- Make sure that you buy beef escalopes and not thin frying steaks. Unlike thin frying steaks, escalopes are lean and not marbled with fat, making them ideal for coating. In addition, they do not have the fine line of chewy connective tissue that some thin steaks have, which needs to be removed before cooking.

SUPER FOOD

OATS
Because they help to stabilise blood glucose levels, oats, if eaten regularly, can lower the risk of developing Type 2 diabetes. As part of a low-fat diet, oats can also help to lower blood cholesterol levels, which may lessen the risk of developing heart disease.

BEEF

Lean beef is an excellent source of high-quality protein – one 50 g serving will provide up to one-third of your daily needs. It also contains only about 5 per cent fat, almost half of which is the healthier monounsaturated type. Rich in iron, zinc and B vitamins, beef helps to boost the immune system and improves the health of your blood.

ITALIAN SUMMER CASSEROLE

Serves 4
Preparation 10 minutes Cooking 40 minutes

Each serving provides • 1017 kJ • 243 kcal • 27 g protein • 12 g fat of which 3 g saturates • 8 g carbohydrates of which 7 g sugars • 2 g fibre

Heat **1 tablespoon olive oil or canola oil** in a flameproof casserole dish over a medium heat. Slice **1 onion** and **1 yellow capsicum** and add them to the dish. Cook for 5 minutes, stirring occasionally. Add **1 chopped clove garlic** and **400 g thinly sliced lean beef steak**. Stir-fry for 2 minutes, or until the meat is lightly browned. Add **400 g canned chopped tomatoes, 1 tablespoon red capsicum pesto, 1 beef stock cube, 100 ml boiling water** and **2 tablespoons chopped fresh parsley**. Bring to the boil, turn down the heat to low, cover and simmer for 20 minutes, stirring halfway through. Remove the lid and cook for a further 5–10 minutes, or until the liquid has reduced to give a moist but not watery result. Scatter over **40 g sliced pitted green olives** and serve.

COOK'S TIPS

● For quick cooking, a cut of beef such as rump or sirloin is best, but less expensive chuck steak is also fine. Trim off any excess fat and increase the cooking time to 1 hour, adding more water to the pan halfway through to prevent the meat from drying out.

● Serve the casserole with new potatoes and a green vegetable, or with wholewheat penne pasta.

BEEF AND VEGETABLE BOLOGNESE SAUCE

Serves 4
Preparation 10 minutes Cooking 1 hour 10 minutes

Each serving provides • 842 kJ • 201 kcal • 23 g protein • 8 g fat of which 2 g saturates • 10 g carbohydrates of which 8 g sugars • 3 g fibre

Heat **1 tablespoon olive oil** in a large frying pan and add **1 large onion, 1 large carrot** and **1 large stick celery**, all finely chopped. Fry over a medium–high heat, stirring occasionally, for 5 minutes, or until the onion softens. Push the vegetables to the edge of the pan and add **350 g lean beef mince**. Turn the heat up and stir-fry the meat for 2 minutes to brown slightly. Stir in **225 g canned chopped tomatoes, 1 tablespoon tomato purée, 1 beef stock cube, 200 ml boiling** water and **2 teaspoons mixed dried herbs**. Season to taste. Bring to the boil, turn down the heat to low, cover and simmer for 1 hour, adding a little water towards the end of cooking if the dish looks dry.

COOK'S TIP

● Serve the bolognese sauce over wholewheat spaghetti or brown rice and top with grated parmesan and some extra ground black pepper.

SPINACH, BEEF AND BEAN SPROUT STIR-FRY

Serves 4
Preparation 10 minutes Cooking 7 minutes

Each serving provides • 803 kJ • 192 kcal
• 26 g protein • 9 g fat of which 3 g saturates
• 3 g carbohydrates of which 2 g sugars • 2 g fibre

Heat **1 tablespoon olive oil or canola oil** in a wok or large frying pan over a high heat. Add **400 g lean beef steak strips** and cook, stirring occasionally, for 1–2 minutes, or until browned. Reduce the heat to medium–high and stir in **1 finely chopped red chilli** and **2 teaspoons grated fresh ginger**. Add **6 chopped spring onions, 150 g baby leaf spinach** and **100 g fresh bean sprouts**. Stir-fry for 2 minutes, or until the spinach has wilted and the bean sprouts are thoroughly cooked. Stir in **2 teaspoons soy sauce, 1 beef stock cube** and **100 ml boiling water** and cook for 1–2 minutes. Transfer the stir-fry to four plates and garnish with **2 tablespoons chopped fresh coriander**.

SWEET POTATO AND MUSHROOM COTTAGE PIE

Serves 4
Preparation 10 minutes Cooking 1 hour 10 minutes

Each serving provides • 1692 kJ • 408 kcal
• 26 g protein • 17 g fat of which 4 g saturates
• 43 g carbohydrates of which 17 g sugars • 7 g fibre

Preheat the oven to 180°C (160°C fan-forced). Bake **600 g unpeeled sweet potatoes** for about 45 minutes, or until tender. Meanwhile, heat **1 tablespoon olive oil or canola oil** in a large saucepan and add **1 finely chopped onion** and **1 diced carrot**. Cook over a medium heat, stirring, for 5 minutes, then add **350 g lean beef mince**. Fry for 2–3 minutes until lightly browned. Stir in **150 g roughly chopped large flat mushrooms, 400 g canned chopped tomatoes, 2 teaspoons mixed dried herbs** and **2 tablespoons tomato purée**. Add **200 ml hot**

beef stock. Bring to the boil, turn down the heat to low, cover and simmer for 30 minutes, stirring occasionally. When the potatoes are cooked, remove from the oven and turn the oven temperature up to 190°C (170°C fan-forced). Carefully scoop the sweet potato flesh into a bowl and mash with **2 tablespoons olive oil** and **50 ml low-fat milk**. Season to taste. Transfer the beef mixture to an ovenproof dish and spread the potato over the top. Bake for 25 minutes and serve.

COOK'S TIP

● Instead of baking the sweet potato in the oven, microwave on high for 8 minutes, or until cooked.

PAPRIKA BEEF FAJITAS

Serves 4
Preparation 5 minutes Cooking 8 minutes

Each serving provides • 803 kJ • 192 kcal
• 26 g protein • 3 g carbohydrates of which 2 g sugars
• 9 g fat of which 3 g saturates • 2 g fibre

Thinly cut **350 g lean beef steak** into 2 cm wide strips and place in a shallow bowl. Sprinkle over **2 teaspoons paprika** and toss well to coat. Thinly slice **1 red onion** and **2 red capsicums**. Heat **1 tablespoon olive oil or canola oil** in a large frying pan over a medium–high heat and fry the onion and capsicum for 5 minutes, stirring regularly, until softened. Add **2 finely chopped jalapeños** or other **mild chillies** for the last 2 minutes of cooking. Season to taste, transfer the vegetables to a plate and keep warm. Heat **1 tablespoon olive oil or canola oil** in the pan, then add the beef strips. Stir fry over a high heat for 2 minutes. Gently warm **4 flour tortillas** in the microwave for 30 seconds on high. Divide the stir-fried beef and cooked vegetables among the tortillas. Add **1 tablespoon mild tomato salsa** and **1 tablespoon reduced-fat sour cream** to each fajita then roll up and serve.

COOK'S TIPS

● Look for ready-sliced stir-fry strips of beef in your local supermarket, which speeds up the preparation.
● Add slices of peeled ripe avocado to the tortillas, before rolling up, for a creamy texture.
● Serve with shredded lettuce.

BEEF AND CAPSICUM BURGERS

Crammed with Mediterranean herbs and vegetables, these juicy burgers are full of both flavour and nutritional value. Serve in toasted buns with your favourite garnishes.

Serves 4
Preparation 15 minutes
Cooking 14 minutes

Each serving provides
- 1723 kJ • 412 kcal • 24 g protein
- 14 g fat of which 3 g saturates
- 44 g carbohydrates of which
4 g sugars • 7 g fibre

2 large carrots
2 spring onions
1 small red capsicum
1 egg
1 medium slice wholemeal bread
2 cloves garlic, crushed
1 teaspoon dried oregano
2 tablespoons tomato purée
50 g rolled oats
250 g lean beef mince
1 tablespoon sunflower oil
4 x 10 cm burger buns
rocket, torn lettuce and tomato
  to serve

ALTERNATIVE INGREDIENTS
- Use pork mince or lamb instead of beef, although lamb has a much higher fat content.
- Try skinned venison sausages instead of beef mince for a richly flavoured low-fat alternative.

SUPER FOOD

RED MEAT

Lean cuts are the healthiest choice for red meat, with any visible fat removed before cooking. Red meat is a key source of haem iron – the iron within the blood pigment haemoglobin – that is easily absorbed by the body and essential for healthy blood. Red meat also contains zinc to boost the immune system.

1 Preheat the grill to medium–high. Finely grate the carrots, thinly slice the spring onions and finely chop the capsicum. Beat the egg in a large bowl. Add the bread and turn the slice in the egg a couple of times. Add the carrots, spring onions, capsicum and garlic but do not mix them in.

2 Stir in the oregano and tomato purée, breaking up the bread. Mix in the oats, beef mince and a little salt and pepper. Use your hands to squeeze, knead and thoroughly bind the ingredients.

3 Line the grill pan with foil. Shape four 10 cm burgers by first rolling balls, then patting them flat. Place the burgers on the foil and brush with ½ tablespoon oil. Grill for 7 minutes, or until sizzling and browned.

4 Carefully turn the burgers using a large spatula, brush with the remaining ½ tablespoons oil and cook for a further 7 minutes. Allow to stand for 2–3 minutes before serving.

COOK'S TIPS

● Make a large batch of burgers and freeze them ready for future use. They will keep for at least 6 months in an airtight container and can be cooked from frozen by grilling slowly for 20–25 minutes, or longer if you prefer them not completely cooked through.
● To make beef mince, put 250 g lean steak into a mincer or food processor and whizz until crumbly.

STEAK AND BEETROOT STROGANOFF

A clever way to lighten classic stroganoff is to use another Russian favourite – beetroot – with yogurt in place of sour cream to cut fat and add calcium. Mouth-watering with noodles or rice.

Serves 4
Preparation 15 minutes
Cooking 17 minutes

1 large onion
350 g button mushrooms
400 g lean frying steak
250 g cooked beetroot
2 tablespoons sunflower oil
1 tablespoon wholegrain mustard
120 g plain yogurt
2 tablespoons fresh thyme
  or oregano leaves

Each serving provides
- 1213 kJ • 290 kcal • 29 g protein
- 14 g fat of which 4 g saturates
- 13 g carbohydrates of which
10 g sugars • 4 g fibre

ALTERNATIVE INGREDIENTS
- Lamb is delicious cooked this way as an alternative to beef. Select fillet or thin leg steaks.
- Lightly cooked carrot strips are tasty with beef in place of beetroot.
- Add tarragon as an alternative to thyme or oregano.

1 Finely slice the onion and mushrooms and cut the steak and beetroot into 2 cm strips. Heat 1 tablespoon of the oil in a large frying pan over a high heat. Fry the onion for 5 minutes, or until beginning to brown. Add the mushrooms and fry for a further 5 minutes, or until softened. Transfer the onion and mushrooms to a bowl and stir in the mustard.

2 Add the remaining 1 tablespoon of oil to the pan and fry the steak over a high heat for 3 minutes. Reduce the heat slightly, if beginning to burn, and continue to cook for 3 minutes until browned. Any juices should have evaporated, leaving the meat moist.

3 Stir in the beetroot and cook for 1 minute. Season to taste and gently stir in the onions and mushrooms. Add 60 g of the yogurt then take the pan off the heat. Stir the mixture, sprinkle with thyme or oregano leaves and divide among four plates. Drizzle each portion with a little yogurt before serving.

COOK'S TIPS
- Ready-prepared stir-fry beef strips are available in supermarkets if you are short on time.
- When buying cooked beetroot, make sure that you choose beetroot in their natural juices and not preserved in vinegar or your meal will have an unpleasant sour taste.

SUPER FOOD

BEETROOT
Fat-free, low-kilojoule and a source of fibre, beetroot is good for maintaining a healthy digestive system. It also contains plenty of folate for heart, circulation and pregnancy benefits, plus some potassium to help to regulate blood pressure.

VEAL ESCALOPES IN BRANDY SAUCE WITH SOUR CHERRIES

The bittersweet flavour of dried sour cherries is superb with lean, tender veal. Add a tantalising brandy sauce to satisfy even the most discerning palate and serve with mashed potatoes.

Serves 4
Preparation 10 minutes
Cooking 10 minutes

1 onion
2 tablespoons olive oil or canola oil
1 clove garlic, crushed
240 g small Swiss brown mushrooms
4 veal escalopes, about 140 g each
100 g dried sour cherries
4 tablespoons brandy
5 tablespoons hot chicken
  or vegetable stock
4 tablespoons chopped fresh parsley,
  to garnish

Each serving provides
• 1054 kJ • 252 kcal • 34 g protein
• 3 g fat of which 1 g saturates
• 23 g carbohydrates of which
22 g sugars • 3 g fibre

ALTERNATIVE INGREDIENTS
• Use beef or pork escalopes instead of veal. Alternatively, lamb steaks or cutlets go nicely with mushrooms. Cook the lamb for 2–4 minutes on each side after browning, depending on how well done you like your meat.
• Try sliced pitted prunes instead of dried sour cherries.
• Unsweetened apple juice can be used instead of brandy.

1 Thinly slice the onion. Heat the oil in a large frying pan over a high heat. Add the sliced onion and garlic and cook, stirring frequently, for 2 minutes, or until softened.

2 Stir in the mushrooms and continue to cook for 2 minutes, or until the onion begins to turn golden. Use a slotted spoon to transfer the mushroom and onion mixture to a dish and set aside.

3 Add the veal to the pan and cook over a high heat for 1 minute on each side, using a spatula to press the meat gently against the bottom of the pan to brown both sides evenly. Reduce the heat to medium or medium–low and cook for a further 2 minutes, or until the meat is cooked.

4 Transfer the veal to four warmed plates. Return the mushroom and onion mixture to the pan and add the cherries and brandy. Increase the heat to high and boil, stirring, for 1 minute. Add the hot stock and boil for a further 1 minute. Divide among the plates. Garnish each serving with 1 tablespoon of parsley.

COOK'S TIPS
● Veal escalopes are thin, tender and quick to cook in a frying pan. Browning the meat, as here, enhances the flavour and minimises the amount of oil used in cooking.
● Dried sour cherries are usually stocked in the baking section or dried fruit aisle at the supermarket.

SUPER FOOD

DRIED CHERRIES
Rich in the plant-based anti-oxidants known as anthocyanins, dried cherries are good for protecting against heart disease. They are also fat free, a good source of fibre and provide an energy boost at any time of the day.

HAM AND SWEET POTATO
BUBBLE AND SQUEAK

Transform a family dinner favourite with generous helpings of juicy ham and creamy-textured sweet potato, all spiked with aromatic fresh sage.

Serves 4
Preparation 15 minutes
Cooking 15 minutes

Each serving provides
• 1105 kJ • 267 kcal • 15 g protein
• 14 g fat of which 3 g saturates
• 22 g carbohydrates of which
8 g sugars • 5 g fibre

1 leek
350 g orange sweet potatoes
200 g lean cooked ham
200 g cabbage, such as savoy
2 tablespoons olive oil
4 large shredded fresh sage leaves

ALTERNATIVE INGREDIENTS
• Try a mixture of parsnip, turnip or regular potato instead of sweet potato.
• As a change to ham, use any cooked poultry or meat, such as corned beef, chicken or leftover roast pork.
• Add diced chorizo in step 2 with the sweet potatoes for a spicy flavour. Alternatively, try diced salami, garlic sausage or frankfurts.
• Bubble and squeak is a great recipe if you want to use up any leftover cooked vegetables, such as carrot, beans, broccoli or cauliflower. Dice the vegetables and add them with, or instead of, the cabbage.

1 Thinly slice the leek, then dice the sweet potatoes and the ham into 1.5 cm pieces and finely shred the cabbage. Heat the oil in a large frying pan over a high heat. Add the leek and stir-fry the mixture for 2 minutes, or until softened.

2 Stir in the sweet potatoes and sage leaves. Reduce the heat to medium, add 3 tablespoons of boiling water and cover the pan. Cook for 8 minutes, shaking the pan occasionally, or until the potatoes are tender and cooked through.

3 Stir in the shredded cabbage and ham. Re-cover the pan and cook for 5 minutes over a medium heat, stirring occasionally and reducing the heat to medium–low if the ingredients stick to the base of the pan. Season to taste and serve.

COOK'S TIP
● When buying sweet potatoes, make sure that they are smooth, plump, dry and clean.

SUPER FOOD

SWEET POTATO
This colourful root vegetable is nutrient-packed with alpha- and beta-carotene – the anti-oxidant pigments that give the sweet potato its bright orange flesh and help to protect against cancer. It also contains vitamin E for heart health and fibre to promote digestive wellbeing.

INDONESIAN SATAY **PORK** WITH **CAPSICUM**

There's a juicy mouthful in every bite with this tempting combination of pork mince, crisp lettuce and peanut sauce. Capsicums and onions help to boost mental alertness.

Serves 4
Preparation 15 minutes
Cooking 12 minutes

2 onions
2 large capsicums (1 red, 1 yellow)
2 tablespoons olive oil or canola oil
400 g lean pork mince
3 cloves garlic
1 tablespoon ground coriander
2 tablespoons soy sauce
4 spring onions
1 crunchy lettuce, such as cos,
    separated into leaves, to serve

For the satay sauce
4 tablespoons smooth peanut butter
1 clove garlic, crushed
1 teaspoon sesame oil
1 teaspoon soy sauce

Each serving provides
• 1732 kJ • 414 kcal • 31 g protein
• 25 g fat of which 5 g saturates
• 18 g carbohydrates of which
14 g sugars • 6 g fibre

ALTERNATIVE INGREDIENTS
• Use 1 green capsicum instead of the red capsicum. Shred a quarter of a Chinese cabbage and add to the mince mixture in step 3 after stir-frying the capsicum for 2 minutes. Finish as above.
• Shred the lettuce instead of using the leaves whole and serve with 2 warmed flour tortillas or similar flatbread wraps per portion. Spread the sauce over the wraps, divide the pork and capsicums among them, then roll up and serve with the lettuce and spring onions on the side.

1 Start by making the satay sauce. Place the peanut butter, 1 crushed clove garlic and the sesame oil in a small bowl. Gradually whisk in 4 tablespoons of boiling water. The mixture will start thick and glossy, then soften after about 1 minute to become pale. Stir in the soy sauce and set aside.

2 Halve and slice the onions, then quarter and slice the capsicums. Heat 1 tablespoon of the oil in a large frying pan over a high heat. Add the pork mince and fry, stirring occasionally, for about 5 minutes, or until the meat is crumbly and browned, and the excess cooking liquid has evaporated.

3 Add the remaining 1 tablespoon oil, the onions and the remaining 2 crushed cloves garlic to the frying pan and stir-fry them for 2 minutes. Stir in the capsicums and coriander and stir-fry for a further 4–5 minutes, or until the capsicums are tender. Remove from the heat and stir in the soy sauce.

4 Trim and slice the spring onions diagonally. Arrange 2–3 lettuce leaves on each plate and divide the pork mixture among them. Spoon over the satay sauce and sprinkle with the spring onion slices.

COOK'S TIPS
● To prepare large capsicums, hold them upright by the stalk end on a board, then slice down to remove the flesh off the core. Slice off three sides, then cut the stalk and remaining seeds away from the fourth side.
● If pork mince is not available at your supermarket or local butcher, put 400 g pork meat, for example a shoulder joint or steak, in a food processor or mincer and grind it until it has an even consistency.

SUPER FOOD

ONION FAMILY
Rich in plant-based substances called phytochemicals that help to prevent and protect against disease, onions and shallots are also a great source of the flavonoid quercetin, a strong anti-oxidant. Some studies have linked quercetin with a lower risk of developing lung cancer.

AROMATIC **PORK** KEBABS

Juicy pieces of pork flavoured with orange zest and coriander make a brilliant match with grilled red capsicums and a crunchy carrot salad. Serve with some warmed pita bread on the side.

Serves 4
Preparation 10 minutes
Cooking 10 minutes

Each serving provides
• 1116 kJ • 267 kcal • 24 g protein
• 11 g fat of which 2 g saturates
• 16 g carbohydrates of which
12 g sugars • 4 g fibre

400 g lean pork cubes
2 large red capsicums
2 large onions
2 tablespoons olive oil or canola oil
grated zest and juice of 1 orange
1 tablespoon finely crushed coriander
   seeds
6 carrots

ALTERNATIVE INGREDIENTS
• Lamb, turkey or chicken breast all work well instead of pork.
• A meaty fish, such as swordfish or tuna, is another good alternative to the pork.
• Coarsely grated zucchini make a quick and easy salad accompaniment. Toss them with a little olive oil and a handful of shredded basil leaves.

1 Preheat the grill to the hottest setting. Line the grill pan with foil. Thread the pork onto metal skewers, leaving a little space between the cubes of meat, and place them on the grill pan. Cut the capsicums into 2 cm wide strips and thinly slice the onions. Arrange the vegetables around the edge of the kebabs.

2 Brush the pork and vegetables with oil. Sprinkle the orange zest and crushed coriander seeds over the pork. Grill for 5 minutes. Grate the carrots, then add the orange juice and mix well.

3 Using an oven glove, carefully turn the pork skewers. Then turn and rearrange the vegetables so that they cook evenly. Grill for a further 5 minutes, until the meat is browned and cooked through and the vegetables are tender.

4 Transfer the kebabs to warmed plates, add a portion of grilled vegetables to each and serve with bowls of carrot salad.

SUPER FOOD

RED CAPSICUMS

Half a fresh red capsicum will provide your total daily vitamin C requirement. Like all vegetables, capsicums are low in kilojoules so are good for weight control.

COOK'S TIPS

● If using wooden skewers, soak them in water for 15 minutes before threading on the pork to prevent them from burning under the grill.
● Use a mortar and pestle to crush the coriander seeds. To prevent the seeds from escaping, put the mortar in a plastic bag, gather the edges around the pestle and hold onto the bag as you pound the seeds. If you do not have a mortar and pestle, put the seeds into a bowl and crush with the end of a rolling pin.

CITRUS FRUIT

You need vitamin C for healthy bones and skin, and few foods give you more of that vital nutrient than citrus fruit such as limes, lemons, oranges, grapefruit and tangerines. Vitamin C also acts as an anti-oxidant, which helps to prevent cell damage, reducing the risk of cancer and other chronic diseases.

FRUIT SALAD

Serves 4
Preparation 20 minutes

Each serving provides • 720 kJ • 172 kcal • 3 g protein • 1 g fat (no saturates) • 41 g carbohydrates of which 41 g sugars • 4 g fibre

Peel **2 blood oranges** and **1 ruby grapefruit**, cut them into segments and place them in a bowl with any juice poured over. Peel **200 g watermelon**, removing all the pips, and cut into 2–3 cm cubes. Add the watermelon to the bowl, together with **100 g seedless red grapes**. Cut any large grapes in half if necessary. Sprinkle **4 teaspoons caster sugar** over the citrus fruit and pour in **800 ml unsweetened breakfast juice** or **orange and raspberry juice**. Stir and chill in the fridge until needed.

COOK'S TIPS

● The easiest way to peel citrus fruit is to remove the top and base with a serrated knife then place the flat base on a board that has a channel around the edge to catch the juices. Hold the fruit at the top while slicing down between peel and flesh, from top to bottom. Move the fruit round a little and continue slicing down until all peel is removed.

● This fruit salad makes a refreshing starter to a fish main course.

CITRUS PANCAKES

Serves 4
Preparation 10 minutes Cooking 12 minutes

Each serving provides • 954 kJ • 228 kcal • 9 g protein • 5 g fat of which 1 g saturates • 40 g carbohydrates of which 20 g sugars • 5 g fibre

Peel **2 large oranges** and slice them into segments, removing all the pith. Put the segments and any juice into a small saucepan with the **juice of 1 lemon** and **2 tablespoons runny honey**. Place the pan over a low heat, stir the mixture and warm through. Put **125 g plain wholemeal flour** and a pinch of salt in a bowl. Add **1 egg** and **250 ml low-fat milk** and beat until the mixture becomes a smooth batter. Brush a non-stick frying pan with a little **olive oil or canola oil** and place over a high heat. When the pan is very hot, spoon one-eighth of the batter into the centre of the pan. Swirl it around to coat the base of the pan and cook for 1 minute, or until the underside is flecked with brown. Turn the pancake with a spatula and cook for a further 30 seconds. Transfer to a plate and keep warm. Repeat with the remaining mixture to make another seven pancakes. Serve with the warm orange mixture spooned over each pancake.

COOK'S TIP

- For a slightly sweeter pancake dish, use 200 g tinned mandarins instead of the segmented oranges and add a light dusting of icing sugar just before serving.

PINK GRAPEFRUIT AND POMEGRANATE SALAD

Serves 4
Preparation 10 minutes

Each serving provides • 996 kJ • 238 kcal
- 1 g protein • 23 g fat of which 3 g saturates
- 7 g carbohydrates of which 7 g sugars • 2 g fibre

Arrange **200 g frisée or other lettuce leaves**, washed and torn if large, in a salad bowl. Peel and segment **1 large pink grapefruit**, then halve the segments and arrange them over the leaves. Remove the seeds from **1 pomegranate** using a small spoon to prise them out. Make a dressing by combining **90 ml olive oil** with **1 tablespoon red wine vinegar, 1 teaspoon balsamic vinegar** and any juice that has run out of the grapefruit. Drizzle the dressing over the salad and toss to combine. Sprinkle the pomegranate seeds over the salad and serve.

COOK'S TIPS

- Frisée lettuce (also known as curly endive) has thin, green, curly leaves that look very decorative. Other attractive salad leaves include sweet lamb's lettuce (mâche) or peppery rocket.
- Use raspberry vinegar instead of red wine vinegar for a fruitier flavour.

PORK FILLETS WITH LIME GREMOLATA

Serves 4
Preparation 10 minutes Marinating 30 minutes
Cooking 10 minutes

Each serving provides • 1021 kJ • 244 kcal
- 27 g protein • 13 g fat of which 3 g saturates
- 2 g carbohydrates of which 1 g sugars • 1 g fibre

In a non-metallic shallow dish, mix **2 tablespoons olive oil, juice of 1 lime, 2 tablespoons dry white wine** and **2 crushed cloves garlic**. Cut **4 pork fillets, 125 g each**,

diagonally in half. Coat with the marinade and leave to marinate for 30 minutes. To make the gremolata, first zest **1 unwaxed lime**. Peel and remove the pith, then cut the lime into small chunks. Combine the lime zest with **1 tablespoon finely chopped fresh parsley** and **2 large finely chopped cloves garlic**. Cook the pieces of pork together with the marinade in a large frying pan over a medium heat for 10 minutes, or until golden and cooked through. Stir in the lime chunks and then add **2 tablespoons low-fat sour cream** and allow to warm through. Serve the pork with the creamy lime sauce and gremolata sprinkled over the top.

COOK'S TIPS

- Serve the pork with pan-fried potato slices and boiled green beans for a taste of summer.
- Other white meats, such as chicken and turkey, also taste great sprinkled with gremolata. Substitute a lemon for the lime for a sharper flavour.

ORANGE AND RED ONION CHUTNEY

Serves 4
Preparation 10 minutes Cooking 10 minutes

Each serving provides • 654 kJ • 156 kcal
- 2 g protein • 10 g fat of which 1 g saturates
- 14 g carbohydrates of which 14 g sugars • 3 g fibre

Preheat the oven to 180°C (160°C fan-forced). Peel **6 small oranges** and cut each fruit across the grain into 4 slices. Transfer the slices to an ovenproof dish, lightly brushed with **1 teaspoon olive oil**. Finely chop **1 red onion** and sprinkle it over the oranges. Drizzle **2 tablespoons olive oil** and **3 teaspoons red wine vinegar** over the mixture, then sprinkle in **1 teaspoon soft dark brown sugar**. Bake for 10 minutes and serve warm with a little extra olive oil drizzled over the top.

COOK'S TIP

- This chutney goes well with grilled chicken, venison sausages or duck breast fillets. Serve with a hearty green salad, as well.

PORK STEAKS WITH BLUEBERRY AND APPLE SAUCE

Brimming with protective anti-oxidants, blueberries also bring colour and sweetness to this quick and easy dish. Serve the pork with stir-fried cabbage and leeks, plus tender baby carrots.

Serves 4
Preparation 10 minutes
Cooking 18 minutes

Each serving provides
- 1289 kJ • 308 kcal • 30 g protein
- 13 g fat of which 3 g saturates
- 18 g carbohydrates of which 18 g sugars • 6 g fibre

2 apples, about 250 g
1 large leek
400 g cabbage
1 tablespoon sugar
150 g blueberries
2 tablespoons olive oil or canola oil
4 lean pork steaks

ALTERNATIVE INGREDIENTS
- Blackberries or sliced plums also taste great with pork. Halve, stone and slice the plums then cook with the apples for 1 minute.
- For a cranberry and apple sauce, cook the cranberries and apples with 3 tablespoons of water until the cranberries have softened. Then add 2 tablespoons sugar and cook gently for 1 minute.
- This fruity sauce also makes a wonderful accompaniment to venison, lamb, turkey steaks and pheasant breast.

1 Peel and coarsely grate the apples. Trim, thinly slice and rinse the leeks then finely shred the cabbage. Place the apples in a saucepan over a high heat. Add the sugar and 1 tablespoon of water and bring to the boil, stirring. Reduce the heat to low, cover and cook for 1–2 minutes, or until the apples soften. Stir in the blueberries to warm through and transfer to a serving bowl.

2 Heat a large frying pan over a high heat until really hot. Pour in 1 tablespoon of the oil and add the pork steaks. Brown for 1 minute on each side, reduce the heat to medium–low and fry for 4 minutes on each side. Transfer the pork to a plate and keep warm.

3 Add the remaining tablespoon of oil to the frying pan, increase the heat to high and stir-fry the leeks for 3 minutes, or until softened. Add the cabbage and stir-fry for a further 2 minutes, or until the cabbage is tender. Transfer the pork and vegetables to four warmed plates and add a large spoonful of blueberry and apple sauce before serving.

COOK'S TIPS
- Make light work of preparing the apples by peeling them whole, then hold them by the core ends and grate directly into the pan.
- The leeks and cabbage reduce rapidly as they soften and cook, so add the cabbage in batches if your pan is small.

SUPER FOOD

CABBAGES
Bursting with nourishment, cabbages of all colours contain high levels of anti-oxidants that work to protect cell membranes from damage by free radicals. As a result, there are studies that link eating cabbages with a lower risk of developing cancer, especially of the digestive tract.

SAUSAGES AND SUPERMASH WITH ONION RELISH

Creamy mashed potato hits new heights with an addition of vitamin-packed carrot and zucchini. Add an easy onion relish and you have the perfect matches for juicy poached sausages. Serve with peas for a dash of colour.

Serves 4
Preparation 15 minutes
Cooking 35 minutes

8 good-quality pork sausages,
  about 450 g
1 kg potatoes
1 zucchini
1 large carrot
4 onions
4 tablespoons olive oil or canola oil
2 tablespoons raw or demerara sugar
2 tablespoons cider vinegar
4 tablespoons low-fat milk

Each serving provides
- 2636 kJ • 630 kcal • 21 g protein
- 34 g fat of which 9 g saturates
- 63 g carbohydrates of which
22 g sugars • 6 g fibre

ALTERNATIVE INGREDIENTS
- Grated celeriac or butternut pumpkin make good alternatives to zucchini.
- Chopped celery, grated carrot and chopped walnuts are another brilliant mixture of complementary flavours for livening up mashed potato.
- Serve grilled, sliced black pudding, good-quality burgers or grilled chicken instead of the sausages.

1 Place the sausages in a saucepan, cover with water and put on a lid. Bring the water to the boil, then reduce the heat to low and poach the sausages for 30 minutes. Meanwhile, peel the potatoes and cut into 3 cm chunks. Transfer to a saucepan, cover with boiling water and simmer for 10 minutes, or until tender. Coarsely grate the zucchini and carrot. Thinly slice the onions.

2 Heat 2 tablespoons of the oil in a saucepan over a medium heat. Add the onions and cook for 5 minutes, stirring once or twice, until softened. Add the sugar and cook for 5–6 minutes, reducing the heat if the onions begin to burn. When the sausages are cooked, carefully remove them with a slotted spoon and dry on paper towel. Dry-fry them in a non-stick frying pan for 3–5 minutes, or until browned all over.

3 Stir the vinegar into the onions, turn up the heat and boil for 1 minute. Reduce the heat to low and simmer for 3–5 minutes, or until the liquid has virtually evaporated and the onions are glazed.

4 Drain the potatoes in a colander. Add the remaining 2 tablespoons of oil, plus the zucchini and carrot, to the empty potato pan and cook over a low heat for 1 minute. Remove from the heat, replace the potatoes, pour in the milk and mash until smooth. Stir up the zucchini and carrot, season and serve with the sausages and onion relish.

COOK'S TIPS
- Make the onion relish when you have a spare moment, up to several hours in advance, then transfer it to a dish and cover until required.
- If you prefer, cook the sausages by grilling them under a high heat for 20 minutes, turning until browned all over and cooked through.

SUPER FOOD

ONIONS
Research indicates that onions, along with other members of the allium family, may protect against stomach cancer. This is because natural phytochemicals in the onions may stimulate enzymes that get rid of harmful chemicals in the body.

FRUITY **PORK STEAKS** WITH GLAZED **PLUMS** AND **RED CABBAGE**

The tangy, sweet-and-sour flavours of ripe plums and red wine vinegar work well with pork and cabbage. Serve with a fibre-rich mixed swede and carrot mash for a real treat.

Serves 4
Preparation 10 minutes
Cooking 25 minutes

2 red onions
400 g red cabbage
8 ripe plums
2 tablespoons olive oil or canola oil
4 lean boneless pork loin chops, about 130 g each
pinch of ground cloves or allspice
100 ml pomegranate juice drink
3 tablespoons raw or demerara sugar
3 tablespoons red wine vinegar

Each serving provides
• 1695 kJ • 405 kcal • 31 g protein
• 17 g fat of which 4 g saturates
• 34 g carbohydrates of which 32 g sugars • 6 g fibre

ALTERNATIVE INGREDIENTS
• Grind 6 juniper berries in a mortar and pestle and use instead of the ground cloves or allspice.
• This recipe also works well with venison or lamb steaks.
• Instead of using fresh fruit, add 150 g thickly sliced pitted prunes or dried apricots in step 2. Stir the dried fruit into the cabbage before replacing the meat. Omit the extra 1 tablespoon sugar and vinegar used to glaze the fruit in step 5.

1 Slice the onions, shred the red cabbage and cut the plums in half. Heat the oil in a large frying pan over a high heat. Add the pork steaks and cook for 3 minutes on each side, or until browned. Reduce the heat to medium, add the onions and cook for a further 5 minutes, stirring occasionally, until the meat is cooked through. Transfer the steaks to a shallow dish, leaving the onions in the pan.

2 Add the cabbage and cloves or allspice to the pan and fry, stirring, for 5 minutes. Pour in the pomegranate juice drink and bring to the boil. Return the pork to the pan with any juices from the dish. Reduce the heat to medium, cover and cook for 3 minutes. Transfer the pork to four plates. Add 1 tablespoon each of sugar and vinegar to the cabbage and boil for 30 seconds, stirring, to glaze the cabbage. Divide among the plates of pork.

3 Add the plums to the pan, cut sides down. Sprinkle in the remaining 2 tablespoons each of sugar and vinegar and cook over a high heat for 4 minutes, shaking the pan so that the sugar dissolves. Season to taste and divide the plums and their glaze among the plates and serve.

COOK'S TIP
● To halve plums, cut around the dimple in the fruit and twist the halves. They will come apart, leaving the stone in one half. Use a small pointed knife to cut out the stone.

SUPER FOOD

PLUMS
The goodness of plums, as with most fruit, is found in or around the skin – so do not peel them. Their nutritional benefits include potassium to help to regulate blood pressure and fibre for keeping the digestive system healthy. Plums also contain anti-oxidants to help to fight the signs of ageing.

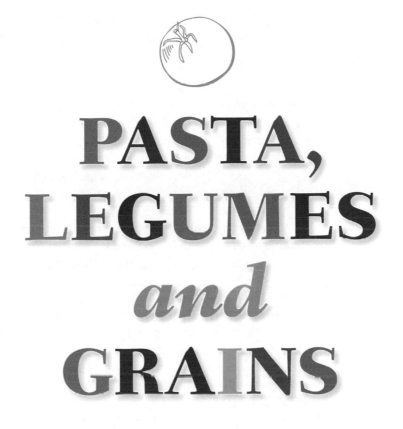

PASTA, LEGUMES *and* GRAINS

ITALIAN SPIRALS WITH **WATERCRESS** AND **OLIVE** DRESSING

Fiery watercress is a great foil for spirali pasta tossed in a gremolata dressing, while crunchy pistachio nuts and a little parmesan enrich the flavour. Serve with cherry tomatoes.

Serves 4
Preparation 10 minutes
Cooking 10 minutes

Each serving provides
• 2460 kJ • 588 kcal • 20 g protein
• 31 g fat of which 7 g saturates
• 61 g carbohydrates of which
5 g sugars • 7 g fibre

300 g pasta shapes, such as spirali
2 small leeks
150 g watercress
50 g shelled pistachios
100 g pimento-stuffed olives
4 tablespoons olive oil
3 cloves garlic, crushed
30 g chopped fresh parsley
grated zest of 1 lemon
60 g grated parmesan

ALTERNATIVE INGREDIENTS
• Enhance the nutty flavour by using a mixture of olive oil and walnut oil. Cook the leeks in 2 tablespoons olive oil, then add 2 tablespoons walnut oil to the pan once the leeks are cooked. Add walnuts instead of pistachios.
• For herb-flavoured pasta, add tarragon or basil to the recipe in addition to the parsley. Chop 2 fresh tarragon sprigs with the parsley. Basil loses its flavour when chopped, so it is best to shred 2–3 large tender sprigs into the pan just before mixing in the olives in step 3.
• Try other cheese, such as gruyère, manchego, pecorino or a strong cheddar, instead of parmesan.

1 Bring a large saucepan of water to the boil. Add the pasta, bring back to the boil and partly cover the pan. Reduce the heat and cook for 10 minutes, or according to the packet instructions, until the pasta is tender but with some bite in the centre. Slice the leeks into rings, cut the rings into quarters and rinse. Chop the watercress and pistachios. Halve the stuffed olives.

2 Halfway through cooking the pasta, heat the oil in a saucepan over a high heat. Add the garlic and leeks then reduce the heat to medium–low. Cover and cook for 5 minutes, stirring once, until the leeks soften.

3 Tip the pasta into a colander and quickly return it to the hot pan without shaking off all the cooking liquid – this way the pasta should be slightly moist and will stay hot. Add the leeks, watercress, parsley, pistachios, lemon zest and stuffed olives. Stir together and divide among four plates. Serve topped with grated parmesan.

COOK'S TIP
● For speed, though the final dish does not look quite as attractive, blend the watercress, parsley and pistachios together in a food processor until finely chopped.

SUPER FOOD

WATERCRESS
Packed with essential nutrients, watercress contains calcium to help to maintain bone strength, iron for preventing anaemia and folate to promote heart health. It is also a good source of anti-oxidants, which may have anti-cancer effects as they protect the body against harmful free radicals.

CREAMY **MUSHROOMS** WITH **TAGLIATELLE**

An indulgent but nutritious sauce coats a fusion of succulent, earthy mushrooms and heart-healthy, anti-oxidant-packed walnuts. They turn a simple bowl of pasta into a hearty meal.

Serves 4
Preparation 10 minutes
Cooking 15 minutes

Each serving provides
- 2407 kJ • 575 kcal • 23 g protein
- 29 g fat of which 3 g saturates
- 55 g carbohydrates of which 9 g sugars • 7 g fibre

250 g tagliatelle
300 g Swiss brown mushrooms
100 g walnuts
2 tablespoons olive oil
3 teaspoons cornflour
400 ml low-fat milk
100 g low-fat cream cheese or ½ cup (50 g) grated low-fat cheddar or tasty-style cheese
4 tablespoons finely chopped fresh parsley
250 g oyster mushrooms
3 tablespoons snipped fresh chives

ALTERNATIVE INGREDIENTS
- Replace the oyster mushrooms with other mushrooms such as shiitake or chanterelle. These can be found in the vegetable or salad section in most large supermarkets.
- Use 300 ml low-fat milk and 100 ml dry sherry instead of all milk. Boil the milk sauce first, then stir in the sherry and simmer.
- Cook 2 sliced spring onions and 1 crushed clove garlic with the mushrooms in step 2.

1 Bring a large saucepan of water to the boil. Add the tagliatelle, bring back to the boil and partly cover the pan. Reduce the heat and cook for 12 minutes, or according to the packet instructions, until the pasta is tender but with some bite in the centre. Meanwhile, slice the Swiss brown mushrooms. Roughly chop the walnuts and set aside 1 tablespoon. Heat 1 tablespoon of oil in another pan and add the Swiss brown mushrooms. Cook over a high heat for 5 minutes, or until softened.

2 Whisk the cornflour with the milk and pour it into the mushroom mixture in the pan. Bring to the boil, stirring, then reduce the heat and simmer for 3 minutes. Stir in the cheese, walnuts and parsley then season to taste.

3 Drain the tagliatelle and stir it into the sauce. Cover and remove from the heat without mixing. Add the remaining 1 tablespoon of oil and oyster mushrooms to the pan you used for the pasta. Fry over a high heat for 1 minute, or until hot and beginning to tinge with brown. Divide the pasta among four bowls and top with the oyster mushrooms and reserved walnuts. Sprinkle with chives and serve.

COOK'S TIP
● If you are using fresh tagliatelle, you will need to reduce the cooking time as fresh pasta cooks much more quickly than dried – usually 2–4 minutes. Check the packet for cooking instructions.

SUPER FOOD

LOW-FAT MILK
Studies show that a diet rich in low-fat dairy foods, alongside other healthy lifestyle choices such as lowering salt intake and exercising regularly, can lower blood pressure in people with hypertension. Low-fat milk may also offer protection against the onset of colon cancer.

FIERY ITALIAN **VEGETABLE** PASTA

Pasta is wonderful at absorbing and enhancing flavours. Combine pasta shapes with colourful vegetables and some feisty chilli for an energising meal.

Serves 4
Preparation 10 minutes
Cooking 20 minutes

300 g pasta shapes, such as shells,
  bows, spirals or tubes
1 onion
1 red chilli
2 cloves garlic
40 g pitted black olives
6 sun-dried tomato halves
2 sticks celery
600 g ripe tomatoes
3 tablespoons olive oil
25 g chopped fresh parsley
finely grated zest of 1 lemon
50 g parmesan, shaved

Each serving provides
- 2033 kJ • 486 kcal • 17 g protein
- 18 g fat of which 5 g saturates
- 68 g carbohydrates of which
11 g sugars • 7 g fibre

ALTERNATIVE INGREDIENTS
- Add sun-dried tomato purée to boost the flavour of the fresh tomatoes instead of using chopped sun-dried tomatoes. Add 1–2 tablespoons purée in step 2, stirring it into the cooked onion mixture before adding the chopped fresh tomatoes.
- Add 50 g anchovy fillets in olive oil, chopped, with the tomatoes and then reduce the oil for cooking the onion to 1 tablespoon.

1 Bring a large saucepan of water to the boil. Add the pasta, bring back to the boil and stir once. Reduce the heat and partly cover the pan. Boil for 12 minutes, or according to the packet instructions, until tender but with some bite in the centre. Drain the pasta in a colander.

2 Meanwhile, finely chop the onion, chilli and garlic. Halve the olives, quarter the sun-dried tomatoes and dice the celery. Chop the fresh tomatoes. Heat the olive oil in a pan and add the onion, chilli, half of the garlic and the celery. Cook over a high heat for 5 minutes, stirring frequently.

3 Stir in the fresh tomatoes, sun-dried tomatoes and olives. Cook the sauce for 3 minutes, then return the pasta to the pan. Stir together and season to taste.

4 Mix the remaining chopped garlic with the parsley and lemon zest. Divide the pasta among four bowls and serve topped with the parsley mixture and shaved parmesan.

COOK'S TIPS
● Roma (plum) tomatoes are ideal for this recipe because they have firm flesh with fewer seeds than other varieties.
● Whether this dish is piquant with a slight heat or fiery in flavour depends on your choice of chilli. A mild chilli will give a gentle warmth to the pasta and vegetables, but if you like it hot then use 2 hot chillies.

SUPER FOOD

CELERY
Crunchy celery helps to maintain a healthy digestive system thanks to the soluble and insoluble fibre it contains. With its folate and potassium, celery is also great for heart health and for regulating blood pressure.

BANANA CHILLIES WITH CHEESY PASTA

Enjoy hearty macaroni with a twist – serve it in lightly grilled red banana chillies. Although they're called chillies, they're not hot – their sweetness cuts through the full-bodied savoury sauce.

Serves 4
Preparation 15 minutes
Cooking 17 minutes

Each serving provides
- 1178 kJ • 281 kcal • 15 g protein
- 11 g fat of which 5 g saturates
- 29 g carbohydrates of which
3 g sugars • 2 g fibre

150 g macaroni
1 small zucchini
4 large red banana chillies
175 g low fat cream cheese or ricotta
2 tablespoons snipped fresh chives
50 g grated parmesan
1 tablespoon olive oil
1 teaspoon paprika

ALTERNATIVE INGREDIENTS
- Use yellow or orange chillies instead of red ones. If you can't get banana chillies, use capsicums and cut each into four pieces.
- Try other pasta shapes instead of macaroni, such as spirals or shells.
- Use 100 g mature cheddar, gruyère or Monterey Jack cheese instead of parmesan, though this will raise the fat content.
- To increase your vegetable intake, add 1 grated carrot with the zucchini in step 2.
- Reduce the quantity of macaroni to 75 g and add 50 g frozen baby peas to the pan for the last 5 minutes of cooking. Bring the water back to the boil after adding the peas.

1 Preheat the grill to the hottest setting. Bring a large saucepan of water to the boil. Add the macaroni, bring back to the boil and stir. Reduce the heat, partly cover the pan and boil for 12 minutes, or according to the packet instructions, until the macaroni is cooked.

2 Meanwhile, finely grate the zucchini and cut the chillies in half lengthwise, scraping out all of the seeds but leaving on the stalks. Combine the cheese, grated zucchini and chives. Reserve 1 tablespoon of parmesan, stir the remainder into the mixture and set aside. Place the chillies on a baking tray and grill, cut sides down, for 3 minutes, or until the skins begin to blister. Turn over and grill for a further 3 minutes, then brush with oil and grill for a final 3 minutes, or until tender.

3 Drain the macaroni, return it to the pan and stir in the cheese and zucchini mixture. Spoon the macaroni into the chilli shells and sprinkle with paprika and the reserved parmesan. Place the chillies back under the grill for 5 minutes to warm through and crisp up on top.

COOK'S TIPS
- During the final grilling, after brushing with a little oil, the chillies may bubble up inside but they will shrink back when removed from the grill. Watch them closely to avoid burning the skins and rims.
- Replace the cheese sauce with a white sauce made with low fat milk, if desired.

SUPER FOOD

LOW-FAT DAIRY FOODS
Reduced-fat and low-fat dairy foods provide valuable protein, phosphorus, some B vitamins, zinc, vitamin A and calcium, which is good for bone health. Three servings of low-fat dairy products per day – along with a diet rich in fibre and fruit and vegetables – helps to reduce high blood pressure and lowers the risk of strokes.

CAPSICUMS

Whether eaten cooked or raw, capsicums are packed full of goodness. They are one of the best sources of vitamin C and are crammed with beneficial carotenes that may protect against lung cancer.

JUICY VEGETABLE KEBABS

Serves 4
Preparation 10 minutes Cooking 20 minutes

Each serving provides • 410 kJ • 98 kcal
• 1 g protein • 8 g fat of which 1 g saturates
• 6 g carbohydrates of which 5 g sugars • 2 g fibre

Preheat the grill to high. Cut **2 red capsicums** in half and place them on the grill pan, skin side up. Brush with **1 tablespoon olive oil** and grill for 15 minutes, turning occasionally, until softened and the skin starts to blister. Turn the grill down to medium. Remove the capsicums, cool slightly and cut into bite-sized squares. Crush **2 medium cloves garlic** with a little salt and pepper then stir in **1 tablespoon olive oil, ½ finely chopped red chilli** and **1 teaspoon balsamic vinegar**. Remove the stalks from **12 small Swiss brown mushrooms**. Use a pastry brush to coat the mushrooms with the flavoured olive oil. Thread the mushrooms and capsicums onto four metal or wooden skewers. Grill for 5 minutes, turning once and basting with any remaining oil.

COOK'S TIPS

● Soak wooden skewers for 30 minutes in cold water before threading the vegetables to prevent the wood from charring under the hot grill.

● Serve the kebabs as a starter on a bed of curly endive or other lettuce with crusty wholemeal bread.

RED CAPSICUM AND TOMATO SAUCE

Serves 4
Preparation 10 minutes Cooking 6 minutes

Each serving provides • 662 kJ • 158 kcal
• 4 g protein • 11 g fat of which 1 g saturates
• 11 g carbohydrates of which 9 g sugars • 3 g fibre

Heat **1 tablespoon olive oil** in a saucepan over a medium heat. Add **1 finely chopped onion** and **2 diced red capsicums** and cook for 5 minutes until softened. Stir in **2 crushed cloves garlic**. Fry for 1 minute, then pour in **200 ml tomato juice**. Transfer to a blender, or to a mixing bowl and use a stick blender, and purée until smooth. Stir in **50 g ground almonds** and blend for a further 5 seconds. Return the sauce to the pan and gently reheat but do not boil. Add salt and pepper to taste before serving.

● This sauce makes a colourful accompaniment to grilled tuna steaks or any robust white fish.

● The sweet flavour of the capsicums and almonds also marries well with roast or grilled chicken.

● Reduce the tomato juice to 25 ml to transform the sauce into a rich dip with a light and refreshing taste. Serve with vegetable crudités and breadsticks or baked cheese straws.

GOLDEN CHICKEN AND AVOCADO SALAD

Serves 4
Preparation 10 minutes Cooking 15 minutes

Each serving provides • 1393 kJ • 333 kcal
• 18 g protein • 26 g fat of which 5 g saturates
• 7 g carbohydrates of which 6 g sugars • 4 g fibre

Preheat the grill to medium–high. Cut **2 yellow capsicums** lengthwise into 5 mm thick slices then halve the slices and transfer them to a large bowl. Pour **3 tablespoons olive oil, juice of ½ lime** and **1 teaspoon runny honey** into a small jug to make a dressing. Stir and season to taste then pour over the capsicum slices. Grill **2 boneless, skinless chicken breasts** for 15 minutes, or until cooked through and lightly golden. Cool for 1–2 minutes then cut into four or five slices. Peel and slice **2 ripe avocados**. Arrange a layer of **mixed salad leaves** on four plates. Layer the capsicum, chicken and avocado slices on top. Drizzle over any remaining dressing and serve.

COOK'S TIP

● Serve the salad as a starter or double the quantity of chicken for a light lunch accompanied with minted new potatoes. Layer the capsicum and avocado slices on top of the salad, then slice 4 grilled chicken breasts and place one breast on each plate.

SESAME-INFUSED CAPSICUM WITH BROCCOLI

Serves 4
Preparation 10 minutes Cooking 10 minutes

Each serving provides • 628 kJ • 150 kcal
• 4 g protein • 13 g fat of which 2 g saturates
• 5 g carbohydrates of which 4 g sugars • 3 g fibre

Heat **2 tablespoons sesame oil** in a frying pan. Thinly slice **2 large capsicums, one green and one orange**. Add the capsicum and **150 g broccoli florets** to the pan. Stir-fry over a medium–high heat for 8 minutes, or until the capsicum softens and turns brown at the edges, but the broccoli is still firm in the centre. Add **1 crushed clove garlic, 1 teaspoon finely chopped fresh ginger, 2 teaspoons light soy sauce** and **2 teaspoons sesame seeds**. Stir for 1 minute. Add salt and pepper to taste and then transfer to four plates. Pour any pan juices over the vegetables and drizzle with **2 teaspoons sesame oil** and an additional **2 teaspoons sesame seeds**.

COOK'S TIPS

● Serve as a healthy side dish with grilled turkey kebabs or a fish fillet. A jacket potato or spoonful of mash makes a filling accompaniment.

● As an alternative to the broccoli, use 150 g sugarsnap peas but omit the ginger and soy sauce.

FETTA, CHILLI AND CAPSICUM SANDWICH SPREAD

Serves 4
Preparation 10 minutes Cooking 10 minutes

Each serving provides • 5954 kJ • 142 kcal
• 6 g protein • 12 g fat of which 6 g saturates
• 3 g carbohydrates of which 3 g sugars • 1 g fibre

Heat **1 tablespoon olive oil** in a small frying pan. Add **1 chopped red or orange capsicum**. Stir over a medium–high heat for 8 minutes, or until softened. Stir in **1 finely chopped fresh jalapeño chilli** and cook for a further 2 minutes before adding **a dash of chilli sauce**. Crumble **150 g fetta** into a bowl. Add the pepper mixture and mash with a fork to form a textured spread.

COOK'S TIPS

● Use a jar of grilled capsicum pieces if fresh capsicums are not available.

● Spread on chunks of crusty bread, or use as a sandwich filling or as a canapé on small squares of toast.

MALAYSIAN LAKSA WITH
PRAWNS AND VEGETABLES

This simple version of a classic Asian recipe is laden with vegetables in a broth just bursting with aromatic spices. Reduced-fat coconut milk provides the authentic background flavour.

Serves 4
Preparation 15 minutes
Cooking 10 minutes

Each serving provides
- 2774 kJ • 663 kcal • 24 g protein
- 21 g fat of which 10 g saturates
- 94 g carbohydrates of which
9 g sugars • 3 g fibre

1 onion
1 red chilli
60 g fresh ginger
300 g Chinese cabbage
¼ cucumber, about 100 g
1 spring onion
200 g bean sprouts
2 tablespoons olive oil or canola oil
2 cloves garlic, crushed
1 teaspoon ground turmeric
4 cups (1 litre) hot fish stock
400 ml can light coconut milk
375 g fine rice noodles
300 g large peeled cooked prawns
8 chopped fresh mint leaves

ALTERNATIVE INGREDIENTS
• Use bok choy or choy sum instead of Chinese cabbage. Alternatively, add any frozen mixed stir-fry vegetables instead of fresh ones.
• For a touch of lemon sharpness, crush 1 piece of lemongrass and add it to the onion mixture in step 1. Remove before serving.

1 Thinly slice the onion, finely chop the chilli and grate the ginger. Shred the cabbage, cut the cucumber into thin strips and finely slice the spring onion. Thoroughly wash the bean sprouts. Heat the oil in a large saucepan over a high heat. Add the garlic, onion and chilli, reduce the heat to medium and cook for 2 minutes.

2 Stir in the ginger, turmeric, hot stock and coconut milk and bring to the boil. Reduce the heat, cover and simmer for 5 minutes. Stir in the rice noodles, Chinese cabbage and bean sprouts and simmer for a further 1 minute before adding the prawns.

3 Continue to cook for 30 seconds to warm the prawns, but do not allow the liquid to boil or the prawns will toughen. Ladle into bowls and sprinkle with cucumber, spring onion and mint before serving.

COOK'S TIP
● Frozen grated ginger is a great ingredient to have on hand. Buy good-quality fresh ginger – look for large, plump, smooth, thin-skinned roots. Peel, chop in a food processor or grate using a metal grater, then spread the ginger on a plastic tray covered in plastic wrap and freeze. When frozen, place the block of ginger in a freezer bag, seal and tap against a work surface to break it into pieces. Use the ginger from frozen.

SUPER FOOD

GARLIC
A member of the onion family, garlic is rich in allyl sulphur compounds, a group of anti-oxidants believed to play a role in reducing the risk of cancer by stimulating enzymes that help the body to get rid of harmful chemicals.

THAI **NOODLES** WITH **CASHEWS** AND STIR-FRIED **VEGETABLES**

Take a wonderfully simple recipe for Thai stir-fry and experiment with shop-bought curry paste, sweet cashew nuts and creamy soybeans for a quick, super-healthy meal any day of the week.

Serves 4
Preparation 10 minutes
Cooking 10 minutes

1 onion
100 g mushrooms
1 red capsicum
200 g bok choy
150 g bean sprouts
2 tablespoons olive oil or canola oil
2 cloves garlic, crushed
75 g unsalted cashew nuts
100 g frozen soybeans
1 tablespoon Thai green curry paste
400 g fresh egg noodles

Each serving provides
• 2715 kJ • 649 kcal • 22 g protein
• 28 g fat of which 5 g saturates
• 82 g carbohydrates of which
7 g sugars • 8 g fibre

ALTERNATIVE INGREDIENTS
• If time is short, cook the garlic and onion then add a 500 g pack of mixed stir-fry vegetables in step 3 instead of the mushrooms, capsicum, bok choy and bean sprouts.
• Try unsalted peanuts as a change from cashew nuts.
• Stir-fry strips of raw chicken or pork with the onion in step 1 and omit the soybeans. The meat strips should be cooked through and lightly browned before adding the curry paste.

1 Finely slice the onion and mushrooms and dice the capsicum. Wash and shred the bok choy and thoroughly wash the bean sprouts. Heat the oil in a large frying pan or wok over a high heat. Add the garlic, onion, mushrooms and capsicum.

2 Stir-fry the vegetables for 2 minutes, then stir in the cashew nuts and continue to cook for a further 3 minutes. Mix in the frozen soybeans and Thai green curry paste. Stir in the noodles, breaking them up with a spoon, then add the bok choy.

3 Stir-fry the mixture for 2 minutes, adding 1–2 tablespoons of cold water if it becomes too dry and the bok choy does not wilt. Stir in the bean sprouts and cook for a final 1 minute before serving.

COOK'S TIPS
● A broad selection of red and green Thai curry pastes is available in the shops. They vary in precise spice mix and chilli heat, so try a few to find your favourite.
● Frozen soybeans are bright green, creamy in flavour and firm. They make a good freezer standby for adding nutrition, great texture and flavour to meat-free meals.

SUPER FOOD

SOYBEANS
Soybeans are rich in vitamins and protein, and packed with nutrients that offer anti-oxidant-boosting and cholesterol-lowering benefits. They are a good source of fibre, vitamin C, iron and the B vitamins thiamin and folate, which help to maintain a healthy heart.

INDONESIAN FRIED **RICE** WITH **EGG** AND **VEGETABLES**

Known as *nasi goreng*, this dish of egg-topped fried rice is a traditional way of using up leftovers. Crunchy water chestnuts, bamboo shoots and bean sprouts complement the soft rice perfectly.

Serves 4
Preparation 15 minutes
Cooking 28 minutes

Each serving provides
- 1816 kJ • 432 kcal • 13 g protein
- 20 g fat of which 3 g saturates
- 54 g carbohydrates of which
10 g sugars • 5 g fibre

200 g brown rice
600 ml hot vegetable stock
2 onions
2 small carrots
225 g can water chestnuts
225 g can sliced bamboo shoots
100 g bean sprouts
3 tablespoons olive oil or canola oil
1 teaspoon sesame oil
3 cloves garlic, crushed
100 g frozen green beans, thawed
½ tablespoon medium curry powder
1 spring onion
3 eggs
3 tablespoons chopped fresh coriander

ALTERNATIVE INGREDIENTS
• Use jasmine rice instead of brown rice and reduce the cooking time to 15 minutes, or according to the packet instructions.
• Use a 500 g pack of fresh mixed stir-fry vegetables instead of the carrots, green beans and bean sprouts.

1 Place the rice in a large saucepan with the hot stock. Cover, bring to the boil and stir once. Reduce the heat and simmer for 25 minutes, or according to the packet instructions, until the rice is tender and the stock has been absorbed. Slice the onions. Thinly slice the carrots at an angle, then drain and slice the water chestnuts, drain the bamboo shoots and wash the bean sprouts.

2 Halfway through cooking the rice, heat 1 tablespoon olive oil or canola oil in a frying pan over a high heat. Add the onions, reduce the heat to medium and fry for 7 minutes, or until browned. Set aside and keep warm. When the rice is almost cooked, heat 1 tablespoon of the olive oil or canola oil in the frying pan. Add the sesame oil, garlic, carrots, water chestnuts, bamboo shoots, green beans and curry powder. Stir-fry for 2 minutes, or until the vegetables are tender. Add the bean sprouts and stir-fry for 1 minute, or until piping hot. Mix the vegetables into the rice and season to taste.

3 Slice the spring onion. Beat the eggs with the spring onion and coriander. Add the remaining 1 tablespoon oil to the frying pan over a high heat. Pour in the egg and cook for 1 minute on each side, or until set. Cut the omelette into thin strips. Divide the rice among four bowls and top with the fried onions and omelette strips.

COOK'S TIP
● Boil the rice uncovered for a few seconds if there is any excess liquid left at the end of cooking in step 1.

SUPER FOOD

BROWN RICE
Wholegrains, including brown rice, consist of three elements – a fibre-rich outer layer (bran), a nutrient-packed inner area (germ) and the central starchy part (endosperm). Brown rice contains the entire grain, keeping all the nutrients intact and so offering full nutritional benefits.

BUTTERNUT PUMPKIN CASSEROLE WITH PAPAYA

Succulent butternut pumpkin, delicate papaya and firm borlotti beans make for a satisfying one-pot meal that helps to keep blood glucose levels steady. Serve with a side salad of mixed leaves.

Serves 4
Preparation 15 minutes
Cooking 10 minutes

½ butternut pumpkin, about 600 g
1 papaya, about 300 g
1 red onion
1 tablespoon olive oil or canola oil
4–6 large fresh sage leaves
1 teaspoon ground cinnamon
juice of 1 large orange, about 100 ml
400 g can borlotti beans, drained

Each serving provides
• 749 kJ • 179 kcal • 7 g protein
• 4 g fat of which 1 g saturates
• 29 g carbohydrates of which
16 g sugars • 9 g fibre

ALTERNATIVE INGREDIENTS
• Try other types of pumpkin if butternut is not available.
• Mango goes well with pumpkin. Select a ripe but firm mango, peel and slice it off the stone and then cut the flesh into chunks. Whereas papaya mellows the flavour of the orange juice, mango accentuates its tanginess.
• Substitute chickpeas or cannellini beans for the borlotti beans.
• For a meaty version of this dish, grill and slice four good-quality sausages and gently stir them into the mixture before serving.

1 Peel and seed the butternut pumpkin and dice the flesh into 2 cm chunks. Seed and peel the papaya (see Cook's Tips below), then slice it and set aside. Thinly slice the onion.

2 Heat the oil in a large pan with a lid. Add the onion and pumpkin and cook over a high heat, stirring occasionally, for 1 minute. Reduce the heat to medium or medium–low, cover the pan and cook for 2 minutes.

3 Shred the sage leaves, then stir them into the pan with the cinnamon and orange juice. Bring to the boil, reduce the heat to low and cover again. Simmer for 5 minutes, stirring once, or until the pumpkin is tender but not soft.

4 Stir in the beans, re-cover the pan and heat gently for 2 minutes. Top with the papaya and serve immediately.

COOK'S TIPS
● To prepare papaya, cut the fruit in half, then scoop out the round black seeds with a spoon. Peel the thin skin off the fruit with a knife.
● Cutting onions in half before slicing them is far easier than slicing them whole as the cut side can be placed flat on a board to prevent it from slipping.

SUPER FOOD

BEANS
A good, low-fat source of protein, beans also have a low glycaemic index (GI) rating, so give a steady energy release without causing spikes in blood glucose levels. The borlotti beans in this recipe are rich in lysine, an essential protein-building amino acid that is often lacking in plant proteins.

MINTED MIXED GRAIN SALAD

Add fresh summery salad stalwarts – plus lots of aromatic parsley, mint and lemon – to plump grains and you have a zesty lunchtime treat that is both refreshing and surprisingly filling.

Serves 4
Preparation 10 minutes,
plus 15 minutes cooling
Cooking 15 minutes

Each serving provides
• 1117 kJ • 267 kcal • 7 g protein
• 13 g fat of which 2 g saturates
• 32 g carbohydrates of which
8 g sugars• 3 g fibre

75 g burghul
75 g quinoa
¼ cucumber
2 large tomatoes
1 large green capsicum
2 spring onions
1 teaspoon sugar
grated zest and juice of 1 lemon
3 teaspoons olive oil
5 chopped large mint sprigs
60 g chopped fresh parsley
1 cos lettuce, to serve

ALTERNATIVE INGREDIENTS
• Use young zucchini instead of cucumber and add a crushed clove garlic in step 2.
• Try the vegetable and herb mixture with rice as a change from burghul and quinoa. Cook jasmine rice for an aromatic salad or sushi rice for a delicious, slightly sticky dish.

1 Place the burghul and quinoa in a saucepan with 1 litre (4 cups) of boiling water. Bring back to the boil, reduce the heat, cover and simmer for 15 minutes, or until the burghul and quinoa are tender. Drain in a sieve if not all of the water has been absorbed. Finely dice the cucumber, tomatoes and capsicum, and thinly slice the spring onions.

2 Mix the sugar, lemon zest and juice in a large bowl, stirring until the sugar dissolves. Whisk in the oil then add the cucumber, tomatoes, capsicum and spring onions. Stir in the cooked burghul and quinoa, then cover and leave to cool for 15 minutes.

3 Stir the mint and parsley into the salad and season to taste just before serving. Divide the salad among four bowls and offer a selection of lettuce leaves for wrapping and scooping.

COOK'S TIPS
● To finely dice cucumber, slice it lengthwise, lay the slices flat together then cut them into strips and cut across the strips to make dice.
● The easiest way to 'chop' herbs is to hold the large leaves in a bundle and shred them finely with scissors.

SUPER FOOD

QUINOA
Perfect in salads, quinoa provides wholegrain, high-fibre goodness to a meal. An excellent source of starchy carbohydrate for energy, quinoa is also rich in iron and zinc for a super-healthy immune system.

SEAFOOD AND VEGETABLE RICE

Vegetables and seafood mix perfectly with savoury rice for a quick alternative to paella. With its vibrant variety of ingredients, the dish also provides an all-round health boost.

Serves 4
Preparation 15 minutes
Cooking 35 minutes

2 onions
2 large capsicums (1 yellow, 1 red)
1 tablespoon olive oil or canola oil
2 large cloves garlic, crushed
2 bay leaves
200 g brown rice
600 ml hot vegetable stock
200 g frozen peas
200 g frozen green beans
350 g frozen cooked mixed seafood
lemon wedges and chopped fresh
    parsley, to garnish

Each serving provides
• 1661 kJ • 397 kcal • 24 g protein
• 9 g fat of which 2 g saturates
• 59 g carbohydrates of which
12 g sugars • 11 g fibre

ALTERNATIVE INGREDIENTS
• Frozen diced capsicums make a good ingredient to have on hand. Add them with the rice at step 2 rather than cooking them with the onions. Frozen mixed vegetables can also be used instead of the peas and beans.
• For a tomato-based version, reduce the stock to 300 ml in step 2, then add a 400 g can chopped tomatoes.
• If you do not like mixed seafood, use 400 g cooked large prawns.

1 Thinly slice the onions and capsicums. Heat the oil in a large frying pan and add the onions, garlic and bay leaves. Add the capsicums and cook, stirring, over a high heat for 2 minutes, or until the vegetables soften slightly.

2 Stir in the rice and pour in the stock. Bring back to the boil and stir to mix the ingredients. Reduce the heat to low so that the liquid simmers. Cover the pan and cook for 20 minutes, or until the liquid has almost evaporated.

3 Use a fork to lightly mix in the frozen peas and beans. Bring back to the boil, reduce the heat and cover the pan. Simmer gently for a further 5 minutes.

4 Sprinkle the frozen cooked seafood over the rice. Re-cover the pan and cook for a final 5 minutes until the rice is tender, but not soft, the seafood is hot and the majority of liquid has evaporated. Garnish with lemon wedges and chopped parsley. Season with ground black pepper before serving.

COOK'S TIPS
● Garnish with mussels in their shells. Rinse and scrub the shells clean, then steam the mussels with 4 tablespoons white wine in a lidded pan for 5–7 minutes, or until the shells open. Throw away any mussels that do not open.
● Serve with a salad of lettuce and cherry tomatoes.

SUPER FOOD

SEAFOOD
Full of goodness, seafood contributes many nutrients to a balanced diet. It contains immune-boosting zinc and the anti-oxidant selenium, which helps to protect against heart disease. It is also a rich source of iodine that is needed for a healthy metabolism.

KEDGEREE WITH SWEETCORN AND BROCCOLI

In an updated classic, the full-on flavour of smoky fish is balanced by refreshing vegetables. Spices add warmth and colour – cumin is pungent and peppery, while turmeric turns the rice golden.

Serves 4
Preparation 15 minutes, plus
5 minutes standing
Cooking 25 minutes

Each serving provides
- 2247 kJ • 537 kcal • 31 g protein
- 17 g fat of which 3 g saturates
- 68 g carbohydrates of which
5 g sugars • 4 g fibre

1 large onion
300 g skinless smoked cod
  or haddock fillet
2 tablespoons olive oil or canola oil
250 g basmati rice
1½ teaspoons cumin seeds
1½ teaspoon turmeric
4 cups (1 litre) hot fish stock
200 g frozen sweetcorn
4 eggs
200 g small broccoli florets
grated zest of 1 lemon
2 tablespoons chopped fresh parsley

ALTERNATIVE INGREDIENTS
- Chunks of fresh salmon are fine in place of smoked fish.
- Omit the uncooked fish in step 2 and serve the rice topped with shredded smoked salmon, allowing 200 g per person, or with smoked mackerel, allowing 300 g per person.
- For a vegetarian kedgeree, leave out the smoked haddock and add 100 g red lentils to the rice. Use vegetable stock in step 1 and increase the quantity to 1.3 litres.

1 Finely chop the onion and cut the smoked fish into 2 cm pieces. Heat the oil in a large saucepan over a high heat. Add the onion and cook for 2 minutes. Reduce the heat and stir in the rice, cumin seeds and turmeric. Pour in the hot stock, bring back to the boil and reduce the heat to low. Cover and simmer for 5 minutes.

2 Add the frozen sweetcorn and bring back to the boil. Mix in the fish, reduce the heat, cover and simmer for 15 minutes, or until the stock has been absorbed by the rice. Meanwhile, cook the eggs for 8 minutes in a pan of boiling water. Remove the rice from the heat and leave it to stand, covered, for 5 minutes.

3 Drain the boiled eggs and rinse them under cold water, then shell and quarter them. Place the broccoli in a saucepan, add boiling water to cover and bring back to the boil. Reduce the heat and simmer for 3 minutes, then drain. Add the broccoli and lemon zest to the kedgeree. Top with the eggs and parsley and season with black pepper.

COOK'S TIPS
- Smoked fish is available either dyed, making it yellow, or undyed and paler, tinged yellow at the edges. Where you can, opt for the natural undyed version.
- Running hard-boiled eggs under cold water stops the cooking process and prevents a grey ring from forming around the egg yolk.

SUPER FOOD

SWEETCORN
As well as containing the naturally occurring phytochemical lutein, good for eye health, sweetcorn is also a useful source of fibre, folate and anti-oxidants. All three of these are associated with a lower risk of cancer.

BACON PILAF WITH BERRIES AND NUTS

The use of brown rice in this pilaf lends a lovely nutty taste and puts wholesome goodness into your meal. The flavours of walnuts, cranberries and bacon combine to make a heart-warming plateful.

Serves 4
Preparation 15 minutes
Cooking 45 minutes

Each serving provides
- 2364 kJ • 565 kcal • 16 g protein
- 26 g fat of which 3 g saturates
- 71 g carbohydrates of which 10 g sugars • 8 g fibre

100 g lean rindless bacon
100 g walnuts
1 onion
2 sticks celery
350 g cabbage
1 tablespoon olive oil
300 g brown rice
4 cups (1 litre) hot chicken stock
50 g dried cranberries
4 tablespoons snipped fresh chives

ALTERNATIVE INGREDIENTS
- Use thin slices of pepperoni or chorizo instead of bacon.
- For a vegetarian pilaf, omit the bacon and dry-fry 100 g pine nuts or roughly chopped macadamia nuts in a frying pan until lightly browned. Remove and set aside, then add with the walnuts in step 4. Use hot vegetable stock in place of the chicken stock.
- Use chopped dried apricots or peaches instead of cranberries.

1 Cut the bacon into thin strips and coarsely chop the walnuts. Finely chop the onion and celery, then shred the cabbage. Put the bacon in a large frying pan over a medium–high heat. Dry-fry for 5 minutes until browned. Add the walnuts, stir-frying them with the bacon for 1 minute. Remove the bacon and walnuts and set aside.

2 Add the oil, onion and celery to the pan and fry over a high heat for 2 minutes, or until the onion softens. Add the rice and continue to cook for 2 minutes, stirring frequently, until the rice grains are opaque.

3 Pour in 2 cups (500 ml) chicken stock, bring to the boil, reduce the heat to medium, cover and simmer for 5 minutes. Add the remaining stock, bring back to the boil and cook for a further 10 minutes.

4 Pile the cabbage on top of the rice, cover and cook over a low heat for 20 minutes, or until the rice is tender and the cabbage is cooked. Add the fried bacon and walnuts plus the cranberries for the last minute of cooking to warm through. Season to taste and divide the pilaf among four plates. Sprinkle with chives and serve.

COOK'S TIPS
- Savoy or any green cabbage works well in this recipe. Spring greens or curly kale are also good choices.
- Take care when adding the first batch of stock to the pan because it will sizzle and steam as the liquid hits the base of the hot pan.

SUPER FOOD

BROWN RICE
Research shows that the risk of both heart disease and Type 2 diabetes may be up to 30 per cent lower in people who regularly eat wholegrains such as brown rice as part of a low-fat diet and healthy lifestyle. It is the combination of health-promoting nutrients working together in brown rice that offers protection against these life-threatening disorders.

GREEK SALAD WITH **CHICKPEAS**

Food does not get much healthier than a salad low in fat, high in fibre and full of anti-oxidants. This dish conjures visions of lazy days in the sun, and delivers on taste with every mouthful.

Serves 4
Preparation 10 minutes

Each serving provides
- 1079 kJ • 258 kcal • 15 g protein
- 14 g fat of which 7 g saturates
- 19 g carbohydrates of which
6 g sugars • 3 g fibre

425 g can chickpeas
1 small onion
1 green capsicum
¼ cucumber
200 g cherry tomatoes
200 g fetta
2 tablespoons olive oil
1 clove garlic, crushed
20 pitted black olives
4 tablespoons chopped fresh parsley
250 g mixed salad leaves
lemon wedges, to garnish

ALTERNATIVE INGREDIENTS
- Try adding miniature new potatoes, either instead of or as well as the chickpeas. Allow 250 g potatoes, cook them in boiling water for 10 minutes until tender and toss with the oil and garlic dressing while still hot.
- Fetta is traditional in Greek salad, but try diced mozzarella for a lighter flavour.

1 Drain the chickpeas and thinly slice the onion. Coarsely dice the capsicum and cucumber. Cut the cherry tomatoes in half and crumble the fetta.

2 Mix the oil, garlic, olives, chickpeas, onion, capsicum and cucumber together in a large bowl. Stir in the tomatoes and parsley. Gently stir in the fetta.

3 Divide the mixed salad leaves among four plates or bowls. Spoon the Greek salad over the leaves and garnish with lemon wedges.

COOK'S TIPS
● Most of this salad can be prepared ahead, apart from adding the tomatoes, parsley and fetta. It can then be covered and set aside for several hours. Once complete, the salad is best served within 2–3 hours.
● If you do not like raw garlic, follow the old-fashioned French method of giving a mild garlic flavour by rubbing a cut clove around the serving bowl before adding the salad. Another alternative is to cook the garlic in a little oil in a small pan over a low heat for 1–2 minutes to mellow its flavour. Cool, then add to the salad in step 1.

SUPER FOOD

OLIVE OIL
For decades, olive oil has been linked to good health. Recent research evidence shows people who follow a Mediterranean diet (olive oil, fruit, vegetables, wholegrains, nuts and fish) do indeed enjoy better health and live longer than people who follow a more traditional meat-based diet.

THREE BEAN SALAD WITH LEMON AND WALNUT DRESSING

A tart dressing transforms a plate of mixed beans into a richly satisfying dish, served either as a main meal or as a side dish. Crisp croutons and lively lemon zest also add texture.

Serves 4
Preparation 10 minutes
Cooking 7 minutes

Each serving provides
- 2021 kJ • 483 kcal • 16 g protein
- 21 g fat of which 2 g saturates
- 62 g carbohydrates of which 16 g sugars • 12 g fibre

8 thick baguette slices
2 tablespoons olive oil
grated zest of 2 lemons and juice of 1 lemon
3 tablespoons honey
1 clove garlic, crushed
3 tablespoons walnut oil
200 g green beans
400 g can red kidney beans
400 g can butter beans

ALTERNATIVE INGREDIENTS
- Try soybeans or chickpeas instead of kidney beans and butter beans.
- Use hazelnut oil as a change from walnut oil.
- Close-textured light rye bread or Italian ciabatta are also good for making croutons.

1 Preheat the grill to the hottest setting. Place the slices of baguette on a grill pan and brush lightly with 1 tablespoon of the olive oil. Toast for about 2 minutes, or until crisp and golden. Turn the slices, brush with the remaining 1 tablespoon olive oil and toast for a further 2 minutes. Cut into chunky croutons and set aside to cool.

2 To make the lemon and walnut dressing, whisk together the lemon zest and juice, honey, garlic and walnut oil in a large bowl. Then trim the green beans and drain the red kidney beans and butterbeans.

3 Place the green beans in a saucepan. Pour in boiling water to cover and bring back to the boil. Reduce the heat slightly and simmer for 3 minutes, or until lightly cooked but still crunchy. Drain the beans, shaking off the cooking water, and toss them in the dressing.

4 Add the red kidney beans and butterbeans to the dressing. Mix well and divide the salad among four bowls, spooning any remaining dressing in the bowl over the beans. Scatter with croutons and serve.

COOK'S TIP
● Canned butterbeans are widely available in all major supermarkets. Alternatively, soak and cook dried butterbeans, following the packet instructions. Drain the cooked beans and pack into freezer bags or containers while still hot, then chill and freeze. Thaw at room temperature before use.

SUPER FOOD

BUTTERBEANS
These large beans are a good source of protein and iron, which play an important role in physical wellbeing. Just 3 tablespoons count as one of your seven-a-day. Butterbeans are also virtually fat free and packed with fibre to promote digestive health.

CHICKEN AND GINGER FRIED RICE

Take a little cooked chicken breast, add some delightfully crunchy vegetables and warming fresh ginger, then combine with rice – and you have a simple dinner that is really hard to beat.

Serves 4
Preparation 10 minutes
Cooking 25 minutes

50 g fresh ginger
350 g cooked boneless, skinless
   chicken breast
225 g can water chestnuts
200 g Chinese cabbage
200 g bean sprouts
4 spring onions
2 tablespoons olive oil or canola oil
2 cloves garlic, crushed
300 g long-grain rice
1 teaspoon sesame oil
4 cups (1 litre) hot salt-reduced
   chicken stock
200 g snow peas

Each serving provides
• 2490 kJ • 595 kcal • 35 g protein
• 18 g fat of which 3 g saturates
• 72 g carbohydrates of which
  8 g sugars • 5 g fibre

ALTERNATIVE INGREDIENTS
• Brown rice works well in this recipe, but allow an additional 200 ml stock and cook it for an extra 10 minutes in step 2.
• Instead of adding the cooked chicken in step 3, add 350 g peeled cooked prawns in step 4, heating them briefly before serving.
• Add a diced red or green capsicum with the snow peas in step 4.
• Try sugarsnap peas instead of snow peas, or add frozen peas or green beans in step 3.
• For vegetarian fried rice, replace the chicken stock with hot vegetable stock and add 350 g Quorn pieces or tofu instead of the chicken.

1 Peel and grate the ginger and slice the chicken into small strips. Drain and slice the water chestnuts and finely shred the Chinese cabbage. Wash the bean sprouts and slice the spring onions.

2 Heat the olive oil or canola oil in a large saucepan over a high heat. Add the ginger, garlic and rice and cook, stirring, for 3 minutes, or until the rice becomes opaque.

3 Pour in the sesame oil and hot stock. Bring back to the boil, reduce the heat to low, cover and simmer for 10 minutes. Add the chicken, water chestnuts and Chinese cabbage, but do not stir them in. Making sure that the stock is simmering, cover the pan and cook gently for a further 7 minutes.

4 Add the snow peas, bean sprouts and spring onions to the pan. Cover and cook for 2 minutes, or until the bean sprouts are piping hot. Fork the ingredients through the rice and serve.

COOK'S TIP
• This is a good recipe for using up leftover roast chicken. Remove all the meat from the bones and cut it into bite-sized pieces, checking that there are no bones. Store cooked chicken in a sealed container in the fridge for up to 3 days.

SUPER FOOD

CHICKEN
Boneless, skinless, chicken breast contains 30 per cent high-quality protein and is low in fat – great for weight control. Chicken also contains some B vitamins, especially niacin, and when eaten with carbohydrate foods, such as rice and pasta, it can help to fight fatigue and improve mood.

ASPARAGUS AND MUSHROOM RICE

Sticky sushi rice is a perfect base for tender Japanese-style vegetables, topped with fibre-packed and mineral-rich seaweed. Serve with sliced chicken.

Serves 4
Preparation 10 minutes, plus
5 minutes standing
Cooking 20 minutes

Each serving provides
- 1414 kJ • 338 kcal • 7 g protein
- 12 g fat of which 1 g saturates
- 46 g carbohydrates of which 5 g sugars • 2 g fibre

200 g sushi rice
4 sheets roasted nori
2 tablespoons Japanese rice vinegar
¼ teaspoon salt
1 tablespoon sugar
3 tablespoons olive oil or canola oil
200 g asparagus tips
100 g shiitake mushrooms
2 tablespoons sake or dry sherry
1 tablespoon soy sauce

ALTERNATIVE INGREDIENTS
- Sprinkle 200 g shredded smoked chicken or ham, or 150 g diced smoked salmon, over the rice instead of, or as well as, asparagus tips.
- Stir-fry 450 g raw large peeled prawns instead of the asparagus tips. Cook for 2–4 minutes, or until they turn pink. Sprinkle them over the rice and omit the asparagus tips.
- You can substitute 2 tablespoons vegetable stock for the sake or sherry if you prefer.

1 Put the rice in a large saucepan and pour in 300 ml of boiling water. Bring back to the boil, stirring once, reduce the heat to low, cover and simmer for 15 minutes, or until the water has been absorbed and the rice is moist.

2 Cut each sheet of nori into four strips, then across into fine shreds and set aside. Mix the vinegar, salt and sugar and stir into the cooked rice. Cover the pan and set aside to infuse for 5 minutes.

3 Meanwhile, heat 1 tablespoon of the oil in a large frying pan over a high heat. Add the asparagus tips and cook for 3 minutes, or until tender. Thinly slice the mushrooms. Heat the remaining 2 tablespoons oil in another pan, add the mushrooms and fry over a high heat for 2 minutes. Add the sake or sherry and soy sauce to the mushrooms and boil for a few seconds, turning the mushrooms in the liquid.

4 Divide the sushi rice among four plates, patting each portion into a neat oblong shape, and top with the asparagus tips. Transfer the mushrooms to the plates and sprinkle with the nori before serving.

COOK'S TIP
● Nori is an edible seaweed. Sheets of roasted, or toasted, nori are available in the international section of most large supermarkets or in Chinese stores. Once opened, store the packet of nori in an airtight bag for 1–2 days, though it is best eaten on the day of opening.

SUPER FOOD

NORI
Rich in fibre, nori is good for aiding digestive health. In addition, it is a good source of protein, iron, vitamin B_{12}, potassium and iodine, which together help to prevent anaemia and regulate blood pressure. Rich in carotenoids, nori has powerful anti-oxidant properties, too.

CAPSICUM **TABOULEH** WITH **CRANBERRIES**

Marjoram, nutmeg and chilli bring a hint of warmth, with dried cranberries adding eye-catching colour, to a light version of a classic Middle Eastern salad. Serve with crisp lettuce leaves and soft tortilla wraps.

Serves 4
Preparation 10 minutes,
plus 30 minutes soaking

Each serving provides
• 1293 kJ • 309 kcal • 6 g protein
• 9 g fat of which 1 g saturates
• 53 g carbohydrates of which
14 g sugars • 2 g fibre

200 g burghul
1 large red capsicum
1 medium-hot red chilli
½ red onion
50 g dried cranberries
1 tablespoon red wine vinegar
2 tablespoons olive oil
4 sprigs fresh marjoram, chopped
pinch of grated nutmeg

ALTERNATIVE INGREDIENTS
• Make a colour change by using an orange capsicum instead of a red one.
• Use walnut oil as an alternative to olive oil for a nuttier tabouleh.
• Dried blueberries are just as tasty as cranberries in this dish. Currants, sultanas and raisins also work well.
• Try sprigs of thyme instead of marjoram. Alternatively, use a mixture of herbs such as parsley and fennel for an aromatic twist.
• For a tangy tabouleh, add the grated zest and juice of 1 orange in step 2.

1 Place the burghul in a heatproof bowl and pour in boiling water to cover – a ratio of one part burghul to two parts water works well. Cover the bowl with plastic wrap and leave it to soak for 30 minutes, or until the burghul is plumped up to double in volume.

2 Meanwhile, finely dice the capsicum and chilli and finely chop the onion. In a large bowl, mix the capsicum, chilli, onion, cranberries, vinegar, oil, marjoram and nutmeg. Cover and set aside until the burghul is ready.

3 Drain the burghul through a sieve to remove any excess water and stir it into the capsicum mixture. Season to taste and serve.

COOK'S TIPS
● The flavour of the tabouleh is enhanced by leaving it to infuse for 2 hours or more before eating. If you have time to plan ahead, prepare and cover the tabouleh, then store it in the fridge until needed – it will stay fresh for up to 2 days when chilled.
● Tabouleh goes well with barbecued food, either as a first course or a side dish. It is also great in packed lunches or picnics.

SUPER FOOD

CRANBERRIES
Similar to other red berries such as raspberries and strawberries, cranberries are rich in a phytochemical called ellagic acid. Some studies have shown that ellagic acid can help to prevent the growth of cancerous cells. With fibre, too, cranberries can lend support to a healthy digestive system.

QUINOA WITH SUMMER VEGETABLES

The creamy, slightly crunchy texture and nutty taste of quinoa make it a great partner for sweet beans and juicy tomatoes. Sprinkle mild gouda cheese on top and serve with salad leaves.

Serves 4
Preparation 5 minutes
Cooking 18 minutes

Each serving provides
- 1393 kJ • 333 kcal • 15 g protein
- 16 g fat of which 5 g saturates
- 35 g carbohydrates of which
7 g sugars • 5 g fibre

200 g quinoa
400 ml hot chicken stock
200 g baby broad beans, thawed
** if frozen**
4 spring onions
400 g cherry tomatoes
2 tablespoons olive oil
6 fresh basil sprigs
60 g gouda cheese, grated or pared

ALTERNATIVE INGREDIENTS
- Try pearl barley if you cannot buy quinoa. Cook pearl barley in boiling water for 30 minutes, allowing 600 ml water to 200 g pearl barley.
- Use frozen soybeans instead of broad beans, adding them to the quinoa from frozen and increasing the cooking time by 2 minutes.
- Look out for firm-textured mature gouda cheese. Alternatively, try Spanish manchego, gruyère or mature cheddar. For a completely different flavour, use smoked cheese or add crumbled fetta.

1 Put the quinoa in a large saucepan and pour in the hot stock. Cover the pan, bring to the boil, reduce the heat to medium and simmer for 10 minutes. Add the baby broad beans to the pan. Re-cover, bring back to the boil and simmer for a further 5 minutes.

2 Turn up the heat and boil the mixture, uncovered, for 1 minute to evaporate excess stock. If any remains in the pan after this time, drain the quinoa through a fine-meshed sieve.

3 Thinly slice the spring onions and cut the tomatoes in half. Pour the oil into a serving bowl and add the spring onions and tomatoes. Shred the basil leaves on top then transfer the cooked quinoa and beans to the mixture and stir to combine. Season to taste, divide among four bowls and top with gouda cheese shavings.

COOK'S TIPS
● Quinoa is cooked when the grains burst open and the germ (inside the grain) has formed into an opaque curl. It should be soft but not stodgy. Quinoa is gluten free, so this recipe is suitable for coeliacs and people sensitive to gluten.
● Baby broad beans can be eaten in their skins, but you may like to pop them out to reveal the delicate bright-green legumes. Larger broad beans benefit from this method as the skins can be quite tough.

SUPER FOOD

QUINOA
Pronounced 'keen-wah', quinoa is a wholegrain with a low glycaemic index (GI) value that produces a slow rise in blood glucose levels and may help to protect against Type 2 diabetes. It is also a source of magnesium, needed for healthy bones, muscle and nerve functions, and high in protein – good news for vegetarians.

PEARL BARLEY PILAF WITH GREEN VEGETABLES

Wholegrain pearl barley is mixed with blueberries and pine nuts for an unusual ensemble that really works. With fresh-flavoured green vegetables, it is as easy on the eye as it is on the palate.

Serves 4
Preparation 10 minutes
Cooking 25 minutes

Each serving provides
- 2469 kJ • 59 kcal • 16 g protein
- 22 g fat of which 3 g saturates
- 79 g carbohydrates of which 17 g sugars • 6 g fibre

200 g pearl barley
1 bay leaf
300 g leeks
3 sticks celery
3 tablespoons olive oil
250 g spinach
1 clove garlic, crushed
50 g pine nuts
70 g dried blueberries

ALTERNATIVE INGREDIENTS
• As a change, use a mix of brown rice and pearl barley, which have similar water absorption and cooking times. Other types of rice that taste good in a pilaf include red rice or wild rice.
• Try raisins or sultanas instead of dried blueberries, and sunflower seeds instead of pine nuts.
• Baby turnips make a tasty alternative to spinach. Thinly slice 400 g baby turnips and cook them in the olive oil in step 3 with the pine nuts and garlic.

1 Place the pearl barley in a large saucepan with the bay leaf and pour in 600 ml of boiling water. Bring back to the boil, stir once, reduce the heat, partly cover the pan and cook for 25 minutes, or until the water has been absorbed and the pearl barley is tender.

2 Meanwhile, thinly slice the leeks and celery. Heat 2 tablespoons of the oil in a frying pan over a high heat. Add the leeks and celery and fry, stirring frequently, for 5 minutes, or until the vegetables are tender. Stir into the cooked barley and season to taste.

3 Pour the remaining 1 tablespoon oil into the pan. Add the spinach and cook over a medium heat for 3 minutes, or until wilted. Add the garlic, pine nuts and dried blueberries and cook for 1 minute. Remove the bay leaf and divide the barley among four plates. Top with spinach, blueberries and pine nuts and serve.

COOK'S TIP

• If you do not have a garlic crusher, peel the garlic, flatten the clove on a board with the side of a large knife blade and then chop it. Whether garlic is crushed, chopped or sliced influences its flavour in the finished dish. Crushed garlic gives the most intense result.

SUPER FOOD

PEARL BARLEY

A member of the grain family, pearl barley contains many nutrients, including B vitamins and folate, which help to produce healthy red blood cells and prevent a type of anaemia known as macrocytic anaemia. Pearl barley also contains some soluble dietary fibre that is effective in lowering cholesterol.

SPINACH

Dark leafy greens, especially spinach, have a rich supply of carotenoids – a group of plant compounds with strong anti-oxidant properties. Eaten often, vegetables that contain carotenoids help to build the body's resistance to diseases. Spinach is also a good source of heart-healthy folate.

PUMPKIN, SPINACH AND HAZELNUT GRATIN

Serves 4
Preparation 15 minutes Cooking 35 minutes

Each serving provides • 1046 kJ • 250 kcal
• 14 g protein • 11 g fat of which 5 g saturates
• 24 g carbohydrates of which 8 g sugars • 6 g fibre

Preheat the oven to 190°C (170°C fan-forced). Peel **1 small butternut pumpkin**, halve lengthwise and remove the seeds, then cut into 1.5 cm slices. Cut **300 g potatoes** into small cubes. Steam the pumpkin and potato together for 8 minutes, or until just tender. Season with ground black pepper. Meanwhile, wilt **500 g fresh spinach** with 1 tablespoon of water in a large saucepan over a medium–high heat, stirring, for 5 minutes. Take off the heat when the spinach leaves have turned dark green, but have not yet disintegrated. Drain off any liquid, stir in **1 teaspoon grated nutmeg** and set aside. Spoon half of the squash and potato mixture into a shallow, oiled baking dish and top with half the spinach. Sprinkle with **2 tablespoons chopped hazelnuts**. Continue layering the dish and top with a creamy sauce made by combining **150 g Greek-style yogurt, 1 beaten egg, 25 g grated parmesan** and **50 g crumbled fetta**. Sprinkle **2 tablespoons wholemeal breadcrumbs** over the top and bake for 25 minutes, or until golden.

COOK'S TIPS

● Try sweet potato instead of white potatoes.
● If you do not have a steamer, place the butternut pumpkin and potatoes in a colander set over a large pan of boiling water. Cover with a lid and steam as above. Alternatively, boil them for 5 minutes then drain, but be sure not to overcook them or the gratin will be mushy.

EGGS FLORENTINE

Serves 4
Preparation 15 minutes Cooking 15 minutes

Each serving provides • 1301 kJ • 311 kcal
• 19 g protein • 22 g fat of which 11 g saturates
• 11 g carbohydrates of which 6 g sugars • 4 g fibre

Preheat the grill to the hottest setting. Make a cheese sauce by melting **20 g butter** in a non-stick pan with **25 g plain flour**. Stir over a medium heat for 2 minutes then gradually beat in **300 ml low-fat milk** until it forms a smooth sauce. Stir in **50 g grated cheddar** and **1 teaspoon French mustard**. Wilt **600 g baby spinach leaves** with 1 tablespoon of water in a large pan over a medium–high heat for 5 minutes. Drain thoroughly and beat in **15 g butter**. Divide among four individual ovenproof dishes, or gratin dishes, and make a hollow in the centre of each portion. Poach **4 eggs** in a pan of simmering water until the whites are cooked, then remove the eggs using a slotted spoon, drain on paper towel and place one in each spinach hollow. Pour the sauce over the spinach and egg, sprinkle each with **1 tablespoon grated cheddar** and grill for 2 minutes, or until golden.

COOK'S TIP

● This dish makes a hearty starter, or serve it as a light supper with crusty bread.

SAVOURY SPINACH WITH PEAS

Serves 4
Preparation 5 minutes Cooking 8 minutes

Each serving provides • 510 kJ • 122 kcal
• 6 g protein • 9 g fat of which 1 g saturates
• 5 g carbohydrates of which 4 g sugars • 8 g fibre

Cook **150 g baby peas** for 3 minutes in a small pan of boiling water. Drain and set aside. Meanwhile, heat **1 tablespoon olive oil** in a large pan. Add **8 chopped spring onions** and fry over a medium heat for about 5 minutes, or until softened. Add **500 g fresh spinach** and an extra **1 tablespoon olive oil**, stirring until wilted. Stir in the peas and the **juice of ½ lemon** and serve.

COOK'S TIP

● As an alternative to baby peas, use fresh shelled peas. They must be sweet and small – large peas contain more starch and can taste floury.

FILLED FILO TARTLETS

Serves 4
Preparation 15 minutes Cooking 20 minutes

Each serving provides • 892 kJ • 213 kcal
• 13 g protein • 14 g carbohydrates of which 3 g sugars • 11 g fat of which 5 g saturates • 3 g fibre

Preheat the oven to 190°C (170°C fan-forced).Wash **500 g baby spinach leaves** in a colander, then shake dry and cook in a large saucepan for 5 minutes over a medium heat, with just the water clinging to the leaves. Drain the spinach, if necessary, then transfer it to a

large bowl with **200 g ricotta, 2 egg yolks** and **1 crushed clove garlic**. Stir to combine, season with ground black pepper and set aside. Chop **2 slices prosciutto** into 1 cm strips. Cut **4 filo pastry sheets** into four squares each and lightly brush with a little **olive oil**. Layer four squares of pastry into four individual metal flan dishes and fill with the spinach mixture. Top each tart with a few slices of prosciutto and sprinkle **1 tablespoon grated parmesan** over each. Bake for 15 minutes, or until the pastry is golden and the filling has set.

COOK'S TIP

● Serve the tarts warm or cold, with a mixed green salad or a tomato and onion salad.

SPINACH AND MUSHROOM PASTA

Serves 4
Preparation 5 minutes Cooking 12 minutes

Each serving provides • 2335 kJ • 558 kcal
• 17 g protein • 29 g fat of which 4 g saturates
• 61 g carbohydrates of which 5 g sugars • 6 g fibre

Cook **300 g penne** in a saucepan of boiling water for 10 minutes, or according to the packet directions, until the pasta is tender but still with some bite in the centre, then drain. Meanwhile, heat **2 tablespoons olive oil** in a large frying pan and then add **2 finely chopped French shallots, 200 g sliced mushrooms** and **2 crushed cloves garlic**. Stir over a medium heat until softened. Add **400 g baby spinach leaves** and **1 teaspoon grated nutmeg**. Stir until the spinach has wilted, then mix in an additional **1 tablespoon olive oil**. Stir the vegetables into the hot pasta and season to taste. Divide among four plates and sprinkle each portion with **½ tablespoon grated parmesan** and **½ tablespoon pine nuts**.

COOK'S TIP

● For a creamy dish, add 100 g low-fat sour cream or low-fat cream cheese instead of the last tablespoon of olive oil.

SUMMER **CHICKEN** RISOTTO WITH GREEN **PEAS**

The creaminess of Italian arborio rice develops with the slow cooking of this mouth-watering and simple dish. The clean sweetness of fresh young peas adds an uplifting final flourish.

Serves 4
Preparation 20 minutes, plus
5 minutes standing
Cooking 28 minutes

1 onion
400 g boneless, skinless chicken
   breasts
400 g fresh peas or 200 g frozen
   baby peas
2 tablespoons olive oil
250 g arborio rice
900 ml hot chicken stock

Each serving provides
• 1925 kJ • 460 kcal • 32 g protein
• 11 g fat of which 2 g saturates
• 60 g carbohydrates of which
4 g sugars • 3 g fibre

ALTERNATIVE INGREDIENTS
• For a richer risotto, try a combination of wine and stock. Add 300 ml dry white wine in step 2 and reduce the chicken stock to 600 ml. Top each portion of risotto with parmesan shavings before serving.
• Asparagus works well instead of peas. Trim off any woody ends from 8 asparagus spears then slice them and add to the pan in step 2 before pouring in the stock.

1 Finely chop the onion and cut the chicken into 2 cm chunks. Shell the peas, if using fresh ones. Heat the oil in a large saucepan over a high heat. Add the onion, reduce the heat to medium and cook for 1 minute. Mix in the chicken and cook, stirring, for 5 minutes, or until the pieces of chicken are firm and white in colour.

2 Add the rice and cook for 1 minute, stirring to coat the rice in the oil. Pour 2 cups (500 ml) of the hot stock into the pan and bring to the boil, stirring once or twice. Reduce the heat to medium or low so that the stock simmers steadily and cook for 10 minutes.

3 Add the peas, if using fresh, and stir in the remaining 400 ml stock. Bring back to the boil, reduce the heat again to medium or low and simmer steadily for 10 minutes. If using frozen peas, add them for the final 5 minutes of cooking time. Stir once or twice to ensure that the rice cooks evenly. By the end of the cooking time, the majority of stock should be absorbed but still with a little excess.

4 Season to taste, cover the pan and remove it from the heat. Leave the risotto to stand for 5 minutes – the rice will finish cooking and absorb the excess liquid, leaving it moist and creamy.

COOK'S TIP
● Simmer the stock gently for an authentic, creamy risotto. Do not allow it to bubble furiously or the stock will evaporate rather than be absorbed by the rice.

SUPER FOOD

PEAS
These little green wonders are bursting with anti-oxidants, including lutein, which can protect your eyesight by lowering the risk of age-related cataract development. Peas are also starchy and high in fibre – good for promoting a healthy heart and digestive system.

HERBED **BURGHUL** WITH **CHORIZO**

Moist grains flavoured with herbs, capsicum and cucumber make a welcome change to everyday salads. A little chorizo adds plenty of punch, with cooling yogurt served on the side.

Serves 4
Preparation 10 minutes,
plus 30 minutes soaking

200 g burghul
400 ml hot chicken stock
½ cucumber
2 red capsicums
125 g cooked chorizo, thinly sliced
4 tablespoons snipped fresh chives
2 tablespoons chopped fresh dill
8 large sprigs fresh mint, leaves
    chopped
120 g natural yogurt

Each serving provides
• 1435 kJ • 343 kcal • 14 g protein
• 12 g fat of which 5 g saturates
• 47 g carbohydrates of which
8 g sugars • 2 g fibre

ALTERNATIVE INGREDIENTS
• Use a variety of cooked meats –
spicy or full-flavoured varieties work
best – such as beef pastrami, garlic
sausage or salami.
• Mixed grains, such as spelt with
barley and buckwheat, make an ideal
change from burghul. Follow the packet
instructions for individual soaking and
cooking times.
• For a meat-free alternative, top the
yogurt with chopped hard-boiled egg,
allowing one egg per portion and
omitting the chorizo and mint. Replace
the chicken stock with vegetable.

1 Place the burghul in a heatproof bowl and pour in the hot stock. Cover with plastic wrap and leave to soak for 30 minutes, or until the burghul is tender and doubled in volume.

2 Meanwhile, dice the cucumber and capsicums and shred the chorizo. Remove any excess liquid from the burghul by draining it through a sieve. Return it to the bowl and stir in the cucumber, capsicum, chives, dill and mint and season to taste.

3 Divide the burghul among four bowls. Top each serving with yogurt and sprinkle with the chorizo.

COOK'S TIPS
● Use kitchen scissors to shred the chorizo into thin strips.
● If you need to measure yogurt, it is helpful to know that the volume in millilitres is equivalent to the weight, so 120 g of yogurt can be measured as 120 ml in a jug.

SUPER FOOD

RED CAPSICUMS
As fibre sources, red capsicums are good for promoting a healthy digestive system, and contain potassium to help regulate blood pressure. They are also packed with powerful anti-oxidant carotenes, which help to protect the body against some cancers.

DESSERTS

RASPBERRY CREAMS WITH MANGO AND HONEY SAUCE

Everyone will love such a lusciously smooth yet quick and healthy dessert. Not only that, its bright jewel-like colours would look great on any dinner-party table.

Serves 4
Preparation 10 minutes

1 cup (250 g) low-fat thick
  Greek-style yogurt or low-fat
  cream cheese
2 tablespoons icing sugar
1 large ripe mango
1 tablespoon honey
260 g raspberries

Each serving provides
- 711 kJ • 170 kcal • 6 g protein
- 2 g fat of which 1 g saturates
- 30 g carbohydrates of which
27 g sugars • 4 g fibre

ALTERNATIVE INGREDIENTS
- Use a variety of fruit instead of raspberries – sliced strawberries, whole blueberries, pitted cherries, halved black or green grapes, kiwi fruit, pineapple chunks or sliced bananas.
- Swap the yogurt or cream cheese for ricotta, beating it thoroughly with the icing sugar in step 1 to remove its 'grainy' texture.
- As a change from mango, try peaches, nectarines or plums to make a tasty purée to complement the raspberries. Use 350 g fruit in total for the purée.

1 Mix together the yogurt or cream cheese with the icing sugar. Cut the mango off the stone, chop into small chunks and purée in a blender or food processor. Stir the honey into the mango purée.

2 Set aside 8 raspberries and reserve 4 teaspoons of the sweetened yogurt or cream cheese. Divide the remainder of the raspberries among four glass dishes and top with the yogurt mixture. Use a knife or the back of a spoon to create an even surface.

3 Spoon the mango purée over the yogurt to cover. Top each portion with 1 teaspoon of the reserved sweetened yogurt and decorate with 2 raspberries.

COOK'S TIP
● To measure runny honey accurately, dip a metal spoon into boiling water, shake off the water and scoop up the honey – it will easily slide off the hot spoon. For set honey, use a round-bladed knife to fill the bowl of a measuring spoon and then to scrape the honey into the mango purée.

SUPER FOOD

RASPBERRIES
Like other berry fruits, raspberries are rich in anthocyanins and ellagic acid, powerful anti-oxidants that protect against cancers and heart disease. Raspberries also have a low glycaemic index (GI) value, which means their natural sugars are released slowly into the bloodstream, helping to keep blood glucose levels steady.

WARM SPICED **PLUMS** WITH **HAZELNUT** YOGURT

Speedy cooking brings out the best in firm plums, especially when they are sprinkled with a little cinnamon. Toasted hazelnuts, mixed with yogurt, add a burst of fibre and vitamin E goodness.

Serves 4
Preparation 10 minutes
Cooking 5 minutes

Each serving provides
- 1566 kJ • 374 kcal • 12 g protein
- 18 g fat of which 3 g saturates
- 39 g carbohydrates of which 33 g sugars • 5 g fibre

100 g chopped toasted hazelnuts
400 g low-fat Greek-style yogurt
2 tablespoons runny honey
1 tablespoon sugar
½ teaspoon cinnamon
500 g firm ripe plums

ALTERNATIVE INGREDIENTS
- Use chopped pecan nuts and maple syrup rather than hazelnuts and honey.
- Grill 8 ripe pear halves in place of plums. Halve 1 pear per portion, remove the cores and place, cut sides up, in the dish. Use a little grated nutmeg instead of the cinnamon, which has too strong a flavour for the pears. Sprinkle the pear halves with the juice of ½ lemon and the spiced sugar before grilling in step 2.
- For a weekend breakfast, serve the plums on heated waffles or pancakes and top with the hazelnut yogurt.

1 Preheat the grill to the hottest setting. Reserve 4 tablespoons of hazelnuts and mix the remaining hazelnuts into the yogurt. Trickle in the honey, mix gently, cover and set aside in the fridge while preparing the plums.

2 Mix the sugar and cinnamon. Halve and stone the plums (see Cook's Tips), cutting the halves in quarters if they are large. Place the plums in an ovenproof dish and sprinkle with the cinnamon sugar. Grill for 5 minutes, or until the sugar has dissolved and the plums begin to brown. The cooking time will depend on the ripeness of the fruit.

3 Divide the plums among four serving plates and pour over any cooking juices. Add a spoonful of hazelnut yogurt and sprinkle with the reserved hazelnuts.

COOK'S TIPS
- To stone plums, cut the fruit in half from the top, following the natural dimple. Twist the halves and they will separate easily, leaving the stone in one half. Use a small pointed knife to cut out the stone.
- To toast your own hazelnuts, place the nuts on a baking tray and roast in the oven for 5 minutes at 220°C (200°C fan-forced), or until browned, checking regularly to make sure they don't burn.
- Prepare the hazelnut yogurt in advance – handy for making an easy weekend breakfast treat.

SUPER FOOD

HAZELNUTS
Highly nutritious, hazelnuts are rich in heart-healthy fats. They are also a good source of some B vitamins, especially thiamine (B_1) and B_6. Full of fibre, the nuts help to maintain digestive health and just a handful will provide your daily dose of vitamin E.

JUICY **APPLES** WITH **OAT** AND **SEED** CRUNCH

A fresh and fibre-rich take on the classic crumble, these lightly stewed apples and prunes with a golden oaty topping are a special treat with a spoonful of yogurt or piping-hot custard.

Serves 4
Preparation 5 minutes
Cooking 8 minutes

450 g cooking apples
100 ml apple juice
100 g pitted prunes
25 g butter
½ cup (50 g) whole rolled oats
25 g sunflower seeds
25 g raw or demerara sugar
¼ cup (60 g) natural yogurt

Each serving provides
• 1142 kJ • 273 kcal • 6 g protein
• 11 g fat of which 4 g saturates
• 41 g carbohydrates of which
31 g sugars • 5 g fibre

ALTERNATIVE INGREDIENTS
• Almost any dried fruit can be used to sweeten the apples instead of prunes: peaches, pears, apricots, sultanas, raisins, cranberries or even mixed dried fruit.
• Add 50 g chopped walnuts with the sugar in step 3.
• Try mixed seeds, such as sesame, sunflower and pumpkin, or use a combination of chopped mixed nuts and seeds.

1 Peel, core and cut the apples into 1 cm slices. Place in a saucepan and pour in the juice. Bring to the boil, reduce the heat and cover the pan with a lid. Simmer for about 5 minutes, stirring occasionally, until soft but not pulpy. Slice the prunes into quarters and gently stir in the pieces. Cover and set aside off the heat.

2 Melt the butter in a frying pan over a medium heat. Add the oats and sunflower seeds, increase the heat to medium–high and cook, stirring, for about 2 minutes, or until the oats and seeds are browned.

3 Add the sugar and stir until it melts and coats the mixture. Remove the pan from the heat. Divide the apple among four dishes and top with the oat mixture. Add 1 tablespoon of yogurt to each dish and serve hot or warm.

COOK'S TIP
● Make double the quantity and freeze in individual portions. You can also do this if you have a surplus of stewed apple. The crunchy topping can be frozen separately and sprinkled over ice cream or yogurt.

SUPER FOOD

APPLES
Fruit is good for heart health as it contains soluble fibre, known to help to lower blood cholesterol. Apples have a low glycaemic index (GI) score, meaning they release glucose steadily rather than rapidly into the bloodstream, which helps to regulate blood glucose levels.

CHOCOLATEY **ORANGE** AND **BLUEBERRY** SOUFFLÉS

A gooey soufflé, with its tempting deep cocoa colour, is baked over a vitamin-filled blueberry base, proving that even such an irresistible dessert can be good for you.

Serves 4
Preparation 10 minutes
Cooking 12 minutes

250 g blueberries
2 eggs
4 tablespoons caster sugar
3 tablespoons plain flour
2 tablespoons unsweetened
  cocoa powder
grated zest and juice of 1 orange
½ teaspoon icing sugar, to dust

Each serving provides
• 870 kJ • 208 kcal • 7 g protein
• 5 g fat of which 2 g saturates
• 35 g carbohydrates of which
23 g sugars • 3 g fibre

ALTERNATIVE INGREDIENTS
• When fresh blueberries are not available, use frozen ones or try frozen mixed berries.

1 Preheat the oven to 220°C (200°C fan-forced). Place four 1 cup (250 ml/9 cm diameter) ramekins on a baking tray and divide the blueberries among them.

2 Separate the eggs, pouring the whites into a thoroughly clean bowl and placing the yolks in a separate bowl. Add the sugar, flour, cocoa powder, orange zest and juice to the egg yolks and beat to form a smooth batter. Whisk the eggwhites until they stand in stiff peaks. Use a large metal spoon to fold the eggwhites into the batter.

3 Spoon the batter over the blueberries, level each surface and bake for 12 minutes, or until the soufflés are risen and set. Dust with icing sugar and serve immediately.

COOK'S TIPS
● When whisking eggwhites, the bowl and beaters must be totally clean and grease-free or the whites will not stiffen.
● If you are preparing this dessert ahead of time, mix the chocolate batter a couple of hours in advance, then cover and set aside until needed. Place the eggwhites in a separate bowl and whisk them just before folding into the batter.

SUPER FOOD

BLUEBERRIES
Acclaimed as one of the ultimate super foods, blueberries are packed full of phytochemicals, especially anthocyanins, which are thought to have anti-inflammatory effects in the body. Researchers believe that the berries may help to protect against some cancers and heart disease.

ORANGE AND BANANA MEDLEY

Cinnamon and orange are a perfect match for banana in a quick, refreshing and filling dessert full of flavour, essential vitamins and minerals. Serve with a dollop of low-fat vanilla ice cream.

Serves 4
Preparation 10 minutes
Marinating 10–15 minutes
Cooking 2 minutes

4 large seedless oranges
50 g raisins or sultanas
1 stick cinnamon
2 large or 4 small bananas

Each serving provides
• 753 kJ • 180 kcal • 4 g protein
• 1 g fat (no saturates) • 43 g carbohydrates of which 41 g sugars
• 6 g fibre

ALTERNATIVE INGREDIENTS
• Use dried cranberries (sometimes sold as 'craisins') or cherries instead of raisins or sultanas.
• Try strawberries as a change from bananas, leaving the strawberries whole or halving large ones.
• Spiced pineapple is a refreshing alternative to banana and orange. Use 1 peeled ripe pineapple, 1 star anise and ¼ teaspoon ground cinnamon.

1 Use a zester to remove the zest of 1 orange, then halve the orange and squeeze out the juice. Add water, if necessary, to make the juice up to 150 ml. Pour the juice into a saucepan. Add the zest, raisins or sultanas, and the cinnamon stick (use just half a stick if long). Bring to the boil, then remove from the heat, cover and set aside.

2 Slice the ends off the remaining 3 oranges, then cut away the peel in wide strips, working down the fruit to remove all the pith. Slice the oranges, discarding any pips.

3 Place the sliced oranges in a serving dish, adding any juices that run out during preparation. Pour the orange juice mixture over the fruit. Cover and set aside for 10–15 minutes.

4 Peel and slice the bananas and add them to the oranges just before serving, mixing to coat the slices in the orange juice mixture so that they do not discolour.

COOK'S TIPS
● The banana and orange medley can also be served warm, especially when using a good-quality fresh cinnamon stick, which will provide plenty of flavour. Prepare the recipe as above but do not set aside the syrup or the fruit in either step 1 or step 3.
● The oranges can be prepared, cooled and chilled overnight in an airtight container.

SUPER FOOD

ORANGES
Oranges are renowned for their high content of vitamin C, which, as well as being a powerful anti-oxidant, is good for eye health and the immune system.

BANANAS

The fibre in bananas, both soluble and insoluble, helps to protect the body against bowel cancer, stabilise blood glucose levels and lower harmful blood cholesterol. Bananas also contain vitamin B$_6$, important for making red blood cells and breaking down protein and fats.

FRUITY TEA BREAD

Makes 8 slices
Preparation 10 minutes Cooking 40 minutes

Each serving provides • 1150 kJ • 275 kcal
• 8 g protein • 14 g fat of which 2 g saturates
• 31 g carbohydrates of which 14 g sugars • 3 g fibre

Preheat the oven to 180°C (160°C fan-forced). Oil a 900 g loaf tin and line it with baking paper. In a bowl, combine **⅔ cup (100 g) self-raising flour, ½ cup (75 g) wholemeal self-raising flour, ⅔ cup (75 g) ground almonds, ½ teaspoon baking powder** and **½ teaspoon ground ginger**. In another bowl, combine **3 mashed very ripe bananas, 2 eggs, 50 ml runny honey** and **100 ml low-fat milk**. Stir the dry ingredients into the wet ingredients, then fold in **75 g chopped pecans**. Pour the mixture into the prepared loaf tin and bake for 40 minutes, or until golden and a skewer comes out clean when pushed into the centre of the tea bread. Cool before slicing.

COOK'S TIP

● This is a healthy alternative for tea time, picnics and lunchboxes. If desired, spread with butter or low-fat spread before serving.

APRICOT AND BANANA CRUMBLE

Serves 4
Preparation 10 minutes Cooking 35 minutes

Each serving provides • 1431 kJ • 342 kcal
• 7 g protein • 12 g fat of which 4 g saturates
• 54 g carbohydrates of which 37 g sugars • 6 g fibre

Preheat the oven to 190°C (170°C fan-forced). Simmer **150 g dried apricots** in sufficient water to cover for 15 minutes, or until tender. Meanwhile, peel and slice **3 bananas** and place in an ovenproof dish. Pour over the juice of **1 lemon**. Drain the apricots, reserving the cooking liquid, chop into quarters and spoon them over the sliced bananas. Pour in 4 tablespoons of the reserved cooking liquid. In a bowl, combine **¾ cup (75 g) rolled oats** with **¼ cup (25 g) chopped mixed nuts** and **1 tablespoon sunflower seeds**. In a small saucepan, add **1 tablespoon honey, 25 g butter** and **1 tablespoon soft brown sugar**. Warm over a medium heat until the sugar has dissolved. Mix together and pour over the dry ingredients, stirring everything together. Spoon the oaty topping over the fruit and bake for 20 minutes, or until the crumble topping is cooked and golden.

● When melting the sugar with the honey and butter, do not place the pan over a high heat or the sugar may burn on the base of the pan and make the crumble topping taste bitter. Stir the mixture regularly.

BANANA SPLIT WITH ICED YOGURT

Serves 4
Preparation 10 minutes, plus 30 minutes cooling
Cooking 5 minutes Freezing 5 hours

Each serving provides • 1715 kJ • 410 kcal
• 13 g protein • 6 g fat of which 3 g saturates
• 81 g carbohydrates of which 79 g sugars • 4 g fibre

To make the iced yogurt, dissolve **100 g caster sugar** in **3 tablespoons hot water** in a saucepan for 5 minutes over a low heat. Remove from the heat and cool for 30 minutes. Combine this sugar syrup with **700 g full-cream natural yogurt** and **½ teaspoon vanilla extract**. Freeze in an ice-cream maker following the manufacturer's instructions, or transfer to a lidded plastic container and freeze for at least 5 hours, removing every hour and beating to prevent ice crystals from forming. In a blender or food processor, whizz **300 g fresh raspberries** with **50 g caster sugar** and the **juice of 1 lemon**. Pass the purée through a fine-meshed sieve to remove the seeds, stirring in 1 tablespoon of water to thin slightly, if necessary. Peel **4 ripe bananas**, halve them lengthwise and arrange in four dishes. Top each banana with a scoop of iced yogurt, **75 g fresh raspberries, 1 tablespoon chopped almonds** and 2 tablespoons of the purée.

COOK'S TIPS

● If short on time, use ready-made raspberry coulis and shop-bought iced yogurt or ice cream.
● For a powerful vanilla boost, try vanilla bean paste instead of vanilla extract.

BANANA SMOOTHIE

Serves 4
Preparation 5 minutes Chilling 30 minutes

Each serving provides • 569 kJ • 136 kcal
• 4 g protein • 1 g fat (no saturates) • 30 g carbohydrates of which 29 g sugars • 1 g fibre

Put **2 ripe bananas** into a blender with **2 tablespoons honey, ½ teaspoon ground cinnamon** and **1 heaped tablespoon wheatgerm**. Blend for 10 seconds, then add **200 ml low-fat natural yogurt, 300 ml orange juice** and the **juice of ½ lemon**. Blend again until smooth. Chill for 30 minutes in the fridge before pouring into four tall glasses.

COOK'S TIPS

● Wheatgerm is a tiny part of the wheat kernel that is high in protein, vitamin E and potassium. You will find it in the cereal aisle in the supermarket, or in health food shops.
● This smoothie is best drunk within an hour of making because it will thicken as the wheatgerm expands and the vitamin C content will begin to deteriorate.

PAN-FRIED BANANAS IN A SWEET CITRUS SAUCE

Serves 4
Preparation 5 minutes Cooking 5 minutes

Each serving provides • 682 kJ • 163 kcal
• 1 g protein • 6 g fat of which 2 g saturates
• 28 g carbohydrates of which 26 g sugars • 1 g fibre

Cut **4 just-ripe bananas** into bite-sized diagonal chunks. Heat **15 g butter** in a large frying pan with **2 teaspoons sunflower oil**. Add the banana chunks to the pan and fry for 3 minutes over a medium heat until golden, then add the **juice of 1 orange, 1 tablespoon soft dark brown sugar** and a **dash of orange liqueur (optional)**. Stir for 2 minutes until bubbling then transfer to four plates and serve with the pan juices spooned over.

COOK'S TIPS

● For an oven-cooked dessert, place 4 whole bananas in an ovenproof dish with the flavourings and bake at 180°C (160°C fan-forced), for 20 minutes, basting once or twice. Remove from the oven and sprinkle with 1 teaspoon desiccated coconut per portion.
● A spoonful of crème fraîche makes a tasty partner to the bananas.

KIWI FRUIT CHEESECAKE WITH LIME HONEY

Sinfully yummy – but not sinfully calorific – this healthy take on traditional cheesecake blends low-fat yogurt or cream cheese with toasted muesli and a fruity combo bursting with vitamin C.

Serves 4
Preparation 10 minutes
Cooking 2 minutes

100 g muesli
250 g low-fat thick Greek-style yogurt
   or low-fat cream cheese
1 teaspoon icing sugar
grated zest of 2 limes and juice
   of 1 lime
2 tablespoons honey
4 ripe kiwi fruit

Each serving provides
• 1032 kJ • 246 kcal • 8 g protein
• 3 g fat of which 1 g saturates
• 47 g carbohydrates of which
32 g sugars • 5 g fibre

ALTERNATIVE INGREDIENTS
• Try 3 crushed chocolate-chip cookies per portion instead of muesli.
• To make a red berry cheesecake, use a handful of raspberries or ripe strawberries per portion and leave out the kiwi fruit.
• For a more substantial dessert, coarsely mash 2 bananas and mix them with the yogurt or cream cheese in step 1.

1 Preheat the grill to the hottest setting. Cover the grill pan with foil and sprinkle the muesli evenly over it. Toast the muesli under the grill for 2 minutes, stirring it once or twice to prevent it from burning. Mix the yogurt or cream cheese with the icing sugar and zest of 1 lime. Stir the lime juice into the honey. Peel and slice the kiwi fruit.

2 Divide half of the toasted muesli among four dessert plates or bowls, spooning the cereal into small mounds. Top with the yogurt or cream cheese and sprinkle with the remaining half of the muesli. Flatten each portion into a 'cake' using a round-bladed knife or the back of a spoon.

3 Arrange the kiwi fruit slices on top of each cheesecake and sprinkle with the remaining zest of 1 lime. Drizzle with the lime and honey mixture just before serving.

COOK'S TIPS
● The exact weight of the muesli may vary slightly depending on the brand and its precise content. As a guide, each cheesecake uses roughly 2 tablespoons of muesli.
● Instead of mounding the cheesecakes on plates, layer the muesli, cheese and fruit into 7 cm cooking rings to form a tidy shape. Remove the rings just before serving.

SUPER FOOD

LIMES
Like all citrus fruit, limes are packed with vitamin C, which is essential for healthy skin, muscles and bones, and a booster for the body's immune system. Vitamin C also offers protection from some cancers and heart disease, and helps the body to absorb essential iron.

WARM **BERRIES** ON TOASTED **BRIOCHE**

A vibrant fruit mix, poured over buttery brioche and served with creamy mascarpone, makes a flavour-drenched dessert. Even better, it is bursting with vitamins and fibre for good health.

Serves 4
Preparation 5 minutes
Cooking 4 minutes

Each serving provides
• 1075 kJ • 257 kcal • 4 g protein
• 12 g fat of which 8 g saturates
• 37 g carbohydrates of which
23 g sugars • 4 g fibre

50 g raw or demerara sugar
40 g butter
4 brioche rolls, about 35 g each
250 g mixed berries, thawed
   if frozen
2 large fresh mint leaves, chopped
120 g mascarpone
4 sprigs mint, to garnish

1 Preheat the grill to the hottest setting. Beat half of the sugar into the butter. Trim the rounded ends off the brioche rolls, then cut each one at a slant into four slices. Toast the slices under the grill on one side.

2 Place the fruit in a small saucepan. Add 2 tablespoons of water and the remaining 25 g of sugar, then bring to the boil over a medium heat, stirring frequently. Cook for 1–2 minutes, or until the sugar dissolves and the fruit releases its juices. Remove the pan from the heat and add the chopped mint.

3 Spread the untoasted sides of the brioche with the sweetened butter. Toast under the grill for 1 minute, or until the sugar melts and the edges of the slices are crisp and browned.

4 Transfer the brioche to four plates and spoon over the hot mixed fruit. Top with a large spoonful of mascarpone and garnish with a sprig of mint before serving.

COOK'S TIPS
● Cook the mixed fruit over a medium rather than high heat to avoid boiling the juices rapidly, which will toughen the skins. Remove the pan from the heat as soon as the juice boils.
● Currants and berries freeze well and can be cooked from frozen if time is short. Allow an extra 3–5 minutes cooking time in step 2 if using frozen fruit. If you grow your own raspberries, strawberries or blackcurrants, rinse and freeze them as soon as possible after picking.

SUPER FOOD

MIXED BERRIES
Vividly coloured berries contain natural compounds called anthocyanins, which can help to counter the effects of potentially damaging free radicals. These are unstable molecules that can alter or damage cells in the body, which may lead to the development of cancer.

STRAWBERRY, GRAPE AND PISTACHIO FLOWERS

What a tempting dessert! Simply arrange fresh strawberry 'petals' around a rosewater and cinnamon-infused grape centre for an enticing bouquet of summertime treats.

Serves 4
Preparation 10 minutes

Each serving provides
• 1143 kJ • 273 kcal • 15 g protein
• 7 g fat of which 4 g saturates
• 36 g carbohydrates of which
32 g sugars • 2 g fibre

¼ teaspoon ground cinnamon
1 teaspoon rosewater
2 tablespoons honey
175 g seedless black grapes
1 tablespoon icing sugar
½ teaspoon vanilla extract
250 g low-fat thick Greek-style yogurt
250 g low-fat cream cheese, softened
300 g strawberries
20 g chopped pistachios

ALTERNATIVE INGREDIENTS
• Use all Greek-style yogurt instead of half yogurt and half low-fat cream cheese for a sharper flavour.
• Try sliced and quartered oranges instead of grapes, removing the bitter pith before mixing them with the cinnamon, rosewater and honey.
• Sliced dried peaches or pears make great alternatives to the grapes. Allow two pieces of dried fruit per portion.

1 Mix together the cinnamon, rosewater and honey in a large bowl. Cut the grapes in half and stir them into the honey mixture.

2 In another bowl, lightly beat the icing sugar and vanilla extract with the yogurt and cream cheese until smooth. Divide among four ice-cream glasses or tall glass dessert dishes. Level the surface of the mixture with the back of a spoon or a round-bladed knife.

3 Hull the strawberries and then chop them in half, slicing any large fruit into smaller pieces. Position the strawberries around the edge of each glass to look like the petals of a flower. Spoon the grape mixture into the centre of each portion and sprinkle with pistachios.

COOK'S TIPS
● Rosewater contributes a flowery flavour that tastes perfect with honey. It is usually stocked in the baking aisle in the supermarket.
● If you cannot buy ready-chopped pistachios, buy whole nuts and whizz them in a food processor for 10 seconds, or until finely chopped.

SUPER FOOD

STRAWBERRIES
A summer favourite, strawberries are rich in vitamin C, helping to boost the body's immune system and protect against ageing. Strawberries also contain ellagic acid, an anti-oxidant found in berry fruits and thought to have anti-cancer properties.

PINEAPPLE AND KIWI FRUIT WITH GINGERNUT CREAM

Mint and preserved ginger are the surprise ingredients in a refreshing exotic fruit dessert. The kiwi fruit and pineapple pieces are sweetly sharp, while crunchy, biscuity cream cheese adds just a hint of indulgence.

Serves 4
Preparation 20 minutes

Each serving provides
• 909 kJ • 217 kcal • 9 g protein
• 5 g fat of which 2 g saturates
• 33 g carbohydrates of which
19 g sugars • 4 g fibre

½ **pineapple**
4 **kiwi fruit**
4 **pieces preserved stem ginger**
6 **large fresh mint leaves**
4 **gingernut biscuits**
200 g **low-fat cream cheese, softened**
4 **sprigs fresh mint, to garnish**

ALTERNATIVE INGREDIENTS
• Instead of kiwi fruit, use 200 g seedless green grapes, cutting them in half first.
• Try ginger or chocolate shortbread biscuits as a change from gingernuts, or use almond macaroons if you want a softer texture.
• Candied ginger is more economical than preserved stem ginger. Use 1 heaped teaspoon chopped candied ginger per portion.

1 Peel, core and slice the pineapple into wedges (see Cook's Tip), then peel and thickly slice the kiwi fruit and cut each slice in half. Thinly slice the preserved stem ginger. Shred the mint leaves and mix them with the pineapple and kiwi fruit.

2 In a bowl or plastic bag, crush the gingernut biscuits with the end of a rolling pin to make fine crumbs. Stir the gingernut crumbs into the cream cheese.

3 Arrange the pineapple and kiwi fruit on four plates with a large spoonful of biscuity cream cheese on the side. Top the cream cheese with sliced ginger and garnish each portion with a mint sprig.

SUPER FOOD

PINEAPPLE
Like all fruit, the tropical pineapple is a low-kilojoule, health-promoting food. It contains fibre and potassium to help to regulate the body's blood pressure and fluid balance. With a glycaemic index (GI) value that is relatively high for a fruit, pineapple is best eaten in combination with low-GI food such as low-fat fromage frais.

COOK'S TIP
● To prepare a whole pineapple, cut off the leafy top and stalk end. Slice off the skin with a sharp knife, working down the fruit to remove any eyes and spines. Divide the pineapple in half lengthwise and remove the tough core from both halves. Slice into semi-circles then cut into wedges.

RED BERRY PANCAKES

Warm fruity pancakes make a feast for any meal, be it brunch, tea time or weekday family desserts. Be generous with the rich red berries, and finish with a little Greek yogurt.

Serves 4
Preparation 15 minutes
Cooking 8 minutes

⅔ cup (100 g) self-raising flour
1 teaspoon sugar
1 egg
75 ml low-fat milk
125 g redcurrants
12 strawberries
25 g unsalted butter
2–3 teaspoons caster sugar
½ cup (125 g) low-fat Greek-style
   yogurt

Each serving provides
- 1109 kJ • 265 kcal • 9 g protein
- 8 g fat of which 5 g saturates
- 39 g carbohydrates of which
17 g sugars • 3 g fibre

ALTERNATIVE INGREDIENTS
- Try fresh or frozen blackcurrants instead of redcurrants.
- Seasonal raspberries, blackberries or pitted cherries make very tasty alternatives to strawberries.
- For a lactose-free dessert, make up the batter with 75 ml unsweetened fruit juice, such as cranberry, apple or orange juice, instead of milk.

1 Sift the flour into a bowl and stir in the sugar. Beat in the egg and a little of the milk to form a thick paste. Gradually add the rest of the milk, beating to remove any lumps until it forms a smooth, thick batter. Pull the stalks off the redcurrants, if necessary, and stir the berries into the batter. Hull and halve the strawberries.

2 Heat a large frying pan over a medium heat and add half the butter to melt. Use shaped moulds (see Cook's Tips) to make the pancakes or cook four heaped dessertspoonfuls of batter, spacing them well apart, for 2 minutes, or until they are firm, set and golden underneath.

3 Flip and cook for a further 1 minute, turning the heat down if the pancakes begin to burn. Transfer the pancakes to a dish and keep warm. Carefully wipe any juice from the berries off the pan with kitchen paper, add the remaining butter and fry four more pancakes using up the rest of the batter. Transfer the pancakes to the dish and keep warm.

4 Add the strawberries to the hot pan for 30 seconds to warm through. Transfer the pancakes to four plates, add the strawberries, sprinkle with a little caster sugar and serve with Greek-style yogurt.

COOK'S TIPS
- To create shaped pancakes, place four heatproof moulds in the frying pan, carefully spoon the batter into each mould, then leave to cook and firm up. Then, carefully remove the moulds and flip the pancakes to cook the other side.
- If using home-grown redcurrants, remove the stalks by gently scraping the fruit against the prongs of a fork, placing a bowl underneath. Shop-bought redcurrants should already have their stalks removed.

SUPER FOOD

REDCURRANTS
This versatile fruit, often used to make jelly, is rich in nutrients and high in health-promoting fibre. Redcurrants also contain potassium, which helps to regulate blood pressure, and vitamin C for healthy bones, teeth and gums.

QUICK MIXED **BERRY** AND **ALMOND** DELIGHTS

A nutty but light topping of fibre-rich almonds and oats transforms a packet of frozen mixed berries into a supercharged dessert that combines comfort eating with healthy treating.

Serves 4
Preparation 10 minutes
Cooking 20 minutes

400 g frozen mixed berries
100 g ground almonds
50 g porridge oats
2 eggs
2 tablespoons runny honey
75 ml low-fat milk
½ teaspoon almond extract

Each serving provides
• 1360 kJ • 325 kcal • 12 g protein
• 19 g fat of which 2 g saturates
• 29 g carbohydrates of which
19 g sugars • 6 g fibre

ALTERNATIVE INGREDIENTS
• Add some frozen cherries to the mixed berries. As they are larger, cherries will need an extra 5 minutes to cook.
• For a lactose-free dish, use apple juice instead of milk.

1 Preheat the oven to 200°C (180°C fan-forced). Divide the frozen berries among four 1 cup (250 ml/9 cm diameter) ramekins.

2 Mix the ground almonds and oats in a bowl and make a well in the centre. Separate the eggs, placing the yolks in the almond mixture and the whites in a separate, clean bowl. Pour the honey, milk and almond extract into the well in the oat mixture and beat the ingredients together to form a soft, dropping consistency (see Cook's Tip).

3 Whisk the eggwhites until stiff and beat one-third of them into the oat mixture. Use a metal spoon to fold in the remaining eggwhites. Spoon the pudding mixture over the frozen berries, levelling the top.

4 Place the ramekins on a baking tray and bake for 20 minutes, or until the mixture browns, rises and is slightly cracked and firm to the touch. Serve hot.

COOK'S TIP
● A dropping consistency is achieved when the mixture drops easily off your spoon when tapped against the side of the bowl. The mixture should be firm and not sloppy.

SUPER FOOD

ALMONDS
There is good evidence that a handful (30 g) of nuts, especially almonds, when eaten daily, can lower harmful cholesterol. Almonds contain 7 g fibre per 100 g, which is good news because high-fibre foods may protect against bowel cancer.

SPICED **RHUBARB** AND **BLUEBERRY** COMPOTE

Ginger delivers a delicious spike to this versatile compote that can be served warm or chilled, for breakfast or dessert – perfect with a scoop of ice cream or yogurt. The fruit provides a mouthwatering cocktail of vitamins.

Serves 4
Preparation 5 minutes
Cooking 10 minutes
Chilling 30 minutes (optional)

600 g rhubarb
3 tablespoons sugar
40 g crystallised stem ginger
125 g blueberries

Each serving provides
• 347 kJ • 83 kcal • 1 g protein
• no fat • 20 g carbohydrates of which 19 g sugars • 3 g fibre

ALTERNATIVE INGREDIENTS
• Frozen blueberries can be used in place of fresh ones, but the rhubarb must be fresh, not canned.
• Strawberries also taste terrific with the rhubarb.
• Serve the rhubarb and blueberry compote with muesli and yogurt for a nutritious breakfast.
• Stone 250–350 g cherries and add them to the rhubarb, omitting the blueberries and ginger and adding an extra tablespoonful of sugar.
• Serve as a healthy topping for pancakes or waffles.

1 Cut the rhubarb into 2–3 cm lengths and place in a large saucepan. Sprinkle the sugar over the fruit and add 1 tablespoon of water. Cook over a high heat for 30 seconds, or until the sugar begins to dissolve.

2 Reduce the heat to medium or medium–low, so that the fruit simmers. Cover the pan and simmer for 5–8 minutes, stirring once, until the rhubarb is tender but not mushy.

3 Cut the crystallised stem ginger into 1–2 mm slices. Remove the pan from the heat and add the ginger and blueberries. Stir gently and divide among four bowls. Serve immediately or chill for 30 minutes.

COOK'S TIPS
● Small, fresh sticks of rhubarb are usually tender and only need the ends of the stalks trimmed and the poisonous leaves discarded. Larger or older sticks should be thinly peeled to remove the skin, which can be stringy.
● Make the stewed rhubarb and keep it in a covered dish in the fridge for up to 3 days. Add the blueberries and ginger just before serving.

SUPER FOOD

RHUBARB
A low sugar content, and therefore a low glycaemic index (GI) rating, means that rhubarb can help to steady blood glucose levels, which is great for weight control and keeping hunger at bay. With fibre and potassium as extra nutritional benefits, rhubarb helps to maintain a healthy digestive system.

BLUEBERRIES

A nutritional supernova, blueberries are bursting with anti-oxidants that can offer protection against long-term health problems such as some cancers and heart disease. As fibre providers, blueberries also do their bit to support a healthy digestive system.

INDIVIDUAL SUMMER PUDDINGS

Serves 4
Preparation 5 minutes Cooking 5 minutes
Chilling 1½ hours

Each serving provides • 732 kJ • 175 kcal
• 5 g protein • 3 g fat of which 1 g saturates
• 35 g carbohydrates of which 20 g sugars • 5 g fibre

Poach **225 g blueberries** and **225 g raspberries** in a saucepan with 3 tablespoons of water, **3 tablespoons caster sugar** and the **juice of 1 lemon** for 5 minutes, or until the juices run free. Line four dariole moulds with plastic wrap. Remove the crusts from **5 thin brown bread slices**, then cut each slice into four squares and use them to line the darioles, placing one square on each base and four around the sides. Spoon the fruit and juice into the lined moulds, wrap in plastic wrap and chill in the fridge for 1½ hours. Lift the summer puddings out of each mould using the plastic wrap and transfer to four plates. Top each pudding with **1 tablespoon reduced-fat crème fraîche** and serve.

COOK'S TIP
● When pouring the fruit juice into the moulds, make sure that it covers as much of the bread as possible.

BERRY ICED YOGURT

Serves 4
Preparation 5 minutes Cooking 15 minutes
Freezing 5 hours

Each serving provides • 1293 kJ • 309 kcal
• 11 g protein • 6 g fat of which 2 g saturates
• 56 g carbohydrates of which 55 g sugars • 3 g fibre

Place **400 g blueberries** in a small saucepan with **25 g caster sugar** and 2 tablespoons of cold water. Bring to the boil over a high heat, lower the heat and simmer the fruit for 5 minutes. Leave to cool. Whisk **2 egg yolks** in a bowl with **75 g caster sugar** and **200 g low-fat Greek-style yogurt**. Transfer to a small saucepan and warm gently over a low heat, stirring continuously, for 10 minutes, or until the mixture thickens slightly. Remove the pan from the heat. Mash **1 ripe banana** with **¼ teaspoon ground cinnamon, juice of ½ lemon** and **200 g low-fat natural yogurt**. Stir this mixture into the pan. Add the blueberries and any juice then stir again. Freeze in an ice-cream maker following the manufacturer's instructions, or transfer to a lidded plastic container and freeze for at least 5 hours, removing from the freezer every hour and beating to remove any ice crystals. When ready to serve, leave the iced yogurt at room temperature for 15 minutes to thaw slightly then cut into slices or scoop into bowls.

COOK'S TIP

● Serve two scoops of iced yogurt in a glass bowl with a crunchy biscuit or wafer per person.

BLUEBERRY CRÈME BRÛLÉE

Serves 4
Preparation 5 minutes Cooking 12 minutes
Chilling 1 hour

Each serving provides • 774 kJ • 185 kcal
• 2 g protein • 13 g fat of which 8 g saturates
• 16 g carbohydrates of which 12 g sugars • 1 g fibre

Preheat the grill to the hottest setting. Place **125 g blueberries**, 1 tablespoon of water and **2 teaspoons caster sugar** in a saucepan over a medium–high heat and simmer for 2 minutes. Spoon the blueberries, and any juice, into four 1 cup (250 ml/9 cm diameter) ramekins. Put **2 digestive biscuits** into a plastic bag and crush them with a rolling pin. Gently beat **300 ml low-fat crème fraîche** with **1 teaspoon vanilla extract** in a bowl and stir in the biscuit crumbs. Spoon the mixture over the blueberries and level the surface. Sprinkle **1 level tablespoon brown sugar** evenly over each ramekin and grill for 10 minutes, or until the sugar caramelises. Cool slightly before transferring to the fridge to chill for 1 hour, or until the tops harden.

COOK'S TIP

● For a nutty crème brûlée, replace the biscuits with 2 tablespoons chopped blanched almonds.

BLUEBERRY AND BUTTERMILK MUFFINS

Makes 6
Preparation 20 minutes, plus 15 minutes cooling
Cooking 25 minutes

Each serving provides • 1200 kJ • 287 kcal
• 9 g protein • 6 g fat of which 1 g saturates
• 52 g carbohydrates of which 18 g sugars • 4 g fibre

Preheat the oven to 180°C (160°C fan-forced). In a large bowl, combine ⅔ **cup (100 g) self-raising flour** with **100 g wholemeal self-raising flour, 1 teaspoon baking powder, zest of ½ lemon** and **50 g soft light brown sugar**. In another bowl, beat **1 egg** and stir in **150 ml buttermilk** and **1 tablespoon sunflower oil**.

Using a large metal spoon, gently stir the wet ingredients into the dry ingredients. Add **125 g blueberries**. Spoon the mixture into six paper muffin cases placed in a muffin tin and bake for 25 minutes, or until risen and golden. Cool in the tin for 15 minutes then transfer to a wire rack.

COOK'S TIPS

● Use low-fat milk or low-fat pouring yogurt if you cannot get buttermilk.
● The muffins will keep fresh for 48 hours in an airtight container but are best eaten soon after baking.

FRUIT EXPLOSION MUESLI

Serves 4
Preparation 10 minutes, plus 15 minutes standing

Each serving provides • 1234 kJ • 295 kcal
• 8 g protein • 12 g fat of which 1 g saturates
• 41 g carbohydrates of which 22 g sugars • 6 g fibre

Place **100 g rolled oats** in a large bowl and then stir in **1 tablespoon sunflower seeds, 1 tablespoon pumpkin seeds, 25 g chopped hazelnuts, 25 g chopped almonds** and **1 tablespoon finely chopped dried apricots**. Add **2 grated apples** with the skins still on and **125 g blueberries**. Pour in **200 ml orange juice**, stir again and leave to soak for 15 minutes. When ready to serve, divide the muesli among four bowls and add **½ teaspoon brown sugar** and **1 heaped tablespoon natural yogurt** to each bowl.

COOK'S TIPS

● For variety, include a mixture of wholegrains, such as wheat or rye flakes, in addition to the rolled oats.
● For a muesli with added crunch, roughly chop the apricots and leave the almonds whole.

POACHED **PEACHES** AND **PEARS** IN A **BLUEBERRY** JUS

Few things are more mouth-watering than a juicy peach and a ripe pear, and poaching is a great way to make them extra delectable. Using nothing but the goodness of fresh fruit and juice guarantees a sweet but healthy dessert.

Serves 4
Preparation 5 minutes
Cooking 30 minutes

Each serving provides
• 812 kJ • 194 kcal • 1 g protein
• no fat • 48 g carbohydrates of which 47 g sugars • 5 g fibre

1 litre blueberry juice drink
2 large firm peaches
2 large pears
120 g blueberries

ALTERNATIVE INGREDIENTS
• A smart way to combine the first pears of the season with late-fruiting raspberries is to use raspberry juice drink instead of blueberry juice drink and top the peaches and pears with 120 g raspberries in place of blueberries.
• Try dried peaches or mango slices instead of fresh peaches. Use 2 dried peach halves per portion or 3 mango slices. Poach the dried fruit with the pears for 5 minutes.

1 Pour the blueberry juice drink into a large saucepan. Halve and stone the peaches, leaving on the skins, then add them to the pan as they are prepared. Peel, halve and core the pears and add them to the pan.

2 Bring the blueberry juice drink to the boil over a high heat, reduce the heat to medium so that the juice is simmering and poach the fruit for 10 minutes, or until tender – test the fruit with the point of a knife. Use a slotted spoon to transfer the fruit to a bowl, then set aside.

3 Increase the heat to high again and boil the blueberry juice drink for 20 minutes, or until it is reduced to a thick glaze. Watch it carefully after 10 minutes to ensure it does not boil over. Divide the fruit among four bowls and spoon a little glaze over each portion. Top with fresh blueberries and serve.

COOK'S TIPS
● Firm peaches do not shed their skins when cooked but become tender and juicy. They also retain their heat better than peeled fruit and should remain warm while the juice drink is boiled down.
● For a healthy breakfast treat, prepare the glazed fruit the day before, then cool, cover and store in the fridge overnight.

SUPER FOOD

PEACHES
Low in kilojoules, peaches make a perfect healthy snack or dessert, with vitamin C to fortify the body's immune system. Peaches also contain beta-carotene, which the body converts to vitamin A for healthy skin and eyes.

CHOCOLATE AND PECAN DIP WITH FRUIT

Rich dark chocolate, crunchy nuts and sticky honey combine for a tempting dip that is actually chock full of healthy fruit. A little goes a long way – so, take it easy and you will be more saint than sinner.

Serves 4
Preparation 10 minutes
Cooking 5 minutes

Each serving provides
- 1550 kJ • 370 kcal • 9 g protein
- 23 g fat of which 9 g saturates
- 32 g carbohydrates of which
31 g sugars • 5 g fibre

120 g dark chocolate
4 teaspoons runny honey
50 g pecans
120 g low-fat cream cheese, softened
    fresh fruit, such as banana,
    pineapple, mandarin segments,
    strawberries, pitted cherries, about
    180 g per person

1 Break the chocolate into 2 cm pieces and place them in a small heatproof bowl. Drizzle in the honey and place the bowl over a saucepan of simmering water set over a low heat for 5 minutes, stirring occasionally, or until the chocolate has melted. Finely chop the pecans.

2 Remove the bowl from the pan and cool slightly. Stir in 2 tablespoons of the cream cheese and the pecans. Gradually stir in the remaining cream cheese and transfer the dipping sauce to one large serving bowl or four individual bowls. Serve the sauce warm with the fresh fruit to dip.

3 Prepare a selection of fresh fruit for serving with the chocolate and nut dipping sauce. Cut the fruit into bite-sized pieces and arrange them on a serving dish.

SUPER FOOD

PECANS
Rich in beneficial cholesterol-lowering unsaturated fats, pecans are good for the heart. In addition, they are high in fibre, omega-3 oils, some B vitamins and vitamin E for healthy skin. Pecans also contain flavonoids, potent plant-based anti-oxidants that may help to protect against cancer.

COOK'S TIP
● To prevent chocolate from splitting when it is being melted, use a small pan that fits neatly under the bowl. It is essential to avoid getting water or steam in the chocolate because this will make the fat separate from the chocolate solids, causing the chocolate to become stiff and grainy. Do not overheat chocolate, as it burns easily.

HOT **FRUIT PUDDINGS** TOPPED WITH HAZELNUT PRALINE

Succulent dried pears, tart apples and luscious raspberries are topped with a layer of creamy yogurt and sprinkled with a crunchy nut praline. Each mouthful promises plenty of vitamins and calcium.

Serves 4
Preparation 5 minutes, plus
2 minutes standing
Cooking 10 minutes
Chilling 30 minutes

350 g tart apples, such as
   granny smith
100 g dried pears
200 g raspberries
500 g low-fat Greek-style yogurt
100 g roasted chopped hazelnuts
50 g sugar

Each serving provides
• 1920 kJ • 459 kcal • 15 g protein
• 20 g fat of which 3 g saturates
• 57 g carbohydrates of which
46 g sugars • 9 g fibre

ALTERNATIVE INGREDIENTS
• Pitted cherries make a succulent replacement for raspberries.
• Flaked almonds are a good alternative to hazelnuts. Buy them ready toasted or grill for 1 minute under a medium–hot heat before adding the sugar.

1 Peel, core and slice the apples into 1 cm wedges and place in a large saucepan. Add 4 tablespoons of boiling water and bring back to the boil over a high heat. Cover the pan, reduce the heat and simmer for 4 minutes, stirring once.

2 Slice the dried pears into 1 cm wedges. Stir the pears into the apples and remove the pan from the heat. Mix in the raspberries and divide the fruit among four bowls. Spoon the yogurt over the fruit. Cover and leave to cool, then chill in the fridge for 30 minutes, ready for finishing with the nut topping.

3 To make the praline, mix the hazelnuts and sugar in a heavy-based frying pan. Place over a high heat for 1–2 minutes, or until the sugar begins to melt. Shake the pan and continue to cook, stirring frequently, for a further 1–2 minutes, or until the sugar turns golden brown.

4 Working quickly so that the sugar does not burn on the hot pan, spoon the praline on top of the desserts. Then leave to stand for 1–2 minutes so the praline is not too hot when served.

COOK'S TIPS
• Praline is a crunchy sweet made by boiling nuts in sugar. If serving the desserts in glass dishes, turn the praline out onto a lightly oiled baking tray to cool slightly, otherwise the heat may crack the glass.
• The praline topping can be made, cooled and stored in an airtight jar. It will keep for several months, ready for sprinkling over fruit compotes or yogurt.

SUPER FOOD

YOGURT
One small pot of yogurt a day provides nearly one third of your daily calcium needs. Bio-yogurt (probiotic) contains lactobacillus and bifido bacteria, which, if eaten regularly, can boost 'friendly' bacteria in the bowel and colon, helping to maintain and promote healthy digestion.

WARM **CHERRY** AND **CHOCOLATE** TRIFLE

Biscotti make a crunchy base for a medley of cherries and blueberries, coated in a smooth chocolate sauce. The fruit bursts with potassium, helping to keep blood pressure under control.

Serves 4
Preparation 10 minutes
Cooking 5 minutes

6 biscotti, about 180 g
425 g can pitted cherries in juice or syrup
150 g blueberries
2 tablespoons cornflour
2 tablespoons cocoa powder
300 ml low-fat milk
1 teaspoon vanilla extract
2 tablespoons sugar
40 g white chocolate chips

Each serving provides
• 2004 kJ • 479 kcal • 9 g protein
• 11 g fat of which 6 g saturates
• 89 g carbohydrates of which 52 g sugars • 2 g fibre

ALTERNATIVE INGREDIENTS
• Use amaretti biscuits or almond macaroons instead of biscotti.

1 Break the biscotti in half and divide them among four dishes (three halves per dish). Drain the cherries using a bowl to catch the juice. Spoon the juice over the biscotti and then leave to soak for 5 minutes before topping with the cherries and blueberries.

2 Whisk the cornflour and cocoa powder with a little of the milk in a small saucepan. Gradually whisk in the remaining milk. Use a spatula to scrape up any cornflour from the bottom of the pan.

3 Put the pan on a medium to medium–high heat and bring the sauce to the boil, whisking continuously. Reduce the heat and simmer, stirring gently, for 2 minutes. Whisk in the vanilla extract and sugar.

4 Pour the sauce over the fruit. Sprinkle with the chocolate chips and use the tip of a knife to swirl the chocolate around as it melts.

COOK'S TIPS
● Try flavoured biscotti, such as almond and chocolate or ones that contain pistachios.
● Check that the cherries are pitted before buying them. Some bottled and canned cherries contain stones.
● Adding sugar to the milk and cocoa sauce at the end of cooking helps to prevent it from browning and sticking to the pan. The milk and cocoa sauce may seem too thick before the sugar is added, but as the sugar melts, your sauce will thin to the correct consistency.
● Instead of chocolate chips, break a bar of chocolate into squares, place in a sturdy plastic bag, then use a rolling pin to crush into tiny pieces.

SUPER FOOD

CHERRIES
High in fibre, cherries are good for digestive health. They are rich in health-protecting anthocyanins, and also contain plenty of potassium that can help to regulate blood pressure.

Copyright © 2013 The Reader's Digest Association, Inc.

Published by
World Publications Group, Inc.
140 Laurel Street
East Bridgewater, MA 02333
www.wrldpub.com

Australian Consultant Suzie Ferrie, Advanced Accredited
Practising Dietitian
Copy Editor Janine Flew
Proofreaders Susan McCreery, Samantha Kent
Production Controller Anne Schwertfeger
Editorial Project Manager General Books Deborah Nixon

READER'S DIGEST GENERAL BOOKS
Editorial Director Lynn Lewis
Managing Editor Rosemary McDonald
Art Director Carole Orbell

ISBN 978-1-4643-0334-0

Printed in China

1 3 5 7 9 10 8 6 4 2